Sketches from Eastern History

THEODORE NÖLDEKE

Sketches
from
Eastern History

translated by
JOHN SUTHERLAND BLACK M.A.
and revised by the Author

LONDON
DARF PUBLISHERS LIMITED
1985

First Published 1892
New Impression 1985

ISBN 1 85077 065 4

Printed and bound in Great Britain by A. Wheaton & Co. Ltd, Exeter

SOME CHARACTERISTICS OF THE SEMITIC RACE.[1]

ONE of the most difficult tasks of the historian is to depict the moral physiognomy of a nation in such a way that no trait shall be lost, and none exaggerated at the cost of the others. The difficulty of the task may be best appreciated by considering how complicated a thing, full of apparent contradictions, individual character is, and that the historian who seeks to define the character of a nation, or perhaps of a race embracing many nations, has to deal with a still more complex phenomenon, made up of widely varying individuals. This difficulty, indeed, is not equally great with all nations. The common characters of the Semitic nations are in many respects so definite and strongly marked, that on the whole they are more easily portrayed than those of the small Greek people, which, although at bottom a unity, embraced a great variety of distinct local types,—Athenians as well as Bœotians, Corinthians as well as Spartans, Arcadians and Ætolians as well as Milesians and Sybarites. And yet it is no very easy matter to form an estimate of the psychical characteristics of the Semites, —witness the contradictory judgments passed on them by such distinguished scholars as Renan and Steinthal. I have no mind to attempt a new portrait of the Semitic type of humanity. All that I intend is to offer a few contributions to the subject, connecting my remarks, whether by way of

[1] Originally published in *Im neuen Reich*, ii. (1872) p. 881 sqq.

agreement or, occasionally, by way of dissent, with a well-written and ingenious essay of the learned orientalist Chwolson, which is mainly directed against Renan.[1]   In this the author is successful in refuting some of Renan's unfavourable criticisms on the Semitic character. But his own judgments are not always strictly impartial; he is himself of Jewish extraction, and in some particulars offers too favourable a picture of the Semitic race, to which he is proud to belong.

Chwolson rightly lays emphasis upon the enormous importance of inborn qualities for nations as well as for individuals; but he is not free from exaggeration in his attempts to minimise the influence of religion and laws on the one hand, of geographical position and of climate on the other. The inhabitants of Paraguay were savage Indians like their neighbours in Brazil and in the Argentine countries; but under the despotic discipline of the Jesuits and their secular successors, they grew into a nation which thirty years ago fought to the death against overwhelming odds for its country and its chief.   Islam, Christianity, and Buddhism have exercised a powerful influence for good or for evil even on the character of nations already civilised.   In like manner, climate and geographical position are very important factors in the formation of national character. Could we observe the first beginnings of nations, they would perhaps be found to be the decisive factors.   Peoples that are, so to speak, adult, and possessed of a developed civilisation, are naturally much less susceptible to such influences than the savage child of nature.   But they are not wholly independent of them: isolated countries in particular, with strongly marked geographical peculiarities, such as elevated mountain regions, lonely islands, and above all desert lands —not to speak of polar regions—exercise this influence in a

[1] *Die Semitischen Völker*, Berlin 1872.

high degree. Ethnologically the Persians and the Hindoos are very closely related, yet their characters differ enormously; and this must be mainly ascribed to the geographical contrast between their seats. The Persians dwell on a lofty plateau, exposed to violent vicissitudes of cold and heat, and in great part unfit for cultivation; the Hindoos in a region of tropical luxuriance. Chwolson points to the enormous difference between the ancient and the modern Egyptians as a convincing proof that race character is little dependent upon local environment; but really we see in Egypt how a country with such marked peculiarities forces its inhabitants into conformity with itself. Munziger, in his day unquestionably the best authority upon North-Eastern Africa, brings out in a few masterly touches the essential likeness of modern to ancient Egypt. I will quote only one of his remarks: "The ancient Egyptians," he says, "were not so far ahead of the modern as we are sometimes ready to imagine; then, as now, hovels adjoined palaces, esoteric science coexisted with crass ignorance," and so forth.[1] In the history of ancient Egypt, extending as it does through millenniums, there naturally occur alternate periods of prosperity and of decay; we may not venture to compare the time of the Mameluke sultans and the Turkish rule with that of the pyramid-builders; but it seems to me a very fair question whether the civilisation of Egypt during the best period of the Fatimids did not stand quite as high as the highest attained under the Pharaohs. The main difference is that the Egyptians in remote antiquity had no neighbours who stood on any sort of equality with them, and thus they received no considerable influences from without; but this was also the reason why their civilisation so soon became stationary.

Chwolson might have made more of the point that peoples

---

[1] *Ostafrikanische Studien*, p. 5 ff.

are not rigid bodies incapable of modification, but organisms
that can develop and assimilate,—organisms offering a varying resistance to external influences, but in the long course
of centuries capable of such transformation that their early
character can only be recognised in some minor features.
Many a touch in the Magyar still reminds us of his Asiatic
origin; yet, on the whole, he has more resemblance to any
one of the civilised peoples of Europe than to his nearest
relations on the Ural.

Similarly, in drawing the character of the Semites, the
historian must guard against taking the Jews of Europe as
pure representatives of the race.   These have maintained
many features of their primitive type with remarkable
tenacity, but they have become Europeans all the same; and,
moreover, many peculiarities by which they are marked are
not so much of old Semitic origin as a result of the special
history of the Jews, and in particular of continued oppression, and of that long isolation from other peoples, which
was partly their own choice and partly imposed upon
them.

Our delineation of the Semites must begin with the
Arabs, Hebrews, and Syrians (Aramæans), the last named of
whom, however, have never constituted a closely - welded
nationality, politically or otherwise.   Of the inner life of the
Phœnicians and some minor Semitic nations of antiquity,
we know very little.   The whole character of the Babylonians and Assyrians, which in many respects differs widely
from that of the other Semites, is steadily coming more and
more to light through the arduous labours of cuneiform
scholars, but we are still far from knowing it nearly so
intimately as we know that of the three first-mentioned
peoples.   Moreover, it still remains undetermined how far
non-Semitic people may have had a share in the commence-
ment of the high and extremely ancient civilisation of

Babylon. To make the picture complete it would be necessary, of course, to bring in also the black Semites of Abyssinia and the adjoining regions; but these to all appearance owe their origin to an intermingling of Arab Semites with Africans; indeed, they are for the most part only Semitised "Hamites," and have accordingly retained much pristine African savagery, especially as they were always strongly exposed to the influence of non-Semitic nations dwelling around and among them. Besides, there is much to be said for neglecting undeveloped or atrophied members when delineating the character of a group of peoples.

The religion of the Semites is the first thing that demands our attention, and that not solely on account of the influence it has exerted on us in Europe. Renan is right in neglecting the beginnings of Semitic religion, and taking the results of their religious development and their tendency to monotheism as the really important thing. The complete victory of monotheism, it is true, was first achieved within historical times among the Israelites; but strong tendencies in the same direction appear also among the other Semitic peoples. Renan is also right in reckoning Christianity as only in part a Semitic religion, for even its origin presupposed a world fructified by Greek ideas, and it was mainly through non-Semitic influences that it became a world-religion; nay, we may almost say that the changes which have taken place in Christianity from the Reformation onwards consist in a more and more complete elimination of its Semitic elements. Islam, on the other hand, in its pure Arabic form, the doctrine of Mohammed and of his disciples, which for a century past has again been preached in its purity by the Wahhabites[1] in the country of its birth, is the logical perfection of Semitic religion, with the importation of only one

[1] See below, p. 103.

fundamental idea, though that is indeed a very important one, namely, the conception of a resurrection and of a life in heaven which had already been adopted by Judaism and Christianity.[1] Islam is infinitely hard and one-sided, but in its crude simplicity strictly logical. Mohammed cannot in strictness be called a great man, and yet the appearance of the religion which found in him such clear and energetic expression—a religion which in one rapid march of conquest first subdued the Semitic world already ripe for the change, and then brought under its sway numerous other peoples both civilised and savage—was the most important manifestation the Semitic genius ever made. In the religious portions of the Old Testament we find that more inward warmth of feeling and that richer fancy which distinguished the ancient Hebrew from the Arab. When we read the Psalms and the Prophets, even without the customary idealising spectacles, we shall place them—and not from the merely æsthetic point of view only—far above the Koran. But the result of the religious development of the Old Testament — the religion of Ezra, of the Pharisees, and of the Rabbins — can hardly be said to stand higher than Islam.

The energy and simplicity of Semitic ideas in religion are not favourable to a complicated mythology. Where anything of the sort is met with among them, it is either of purely foreign provenance, or has arisen through admixture with foreign elements. This holds good perhaps even of the Babylonian mythology (which, for the rest, is somewhat formless), certainly of all the variety of Gnostic sects, and in a large measure also of the official Christianity as it is found among Semites. Mystical doctrines with them easily degenerate into crudeness; compare, for example, the reli-

[1] Strictly speaking, this idea is itself but a conglomerate of Persian religious teachings and Greek thought with Semitic accretions.

gion of the purely Semitic Druses with analogous phenomena of Persian and Indian origin.

Even in the field of religion the nations of Indo-European civilisation display a richer genius than the Semites; but they lack that tremendous energy which produced the belief in the unity of God, not as a result of scientific reflection, but as a moral demand, tolerating no contradiction. This strength of faith, which has subdued the world, is necessarily associated with much violence and exclusiveness. Nowhere is the uncompromising spirit of the Old Testament more impressive than in its half-mythical and yet thoroughly historical portrait of Elijah, that magnificent ideal of prophecy in its zeal for the Lord. I cannot understand how Chwolson will scarcely admit the existence of religious ecstasy among the Semites, when the Old Testament is full of evidences of high imaginative exaltation in its prophets as well as in those of Baal; nay, in Hebrew the very word "to behave as a prophet" (*hithnabbê*) also means simply "to behave madly, to rave." Ecstasy, the condition in which the religiously-inspired man believes himself to hold immediate converse with God, was to the prophets themselves the subjective attestation of their vocation. Not less deeply rooted in their religion is that Semitic fanaticism which Chwolson would also fain deny. "Take heed to thyself lest thou make a covenant with the inhabitants of the land whither thou goest, lest it be for a snare in the midst of thee; but ye shall break down their altars, and dash in pieces their images, and ye shall cut down their groves" (Ex. xxxiv 12, 13)—in such or similar terms run those strict commands, which were indeed justifiable at the time, but none the less bear witness to frightful exclusiveness and rigid fanaticism. In the same spirit the followers of Baal destroy the altars of Jehovah and slay His prophets (1 Kings xix. 10). The captives and property taken by the Israelites from their enemies were often devoted to destruction in honour of Jehovah (*herem*). By the inscription of king Mesha we now know that the Moabites practised the same thing on a large scale, in honour of their god Chemosh. The Greek translation of *herem* is *anathema*, properly "a dedicatory gift;" the cry, "Anathema sit," so often heard in Christendom, is an inheritance from the Semites. I grant that religious fanaticism has been powerful elsewhere, and particularly where there has been a strong priestly class, as in India; but for the Semitic religions, fanaticism is characteristic. Among the Persian priests of the Sásánian period it first became powerful under Semitic influence and in conflict with Semitic religion. The same trait is conspicuous in Islam. There, indeed, it is more deeply rooted, and of stricter inward necessity, than in Christianity, though it has seldom risen to such heights of atrocity as it has sometimes reached in the latter. When all has been said, Moslems are bound to regard all peace with unbelievers as a truce merely—an obligation at this day much more vividly present to the minds of the vast majority of Mohammedans than Europeans usually suspect.

Another side of their religious narrowness is shown in the wide diffusion which human sacrifice continued to have amongst highly civilised Semites. Amongst the ancient Hebrews, indeed, only isolated traces of it continue to be met with (as also among the Greeks); but as king Mesha sacrificed his son in his need (2 Kings iii. 27), so also did Carthaginian generals centuries afterwards. In fact, extensive human sacrifices were offered to a god in Carthage every year, and as late as the fourth century B.C., the distress into which Agathocles brought the city (in 310) was attributed to the wrath of the deity because the rich had begun to cause purchased children to be offered instead of their own; on this account the horrible custom was again re-established in all its simplicity (Diodor. xx. 14). Among the Arabs also we meet with human sacrifice; only a century before Mohammed, the Arab prince of Híra, a town that contained a large Christian population, sacrificed four hundred nuns whom he had taken in war to his goddess Ozza (the planet Venus). In the Semitic religions occasional traces of primitive rudeness in ideas and manners are continually cropping up. In Mecca reverence is still paid to the black stone, a relic of the once widely-diffused worship of stone-fetishes, of which traces are found even in the Old Testament. To the same category belongs the retention, both in Judaism and in Mohammedanism, of the old custom of circumcision. As the unchaste worship of female goddesses was specially in vogue among the ancient Semites, so even now it happens in Arab countries, that amongst people who pass for thoroughly holy and world-weaned (often simply insane) the grossest excesses are regarded as holy deeds; this, to be sure, is only popular belief, and has never been sanctioned by orthodox theologians. It is a high prerogative of the Old Testament that, surrounded by unchaste religious services, it sternly banishes all such immorality from its worship of Jehovah.

In denying to the Semites in general any tendency to asceticism and monkery, Chwolson is not entirely wrong, but neither is he perfectly right. In the first place, it is fair to say that such a tendency is hardly in any instance characteristic of a nation as a whole. And then, again, the Old Testament does look upon the Nazirate (and also the rule of the Rechabites, who, amongst other things, abstained from wine) as something meritorious; the Jewish Essenes were neither more nor less than a monastic order; and the Old Testament and the Koran alike contain some precepts either wholly or partially ascetic in their character. It must, however, be conceded that the precepts are not exorbitant, and that some of them (such as the prohibition of wine) are

very suitable for Asiatic and African countries. Yet it must
always be remembered that in all Christendom, Egypt apart,
it will be difficult to find such an insane and soul-destroying
asceticism as was practised by the purely Semitic Syrians
from about the fourth to the seventh century.[1]

The Old Testament almost everywhere breathes a purely
ethical spirit, and seeks to conceive of the Godhead as morally
perfect; but this view is not wholly strange to other nations.
The Roman "Jupiter optimus maximus" is surely intended
to express moral perfection as well as the highest power;
and amongst the Greeks there arose, at a tolerably early
date, a view which freed the gods of the objectionable
features attributed to them by the ancient myths. But if
the Israelite (like other Semitic peoples) regards his God as
the merciful and gracious One, it by no means follows that
he is disposed to allow this mercy and grace to extend to
other men. The ethical prescriptions of the Old Testament
are often unduly idealised. The command to love one's
neighbour has reference, in the Old Testament, only to people
of one's own nation. Cosmopolitan ideas appear occasionally
in some of the prophets, but only in germ, and always in
such a way that Israel and Israel's sanctuary remain exalted
above all peoples. The cosmopolitanism without which
Christianity would be inconceivable, could not gain any
strength until after Hellenic and Oriental ideas had begun
to combine. Whether the precepts in Deuteronomy, which
enjoin humanity in war and otherwise, give as favourable a
testimony to the mild disposition of the ancient Israelites as
is sometimes supposed, is very doubtful. Perhaps they
indicate the very contrary. Chwolson himself points out
that among the lying Persians the duty of truthfulness has
from of old been specially insisted on; and I believe it
would be possible to prove that the hot - blooded ancient

[1] See below, "Some Syrian Saints."

Semites had a strong vein of ferocity. The great humanity and benevolence of the Jews of to-day, a result of their peculiar history, can certainly not be adduced as evidence to the contrary.

In political life the Semites have done more than is commonly supposed. It is true that we find among them, on the one hand, a lawless and highly-divided state of society, in which even the rudiments of political authority are hardly known (as among the ancient and modern Bedouins), and, on the other, unlimited despotism. In the first century of Islam the former of these conditions was almost immediately replaced by the latter. Chwolson ought not to deny the despotic character of the Omayyad caliphate, which was purely Semitic, and not half-Persian, like that of the Abbásids in Bagdad. The Arabs of that age, in fact, could hardly think of a ruler at all as without absolute authority. Even the individual governor or general, as long as he is in office, has full and unlimited power. Even those radical fanatics, the Kharijites, who recognised only a perfect Moslem as ruler, whether great or small,[1] gave absolute authority to their leader, if only he did not apostatise from the faith. If, indeed, he did this—and the decision on this point of fact each reserved for himself—they deposed him, and at that period the actual rulers and chiefs had to reckon very strictly with the views and wishes of their fighting subjects; but in theory they were unrestricted in their actions, and a strong and capable prince in some degree actually was so. It was otherwise, however, in ancient Israel. We can still discern that in both kingdoms the sovereigns were in many points limited by survivals of the old aristocratic constitution. To get rid of Naboth, queen Jezebel required the sentence of a public assembly, which she secured by false witnesses (1 Kings xxi.). The narrator

[1] See below, p. 80.

therefore gives us to understand that the heads of the commune retained the power of life and death in their own hands, although the monarchy was even then an old institution. The kings of Edom appear in very early times to have been elective princes. And the Phœnicians (including the Carthaginians) present a very large variety of political constitution, which reminds one of Greece. Amongst the Phœnicians we find also, at least in times of the direst need, a self-sacrificing patriotism, as is witnessed by the wars against Rome, in which Carthage perished, and the mortal struggle of Tyre against Alexander (although in the latter religious motives seem to have played a part). But, in general, individualism preponderates among the Semites so greatly that they adapt themselves to a firmly settled state only at the call of great religious impulses, or under the pressure of despotic authority; and, even when it is established, they have no real attachment to it. The still untamed Arab is much more strongly attached to the family, the clan, the tribe; so also among the Israelites of the older time, clanship seems to have been a bond of very great strength. But it is an error to try to see in this absence of formed national feeling, as contrasted with the patriotism of the Greeks, any approach to the freer modern conception of the State.

It is also quite a mistake to attribute to the Semites democratic inclinations. No people has ever laid so much stress upon genealogies as the two Semitic nations with which we are best acquainted, the Hebrews and the Arabs, have done. The genuine Arab is thoroughly aristocratic. Many a feud turns upon the precedence of one family or tribe over another. In the first two centuries after Mohammed bloody wars were waged on such rivalries. Even now it is with a heavy heart that the Arab sees set over him a man of less noble extraction than himself. The deeds of ancestors are accepted as legitimation, but are also the spur of emulation. In the councils of the tribe or of the community, it is difficult for the man of humble origin to acquire influence. Even a caliph so early as the third in the series owed his throne to the influence of his clan, the Omayyads, who yet shortly before had been the bitterest enemies of the Prophet, but nevertheless, after their subjection, retained the position of greatest prominence in Mecca, and so in the new State. But for the consideration in which his family was held, Moáwiya, the real founder of the Omayyad dynasty, with all his talent and all his services to the empire, would never have attained to the supreme command. In this matter, indeed, Islam has gradually effected a mighty change. At his first appearance Mohammed gave offence to the upper-class Meccans by admitting to the number of his followers slaves, freedmen, and other people of no family or account. The might of the religious idea triumphed over old prejudices. In presence of the almighty extra-mundane God all mortals are on an absolute equality; whosoever went over to Islam received the same rights, and undertook the same duties as the highest and the meanest believer. But, in spite of all this, Mohammed himself made many concessions to the aristocratic temper, and this temper continued for a long time after to be a great power; it was the complete development of the despotism, after the old Oriental fashion, that levelled all subjects. But even to this day aristocratic ideas prevail among the Arabs of the desert, and also among the sedentary Arabs in remoter regions. The genuine Arab has in connection with his aristocratic notions a sense of chivalry, a fine feeling for points of honour (not necessarily the same as we ourselves take), but also a strong propensity to vanity and boasting. There are many evidences that in the communities of ancient Israel also an aristocratic rule (elders and nobles) prevailed. That the constitution of Carthage was in its essential features aristocratic is well known. The same is true of the Syrian city of Palmyra, though its constitution was modified by the general conditions of the Roman empire, to which it had to accommodate itself.

As the Semite can hardly be induced, voluntarily, to submit to a strict discipline, he does not, on the whole, make a good soldier. Skirmishes and little surprises are what the Arab finds inspiriting; of the adventures of his heroes and robbers he tells stories, as the Hebrews before him did about Samson. Like all vigorous nations with an exuberant vitality, the Arabs delight in narratives of battle and victory, especially if these are properly exaggerated and flatter their pride of family or race. The Old Testament speaks less of heroes than of saints, but then it is a religious book; its many tales of the "wars of the Lord" nevertheless bear witness that the peaceful Hebrew could also be thoroughly warlike. How could it possibly have been otherwise in a land that had been conquered with the sword, and very often required to be similarly defended? When Chwolson tries to demonstrate the absolutely peaceable disposition of the Israelites by reference to the ideal kingdom of peace which was the object of their hopes, it can be argued on the other side that the very prophet who promises the beating of swords into ploughshares, and of spears into pruning-hooks, depicts the daughter of Zion as trampling on the nations or wasting the land of Assyria with the sword (Micah iv., v.). But Semitic armies have seldom done anything great. This might be ascribed to the circumstance that among the Semites the power of taking in complex unities at a glance, the talent for arrangement, is rare, and that therefore they have had no generals; but we have only to think of Hannibal and other great Carthaginians to reject this view. These, however, carried on their campaigns with foreign troops. For it is quite undeniable that the Semites do not readily make good soldiers. For moulding the Arabs into powerful armies in the early years of Islam, unusual impulses were required: the enthusiasm generated by a new national religion which promised a heavenly reward, and the allurements which the prospects of booty and of settlement in rich lands offered to the inhabitants of the sterile wilderness. Over and above all this there was a wonderful intellectual outburst which showed itself in the appearance of a singular series of highly gifted generals, statesmen, and men of eminence in various directions. And these were precisely the men who then stood at the head of the nation. To subsequent generations the youth of Islam, the true prime of the Arabs, is unintelligible. They are unable to appreciate the great spiritual forces which, either in conjunction with, or in hostile opposition to, each other, were then unfolded. The theological school discerns everywhere only theological battles, and this school dominates the view of later Moslems. This is the chief reason why the names of the great warriors and statesmen of that period have long been almost forgotten in the East, while those of theologians and saints are popular. The later Jews also often fought with the utmost bravery, but only when the defence of their religion was in question. To become subject to a stern discipline, and to encounter death merely for the sake of freedom and fatherland, was not a thought that came naturally to them. Chwolson seems to prefer the enthusiasm of religion to the enthusiasm of patriotism; but I take it that the heroes of Marathon laid the world under a debt of obligation by no means less deep than did the armies of the Maccabees.

In religion the one-sidedness of the Semitic mind was a creative power; but it was highly prejudicial to the development of science. A keen eye for particulars, a sobriety of apprehension (justly dwelt on by Chwolson), are undoubtedly talents of great service in the beginnings of science. Ac-

cordingly we find at a comparatively early period amongst
Hebrews and Arabs an intelligent system of chronicles such
as was never attained by (let us say) the dreamy Hindoos;
and from the firm lapidary style in which king Mesha
recounts his exploits we can infer that in his time (about
900 B.C.) some beginnings of historic narrative existed even
in that remote land. But, as already remarked, the Semite
is deficient in the power of taking a general view, in the
gift of comprehensive intelligence, of large and, at the same
time, logical thought, and therefore, speaking generally, he
has only in a few cases contributed anything of importance to science. The ideas of monotheism and of a creation
are by no means products of philosophical reflection; the
naive intelligence of the Israelite has not the faintest suspicion of the enormous difficulties which the assumption of a
creation out of nothing presents to the reflecting mind; to
him the proposition is self-evident. The speculation of the
Arabs on the freedom of the will and similar subjects, continued to be very unsystematic and unscientific as long as
it was only superficially affected by Greek thought. And
even after they had been trained by Greek philosophy, the
Arabs, so far as I am able to judge from what I freely confess to be a very limited knowledge, produced little that was
new in this field. On the whole, it becomes increasingly
apparent that the Syrians and Arabs, whatever their merit
in keeping up and handing on the sciences of the Greeks,
were not very fruitful in their own cultivation of these,
though it must be admitted that the Arabs at least made
advances in some matters of detail. Besides, we must not
assume that everything written in Arabic must necessarily
be Arab and Semitic; one might as well ascribe all the
Latin literature of the Middle Ages to the Italians. There
are, however, undeniably certain fields of knowledge in which
the Arabs distinguished themselves without stimulus from

without; Arabian philology in particular, in its various branches, is a brilliant achievement. Many Persians, it is true, had a share in it, but it is almost entirely Arabian in its first origin, and thoroughly so in spirit. It evinces an exceedingly keen observation of the phenomena of language, and though breadth of view and genuine systematic method are frequently wanting, and the wisdom of the school seeks to improve upon the facts, the Arabic language (of course the Arabic only) is examined from all sides with a subtlety worthy of all admiration. But how any one could ever have thought of finding among the ancient Israelites long before Aristotle's time anything of the nature of natural science is, I confess, incomprehensible to me. When we read that Solomon "spake of trees" and of animals (1 Kings iv. 33; [Heb. v. 13]), the expression admits perhaps of more than one interpretation, but certainly we are not to understand that botany and zoology are meant. Neither should I be disposed to reckon under Semitic science the agricultural treatises of the Carthaginian Mago. We shall be safe in asserting that these did not stand on a higher level than the corresponding Roman and Greek works on that subject, which were directed exclusively to practical ends; but if we are to regard such writings as scientific, we must do the same with cookery books. The discovery of the alphabet, or rather the separation of a true alphabet out of a highly complicated system of writing, has proved infinitely important for science, and bears decisive testimony to the intellectual powers of the Semites,[1] but I hesitate to call this an achievement of science in the proper sense of the word. The science of the Babylonians, on the other hand, deserves high recognition. What they did for astronomy

---

[1] It may now be regarded as tolerably certain that the Semitic alphabet, from which all those of Europe had their origin, was reached by simplification of the extremely unpractical writing of the Egyptians.

and the measurement of time in particular at a very early
period is of the very greatest value, and is even now not
wholly out of date; just as, in another aspect, the astrological
superstition connected with it dominated succeeding ages.
The conspicuous services to science of modern Jewish *savants*
clearly cannot come into the account here; for these men
belong to civilised Europe.

All qualified judges are pretty unanimous about Semitic
poetry and art. A keen eye for particulars, great subject-
ivity, a nervous restlessness, deep passion and inwardness of
feeling, and, finally, a strong tendency to follow older models
and keep to traditional forms of presentation, mark their
excellences as well as their defects. I shall not here repeat
the remarks so often made on Arabic and Hebrew poetry,
as to the want of a Semitic epic and so on. I only observe
that the few remains we possess of Hebrew poetry, though
mainly of a religious character, reveal many-sidedness in a
far higher degree, and also, on the whole, more of depth and
freshness, than does the very uniform if formally perfect
poetry of the Arabs, of which, notwithstanding many losses,
we still possess a very large quantity. From the Syrians
much verse has come to us, but hardly anything truly
poetical apart from some quite short popular songs of the
modern Syrians of the extreme north-east. For the rest,
the want of an epos is compensated among the Hebrews and
Arabs (as also among some Indo-European peoples) by talent
for lively and attractive prose narration. Essentially, as a
result of the peculiar structure of their language, the Arabs
have naturally a strong tendency to a pointed manner of
speech, varying between epigrammatic brevity and ornate
tautology. Even the Bedouins in the desert spoke in this
way; and this was the style employed by the princes and
generals of the first period of Íslam in their public addresses
as well as in their letters. This artificial and ornate style

inevitably degenerated into a mannerism, and finally issued in a meaningless jingle of words and the well-known oriental inflation which we find so intolerable, especially in Persian and Turkish imitations. The counterpart of this love for a striking and elegant manner of speech was, of course, a great sensibility to style on the part of hearers and readers. Eloquence was a highly - prized gift before Mohammed's time. The 'pleasure which the Arabs took in beauty of language is one of the principal causes which led to their peculiar success in philology. A taste for well-arranged, striking, and sonorous words existed among the ancient Hebrews also, though not in so highly-developed a form.

Every one admits that, apart from the Babylonians and Assyrians, the Semites have had little success in the plastic arts. The statements of the Old Testament give us a very moderate idea of the architectural performances of the Hebrews. In all essential respects the Phœnicians appear to have copied Egyptian, and afterwards Greek models. The extensive ruins of Palmyra, Petra, Baalbec (Heliopolis), and other towns of Syria, are in a Greek style, only slightly modified by oriental influences. The Arabs, also, have mainly followed foreign patterns. Arab buildings some- times, indeed, show extraordinary beauty of detail, wonderful ornamentation, splendid colour; but in this department, also, there is a want of sense for totality, of articulate unity of plan. It must, moreover, be noted, that many buildings of the Arabs—the very famous Omayyad mosque at Damas- cus, among others—were in whole or in part executed by foreigners. It is characteristic of the Arabs that they reckon caligraphy among the fine arts; and certainly any one who has seen finished examples of the work of Arab penmen must acknowledge that there is in them something more than mere dexterity and elegance,—that these wonderfully free and pure forms are controlled by the same feeling for nobility of outline which appears in all branches of Arab decorative art.[1] In Arabian art we everywhere find a delicate sense for detail, but nowhere large apprehension of a great and united whole. That most Semites have effected nothing in sculpture, and very little in painting strictly so called, is partly to be accounted for, no doubt, by religious considerations; but at bottom it has its explanation in want of aptitude for these arts. It is only among the Babylonians and Assyrians that an original sculpture has flourished. Among the remains of Nineveh some notable works of art occur, alongside of many pieces of excellent but purely conventional workmanship.

Our general conclusion, then, is that the genius of the Semites is in many respects one-sided, and does not reach the level of some Indo-European nations, especially the Greeks; but it would be most unjust to deny their claim to one of the highest places among the races of mankind. Among the pure Semites of the present day, indeed, we discover extraordinarily few indications of natural or vigorous progress; much points to the conclusion that this group of nations has long since passed its prime. Whether modern European culture may be able really to lay hold of them, and awaken them to a new and strenuous life, is a question which will not be answered in the immediate future.

[1] Some of the Phœnician inscriptions also, in their slender straight lines, show a fine caligraphic taste.

II.

THE KORAN.[1]

THE Koran (*Ḳor'ấn*) is the foundation of Islam. It is the
sacred book of more than a hundred millions of men, some
of them nations of immemorial civilisation, by all whom
it is regarded as the immediate word of God. And since the
use of the Koran in public worship, in schools and otherwise, is much more extensive than, for example, the reading
of the Bible in most Christian countries, it has been truly
described as the most widely-read book in existence. This
circumstance alone is sufficient to give it an urgent claim
on our attention, whether it suit our taste and fall in with
our religious and philosophical views or not. Besides, it is
the work of Mohammed, and as such is fitted to afford a
clue to the spiritual development of that most successful of
all prophets and religious personalities. It must be owned
that the first perusal leaves on a European an impression
of chaotic confusion,—not that the book is so very extensive,
for it is not quite so large as the New Testament. This
impression can in some degree be modified only by the
application of a critical analysis with the assistance of
Arabian tradition.

To the faith of the Moslems, as has been said, the Koran
is the word of God, and such also is the claim which the
book itself advances. For except in sur. i.—which is a
prayer for men—and some few passages where Mohammed

[1] Originally published in the *Encyclopædia Britannica*, 9th ed., vol. xvi.,
p. 597 sqq.

(vi. 104, 114, xxvii. 93, xlii. 8), or the angels (xix. 65, xxxvii. 164 sqq.), speak in the first person without the intervention of the usual imperative " say " (sing. or pl.), the speaker throughout is God, either in the first person singular, or more commonly the plural of majesty " we." The same mode of address is familiar to us from the prophets of the Old Testament; the human personality disappears, in the moment of inspiration, behind the God by whom it is filled. But all the greatest of the Hebrew prophets fall back speedily upon the unassuming human " I "; while in the Koran the divine " I " is the stereotyped form of address. Mohammed, however, really felt himself to be the instrument of God; this consciousness was no doubt brighter at his first appearance than it afterwards became, but it never entirely forsook him. We might therefore readily pardon him for giving out, not only the results of imaginative and emotional excitement, but also many expositions or decrees which were the outcome of cool calculation, as the word of God, if he had only attained the pure moral altitude which in an Isaiah or a Jeremiah fills us with admiration after the lapse of ages.

The rationale of revelation is explained in the Koran itself as follows:—In heaven is the original text (" the mother of the book," xliii. 3; " a concealed book," lv. 77; " a well-guarded tablet," lxxxv. 22). By a process of " sending down " (*tanzíl*), one piece after another was communicated to the Prophet. The mediator was an angel, who is called sometimes the " Spirit " (xxvi. 193), sometimes the " holy Spirit " (xvi. 104), and at a later time " Gabriel " (ii. 91). This angel dictates the revelation to the Prophet, who repeats it after him, and afterwards proclaims it to the world (lxxxvii. 6, etc.). It is plain that we have here a somewhat crude attempt of the Prophet to represent to himself the more or less unconscious process by which his ideas

arose and gradually took shape in his mind. It is no wonder
if in such confused imagery the details are not always self-
consistent. When, for example, this heavenly archetype is
said to be in the hands of an exalted "scribe" (lxxx. 13 sqq.),
this seems a transition to a quite different set of ideas,
namely, the books of fate, or the record of all human actions
—conceptions which are actually found in the Koran. It is
to be observed, at all events, that Mohammed's transcend-
ental idea of God, as a Being exalted altogether above the
world, excludes the thought of direct intercourse between
the Prophet and God.

It is an explicit statement of the Koran that the sacred
book was revealed ("sent down") by God, not all at once,
but piecemeal and gradually (xxv. 34). This is evident from
the actual composition of the book, and is confirmed by
Moslem tradition. That is to say, Mohammed issued his
revelations in fly-leaves of greater or less extent. A single
piece of this kind was called either, like the entire collection, kor'án, i.e. "reading," or rather "recitation;" or kitáb,
"writing;" or súra, which is the late-Hebrew shúrá, and
means literally "series." The last became, in the lifetime
of Mohammed, the regular designation of the individual
sections as distinguished from the whole collection; and
accordingly it is the name given to the separate chapters of
the existing Koran. These chapters are of very unequal
length. Since many of the shorter ones are undoubtedly
complete in themselves, it is natural to assume that the
longer, which are sometimes very comprehensive, have arisen
from the amalgamation of various originally distinct revelations. This supposition is favoured by the numerous
traditions which give us the circumstances under which
this or that short piece, now incorporated in a larger section,
was revealed; and also by the fact that the connection of
thought in the present súras often seems to be interrupted.

And in reality many pieces of the long súras have to be severed out as originally independent; even in the short ones parts are often found which cannot have been there at first. At the same time we must beware of carrying this sifting operation too far,—as I now believe myself to have done in my earlier works, and as Sprenger in his great book on Mohammed also sometimes seems to do. That some súras were of considerable length from the first is seen, for example, from xii., which contains a short introduction, then the history of Joseph, and then a few concluding observations, and is therefore perfectly homogeneous. In like manner, xx., which is mainly occupied with the history of Moses, forms a complete whole. The same is true of xviii., which at first sight seems to fall into several pieces; the history of the seven sleepers, the grotesque narrative about Moses, and that about Alexander " the Horned," are all connected together, and the same rhyme runs through the whole súra. Even in the separate narrations we may observe how readily the Koran passes from one subject to another, how little care is taken to express all the transitions of thought, and how frequently clauses are omitted, which are almost indispensable. We are not at liberty, therefore, in every case where the connection in the Koran is obscure, to say that it is really broken, and set it down as the clumsy patchwork of a later hand. Even in the old Arabic poetry such abrupt transitions are of very frequent occurrence. It is not uncommon for the Koran, after a new subject has been entered on, to return gradually or suddenly to the former theme,—a proof that there at least separation is not to be thought of. In short, however imperfectly the Koran may have been redacted, in the majority of cases the present súras are identical with the originals.

How these revelations actually arose in Mohammed's mind is a question which it is almost as idle to discuss as it would be to analyse the workings of the mind of a poet. In his early career, sometimes perhaps in its later stages also, many revelations must have burst from him in uncontrollable excitement, so that he could not possibly regard them otherwise than as divine inspirations. We must bear in mind that he was no cold systematic thinker, but an Oriental visionary, brought up in crass superstition, and without intellectual discipline; a man whose nervous temperament had been powerfully worked on by ascetic austerities, and who was all the more irritated by the opposition he encountered, because he had little of the heroic in his nature. Filled with his religious ideas and visions, he might well fancy he heard the angel bidding him recite what was said to him. There may have been many a revelation of this kind which no one ever heard but himself, as he repeated it to himself in the silence of the night (lxxiii. 4). Indeed the Koran itself admits that he forgot some revelations (lxxxvii. 7). But by far the greatest part of the book is undoubtedly the result of deliberation, touched more or less with emotion, and animated by a certain rhetorical rather than poetical glow. Many passages are based upon purely intellectual reflection. It is said that Mohammed occasionally uttered such a passage immediately after one of those epileptic fits which not only his followers, but (for a time at least) he himself also, regarded as tokens of intercourse with the higher powers. If that is the case, it is impossible to say whether the trick was in the utterance of the revelation or in the fit itself.

How the various pieces of the Koran took literary form is uncertain. Mohammed himself, so far as we can discover, never wrote down anything. The question whether he could read and write has been much debated among Moslems, unfortunately more with dogmatic arguments and spurious traditions than authentic proofs. At present, one is inclined to say that he was not altogether ignorant of these arts, but that from want of practice he found it convenient to employ some one else whenever he had anything to write. After the emigration to Medina (A.D. 622) we are told that short pieces — chiefly legal decisions — were taken down immediately after they were revealed, by an adherent whom he summoned for the purpose; so that nothing stood in the way of their publication.   Hence it is probable that in Mecca, where, as in a mercantile town, the art of writing was commoner than in Medina, a place of agriculture, he had already begun to have his oracles committed to writing. That even long portions of the Koran existed in written form from an early date, may be pretty safely inferred from various indications; especially from the fact that in Mecca the Prophet had caused insertions to be made, and pieces to be erased, in his previous revelations.   For we cannot suppose that he knew the longer súras by heart so perfectly that he was able after a time to lay his finger upon any particular passage.   In some instances, indeed, he may have relied too much on his memory.   For example, he seems to have occasionally dictated the same súra to different persons in slightly different terms.   In such cases, no doubt, he may have partly intended to introduce improvements; and so long as the difference was merely in expression, without affecting the sense, it could occasion no perplexity to his followers.   None of them had literary pedantry enough to question the consistency of the divine revelation on that ground.   In particular instances, however, the difference of reading was too important to be overlooked.   Thus the Koran itself confesses that the unbelievers cast it up as a reproach to the Prophet that God sometimes substituted one verse for another (xvi. 103).   On one occasion, when a dispute arose between two of his own followers as to the true reading of a passage which both had received from the

Prophet himself, Mohammed is said to have explained that the Koran was revealed in seven forms. In this dictum, which perhaps is genuine, seven stands, of course, as in many other cases, for an indefinite but limited number. But one may imagine what a world of trouble it has cost the Moslem theologians to explain the saying in accordance with their dogmatic beliefs. A great number of explanations are current, some of which claim the authority of the Prophet himself; as, indeed, fictitious utterances of Mohammed play throughout a conspicuous part in the exegesis of the Koran. One very favourite, but utterly untenable interpretation is that the "seven forms" are seven different Arabic dialects.

When such discrepancies came to the cognisance of Mohammed it was doubtless his desire that only one of the conflicting texts should be considered authentic; only he never gave himself much trouble to have his wish carried into effect. Although in theory he was an upholder of verbal inspiration, he did not push the doctrine to its extreme consequences; his practical good sense did not take these things so strictly as the theologians of later centuries. Sometimes, however, he did suppress whole sections or verses, enjoining his followers to efface or forget them, and declaring them to be "abrogated." A very remarkable case is that of the two verses in liii., when he had recognised three heathen goddesses as exalted beings, possessing influence with God. This he had done in a moment of weakness, to win his countrymen by a compromise which still left Allah in the highest rank. He attained his purpose indeed, but was soon visited by remorse, and declared the words in question to have been inspirations of the Evil One.

So much for abrogated readings; the case is somewhat different when we come to the abrogation of laws and directions to the Moslems, which often occurs in the Koran.

There is nothing in this at variance with Mohammed's idea
of God. God is to him an absolute despot, who declares a
thing right or wrong from no inherent necessity, but by His
arbitrary fiat. This God varies His commands at pleasure,
prescribes one law for the Christians, another for the Jews,
and a third for the Moslems; nay, He even changes His
instructions to the Moslems when it pleases Him. Thus,
for example, the Koran contains very different directions,
suited to varying circumstances, as to the treatment which
idolaters are to receive at the hands of believers. But
Mohammed showed no anxiety to have these superseded
enactments destroyed. Believers could be in no uncertainty
as to which of two contradictory passages remained in force;
and they might still find edification in that which had become obsolete. That later generations might not so easily
distinguish the "abrogated" from the "abrogating" did not
occur to Mohammed, whose vision, naturally enough, seldom
extended to the future of his religious community. Current
events were invariably kept in view in the revelations. In
Medina it called forth the admiration of the Faithful to
observe how often God gave them the answer to a question
whose settlement was urgently required at the moment.
The same *naïveté* appears in a remark of the Caliph Othmán
about a doubtful case: "If the Apostle of God were still
alive, methinks there had been a Koran passage revealed on
this point." Not unfrequently the divine word was found
to coincide with the advice which Mohammed had received
from his most intimate disciples. "Omar was many a time
of a certain opinion," says one tradition, "and the Koran was
then revealed accordingly."

The contents of the different parts of the Koran are
extremely varied. Many passages consist of theological or
moral reflections. We are reminded of the greatness, the
goodness, the righteousness of God as manifested in Nature,

in history, and in revelation through the prophets, especially through Mohammed. God is magnified as the One, the All-powerful. Idolatry and all deification of created beings, such as the worship of Christ as the Son of God, are unsparingly condemned. The joys of heaven and the pains of hell are depicted in vivid sensuous imagery, as is also the terror of the whole creation at the advent of the last day and the judgment of the world. Believers receive general moral instruction, as well as directions for special circumstances. The lukewarm are rebuked, the enemies threatened with terrible punishment, both temporal and eternal. To the sceptical the truth of Islam is held forth; and a certain, not very cogent, method of demonstration predominates. In many passages the sacred book falls into a diffuse preaching style, others seem more like proclamations or general orders. A great number contain ceremonial or civil laws, or even special commands to individuals down to such matters as the regulation of Mohammed's harem. In not a few, definite questions are answered which had actually been propounded to the Prophet by believers or infidels. Mohammed himself, too, repeatedly receives direct injunctions, and does not escape an occasional rebuke. One súra (i.) is a prayer, two (cxiii., cxiv.) are magical formulas. Many súras treat of a single topic, others embrace several.

From the mass of material comprised in the Koran—and the account we have given is far from exhaustive—we should select the histories of the ancient prophets and saints as possessing a peculiar interest. The purpose of Mohammed is to show from these histories how God in former times had rewarded the righteous and punished their enemies. For the most part the old prophets only serve to introduce a little variety in point of form, for they are almost in every case facsimiles of Mohammed himself. They preach exactly like him, they have to bring the very same charges against their opponents, who on their part behave exactly as the unbelieving inhabitants of Mecca. The Koran even goes so far as to make Noah contend against the worship of certain false gods, mentioned by name, who were worshipped by the Arabs of Mohammed's time. In an address which is put in the mouth of Abraham (xxvi. 75 sqq.) the reader quite forgets that it is Abraham, and not Mohammed (or God Himself), who is speaking. Other narratives are intended rather for amusement, although they are always well seasoned with edifying phrases. It is no wonder that the godless Koraishites thought these stories of the Koran not nearly so entertaining as those of Rostam and Ispandiár related by Nadr the son of Hárith, who, when travelling as a merchant, had learned on the Euphrates the heroic mythology of the Persians. But the Prophet was so exasperated by this rivalry that when Nadr fell into his power after the battle of Badr, he caused him to be executed; although in all other cases he readily pardoned his fellow-countrymen.

These histories are chiefly about Scripture characters, especially those of the Old Testament. But the deviations from the Biblical narratives are very marked. Many of the alterations are found in the legendary anecdotes of the Jewish Aggádá and the New Testament Apocrypha; but many more are due to misconceptions such as only a listener (not the reader of a book) could fall into. The most ignorant Jew could never have mistaken Haman (the minister of Ahasuerus) for the minister of Pharaoh, or identified Miriam the sister of Moses with Mary (=Miriam) the mother of Christ. In addition to such misconceptions there are sundry capricious alterations, some of them very grotesque, due to Mohammed himself. For instance, in his ignorance of everything out of Arabia, he makes the fertility of Egypt —where rain is almost never seen and never missed—depend on rain instead of the inundations of the Nile (xii. 49). The strange tale of "the Horned" (*i.e.* Alexander the Great, xviii. 82 sqq.) reflects, as has been lately discovered, a rather absurd story, written by a Syrian in the beginning of the sixth century; we may believe that the substance of it was related to the Prophet by some Christian. Besides Jewish and Christian histories, there are a few about old Arabian prophets. In these he seems to have handled his materials even more freely than in the others.

The opinion has already been expressed that Mohammed did not make use of written sources. Coincidences and divergences alike can always be accounted for by oral communications from Jews who knew a little and Christians who knew next to nothing. Even in the rare passages where we can trace direct resemblances to the text of the Old Testament (comp. xxi. 105 with Ps. xxxvii. 29; i. 5 with Ps. xxvii. 11) or the New (comp. vii. 48 with Luke xvi. 24; xlvi. 19 with Luke xvi. 25), there is nothing more than might readily have been picked up in conversation with any Jew or Christian. In Medina, where he had the opportunity of becoming acquainted with Jews of some culture, he learned some things out of the Mishna, *e.g.* v. 35 corresponds almost word for word with Mishna *Sanh.* iv. 5; compare also ii. 183 with Mishna *Ber.* i. 2. That these are only cases of oral communication will be admitted by any one with the slightest knowledge of the circumstances. Otherwise we might even conclude that Mohammed had studied the Talmud; *e.g.* the regulation as to ablution by rubbing with sand, where water cannot be obtained (iv. 46), corresponds to a Talmudic ordinance (*Ber.* 15a). Of Christianity he can have been able to learn very little even in Medina; as may be seen from the absurd travesty of the institution of the Eucharist in v. 112 sqq. For the rest, it is highly improbable that before the Koran any real literary

production—anything that could be strictly called a book—
existed in the Arabic language.

In point of style and artistic effect, the different parts of
the Koran are of very unequal value. An unprejudiced and
critical reader will certainly find very few passages where
his æsthetic susceptibilities are thoroughly satisfied. But
he will often be struck, especially in the older pieces, by a
wild force of passion, and a vigorous, if not rich, imagination.
Descriptions of heaven and hell, and allusions to God's working in Nature, not unfrequently show a certain amount of
poetic power. In other places also the style is sometimes
lively and impressive; though it is rarely indeed that we
come across such strains of touching simplicity as in the
middle of xciii. The greater part of the Koran is decidedly
prosaic; much of it indeed is stiff in style. Of course, with
such a variety of material, we cannot expect every part to
be equally vivacious, or imaginative, or poetic. A decree
about the right of inheritance, or a point of ritual, must
necessarily be expressed in prose, if it is to be intelligible.
No one complains of the civil laws in Exodus or the sacri-
ficial ritual in Leviticus, because they want the fire of Isaiah
or the tenderness of Deuteronomy. But Mohammed's
mistake consists in persistent and slavish adherence to the
semi-poetic form which he had at first adopted in accordance
with his own taste and that of his hearers. For instance,
he employs rhyme in dealing with the most prosaic subjects,
and thus produces the disagreeable effect of incongruity
between style and matter. It has to be considered, however,
that many of those sermonising pieces which are so tedious
to us, especially when we read two or three in succession
(perhaps in a very inadequate translation), must have had a
quite different effect when recited under the burning sky
and on the barren soil of Mecca. There, thoughts about
God's greatness and man's duty, which are familiar to us

from childhood, were all new to the hearers—it is hearers we have to think of in the first instance, not readers—to whom, at the same time, every allusion had a meaning which often escapes our notice. When Mohammed spoke of the goodness of the Lord in creating the clouds, and bringing them across the cheerless desert, and pouring them out on the earth to restore its rich vegetation, that must have been a picture of thrilling interest to the Arabs, who are accustomed to see from three to five years elapse before a copious shower comes to clothe the wilderness once more with luxuriant pastures. It requires an effort for us, under our clouded skies, to realise in some degree the intensity of that impression.

The fact that scraps of poetical phraseology are specially numerous in the earlier súras, enables us to understand why the prosaic mercantile community of Mecca regarded their eccentric townsman as a "poet," or even a "possessed poet." Mohammed himself had to disclaim such titles, because he felt himself to be a divinely-inspired prophet; but we too, from our standpoint, shall fully acquit him of poetic genius Like many other predominantly religious characters, he had no appreciation of poetic beauty; and if we may believe one anecdote related of him, at a time when every one made verses, he affected ignorance of the most elementary rules of prosody. Hence the style of the Koran is not poetical but rhetorical; and the powerful effect which some portions produce on us is gained by rhetorical means. Accordingly the sacred book has not even the artistic form of poetry; which, among the Arabs, includes a stringent metre, as well as rhyme. The Koran is never metrical, and only a few exceptionally eloquent portions fall into a sort of spontaneous rhythm. On the other hand, the rhyme is regularly maintained; although, especially in the later pieces, after a very slovenly fashion. Rhymed prose was a favourite form

3

of composition among the Arabs of that day, and Mohammed
adopted it; but if it imparts a certain sprightliness to some
passages, it proves on the whole a burdensome yoke. The
Moslems themselves have observed that the tyranny of the
rhyme often makes itself apparent in derangement of the
order of words, and in the choice of verbal forms which
would not otherwise have been employed; *e.g.* an imperfect
instead of a perfect. In one place, to save the rhyme, he
calls Mount Sinai *Sínín* (xcv. 2) instead of *Síná* (xxiii. 20);
in another Elijah is called *Ilyásín* (xxxvii. 130) instead of
Ilyás (vi. 85, xxxvii. 123). The substance even is modified
to suit exigencies of rhyme. Thus the Prophet would
scarcely have fixed on the unusual number of *eight* angels
round the throne of God (lxix. 17) if the word *thamániyah,*
"eight," had not happened to fall in so well with the rhyme.
And when lv. speaks of *two* heavenly gardens, each with *two*
fountains and *two* kinds of fruit, and again of *two* similar
gardens, all this is simply because the dual termination (*án*)
corresponds to the syllable that controls the rhyme in that
whole súra. In the later pieces, Mohammed often inserts
edifying remarks, entirely out of keeping with the context,
merely to complete his rhyme. In Arabic it is such an easy
thing to accumulate masses of words with the same termination, that the gross negligence of the rhyme in the Koran is
doubly remarkable. One may say that this is another mark
of the Prophet's want of mental training, and incapacity for
introspective criticism.

On the whole, while many parts of the Koran undoubtedly
have considerable rhetorical power, even over an unbelieving
reader, the book, æsthetically considered, is by no means a
first-rate performance. To begin with what we are most
competent to criticise, let us look at some of the more
extended narratives. It has already been noticed how
vehement and abrupt they are where they ought to be

characterised by epic repose. Indispensable links, both in expression and in the sequence of events, are often omitted, so that to understand these histories is sometimes far easier for us than for those who heard them first, because we know most of them from better sources. Along with this, there is a great deal of superfluous verbiage; and nowhere do we find a steady advance in the narration. Contrast, in these respects, "the most beautiful tale," the history of Joseph (xii.), and its glaring improprieties, with the story in Genesis, so admirably conceived and so admirably executed in spite of some slight discrepancies. Similar faults are found in the non-narrative portions of the Koran. The connection of ideas is extremely loose, and even the syntax betrays great awkwardness. Anacolutha are of frequent occurrence, and cannot be explained as conscious literary devices. Many sentences begin with a "when" or "on the day when," which seems to hover in the air, so that the commentators are driven to supply a "think of this" or some such ellipsis. Again, there is no great literary skill evinced in the frequent and needless harping on the same words and phrases; in xviii., for example, "till that" (*hattá idhá*) occurs no fewer than eight times. Mohammed, in short, is not in any sense a master of style. This opinion will be endorsed by any European who reads through the book with an impartial spirit and some knowledge of the language, without taking into account the tiresome effect of its endless iterations. But in the ears of every pious Moslem such a judgment will sound almost as shocking as downright atheism or polytheism. Among the Moslems, the Koran has always been looked on as the most perfect model of style and language. This feature of it is in their dogmatic the greatest of all miracles, the incontestable proof of its divine origin. Such a view on the part of men who knew Arabic infinitely better than the most accomplished European Arabist will ever do, may well

startle us. In fact, the Koran boldly challenged its opponents
to produce ten súras, or even a single one, like those of the
sacred book, and they never did so. That, to be sure, on
calm reflection, is not so very surprising. Revelations of the
kind which Mohammed uttered, no unbeliever could produce
without making himself a laughing-stock. However little
real originality there is in Mohammed's doctrines, as against
his own countrymen he was thoroughly original, even in the
form of his oracles. To compose such revelations at will was
beyond the power of the most expert literary artist; it would
have required either a prophet or a shameless impostor. And
if such a character appeared *after* Mohammed, still he could
never be anything but an imitator, like the false prophets
who arose about the time of his death and afterwards. That
the adversaries should produce any sample whatsoever of
poetry or rhetoric equal to the Koran is not at all what the
Prophet demands. In that case he would have been put to
shame, even in the eyes of many of his own followers, by the
first poem that came to hand. Nevertheless, it is on such a
false interpretation of this challenge that the dogma of the
incomparable excellence of the style and diction of the Koran
is based. The rest has been accomplished by dogmatic prejudice, which is quite capable of working other miracles
besides turning a defective literary production into an
unrivalled masterpiece in the eyes of believers. This view
once accepted, the next step was to find everywhere evidence
of the perfection of the style and language. And if here
and there, as one can scarcely doubt, there was among the
old Moslems a lover of poetry who had his difficulties about
this dogma, he had to beware of uttering an opinion which
might have cost him his head. We know of at least one
rationalistic theologian who defined the dogma in such a way
that we can see he did not believe it (Shahrastání, p. 39).
The truth is, it would have been a miracle indeed if the style

of the Koran had been perfect. For although there was at that time a recognised poetical style, already degenerating to mannerism, a prose style did not exist. All beginnings are difficult; and it can never be esteemed a serious charge against Mohammed that his book, the first prose work of a high order in the language, testifies to the awkwardness of the beginner. And further, we must always remember that entertainment and æsthetic effect were at most subsidiary objects. The great aim was persuasion and conversion; and, say what we will, that aim has been realised on the most imposing scale.

Mohammed repeatedly calls attention to the fact that the Koran is not written, like other sacred books, in a strange language, but in Arabic, and therefore is intelligible to all. At that time, along with foreign ideas, many foreign words had crept into the language, especially Aramaic terms for religious conceptions of Jewish or Christian origin. Some of these had already passed into general use, while others were confined to a more limited circle. Mohammed, who could not fully express his new ideas in the common language of his countrymen, but had frequently to find out new terms for himself, made free use of such Jewish and Christian words, as was done, though perhaps to a smaller extent, by certain thinkers and poets of that age who had more or less risen above the level of heathenism. In Mohammed's case this is the less wonderful, because he was indebted to the instruction of Jews and Christians whose Arabic—as the Koran pretty clearly intimates with regard to one of them— was very defective. Nor is it very surprising to find that his use of these words is sometimes as much at fault as his comprehension of the histories which he learned from the same people—that he applies Aramaic expressions as incorrectly as many uneducated persons now employ words derived from the French. Thus, *forkán* means really

" redemption," but Mohammed (misled by the Arabic meaning of the root *frk*, " sever," " decide ") uses it for " revelation." *Milla* is properly " Word," but in the Koran " religion." *Illíyún* (lxxxiii. 18, 19) is apparently the Hebrew name of God, *Elyón*, " the Most High ; " Mohammed uses it of a heavenly book (see S. Fraenkel, *De vocabulis in antiquis Arabum carminibus et in Corano peregrinis*, Leyden 1880, p. 23). So again the word *mathání* is, as Geiger has conjectured, the regular Arabic plural of the Aramaic *mathníthá*, which is the same as the Hebrew *Mishna*, and denotes, in Jewish usage, a legal decision of some of the ancient Rabbins. But in the Koran " the seven *Mathání* " (xv. 87) are probably the seven verses of súra i., so that Mohammed appears to have understood it in the sense of " saying " or " sentence " (comp. xxxix. 24). Words of Christian origin are less frequent in the Koran. It is an interesting fact that of these a few have come over from the Abyssinian, such as *hawáríyún*, " apostles," *máida*, " table," and two or three others ; these all make their first appearance in súras of the Medina period. The word *shaitán*, " Satan," which was likewise borrowed, at least in the first instance, from the Abyssinian, had probably been already introduced into the language. Sprenger has rightly observed that Mohammed makes a certain parade of these foreign terms, as of other peculiarly constructed expressions ; in this he followed a favourite practice of contemporary poets. It is the tendency of the imperfectly educated to delight in out-of-the-way expressions, and on such minds they readily produce a remarkably solemn and mysterious impression. This was exactly the kind of effect that Mohammed desired, and to secure it he seems even to have invented a few odd vocables, as *ghislín* (lxix. 36), *sijjín* (lxxxiii. 7, 8), *tasním* (lxxxiii. 27), and *salsabíl* (lxxvi. 18). But, of course, the necessity of enabling his hearers to understand ideas which they must have found sufficiently novel in themselves, imposed tolerably narrow limits on such eccentricities.

The constituents of our present Koran belong partly to the Mecca period (before A.D. 622), partly to the period commencing with the emigration to Medina (from the autumn of 622 to 8th June 632). Mohammed's position in Medina was entirely different from that which he had occupied in his native town. In the former he was from the first the leader of a powerful party, and gradually became the autocratic ruler of Arabia; in the latter he was only the despised preacher of a small congregation. This difference, as was to be expected, appears in the Koran. The Medina pieces, whether entire súras or isolated passages interpolated in Meccan súras, are accordingly pretty broadly distinct, as to their contents, from those issued in Mecca. In the great majority of cases there can be no doubt whatever whether a piece first saw the light in Mecca or in Medina; and, for the most part, the internal evidence is borne out by Moslem tradition. And since the revelations given in Medina frequently take notice of events about which we have pretty accurate information, and whose dates are at least approximately known, we are often in a position to fix their date with, at any rate, considerable certainty; here, again, tradition renders valuable assistance. Even with regard to the Medina passages, however, a great deal remains uncertain, partly because the allusions to historical events and circumstances are generally rather obscure, partly because traditions about the occasion of the revelation of the various pieces are often fluctuating, and often rest on misunderstanding or arbitrary conjecture. But, at all events, it is far easier to arrange in some sort of chronological order the Medina súras than those composed in Mecca. There is, indeed, one tradition which professes to furnish a chronological list of all the súras. But not to mention that it occurs in several divergent

forms, and that it takes no account of the fact that our
present súras are partly composed of pieces of different dates,
it contains so many suspicious or undoubtedly false statements, that it is impossible to attach any great importance
to it. Besides, it is *à priori* unlikely that a contemporary of
Mohammed should have drawn up such a list; and if any
one had made the attempt, he would have found it almost
impossible to obtain reliable information as to the order of
the earlier Meccan súras. We have in this list no genuine
tradition, but rather the lucubrations of an undoubtedly
conscientious Moslem critic, who may have lived about a
century after the emigration.

Among the revelations put forth in Mecca there is a considerable number of (for the most part) short súras, which
strike every attentive reader as being the oldest. They are
in an altogether different strain from many others, and in
their whole composition they show least resemblance to the
Medina pieces. It is no doubt conceivable—as Sprenger
supposes—that Mohammed might have returned at intervals
to his earlier manner; but since this group possesses a
remarkable similarity of style, and since the gradual formation of a different style is on the whole an unmistakable
fact, the assumption has little probability; and we shall
therefore abide by the opinion that these form a distinct
group. At the opposite extreme from them stands another
cluster, showing quite obvious affinities with the style of the
Medina súras, which must therefore be assigned to the later
part of the Prophet's work in Mecca. Between these two
groups stand a number of other Meccan súras, which in
every respect mark the transition from the first period to
the third. It need hardly be said that the three periods—
which were first distinguished by Professor Weil—are not
separated by sharp lines of division. With regard to some
súras, it may be doubtful whether they ought to be reckoned

amongst the middle group, or with one or other of the
extremes. And it is altogether impossible, within these
groups, to establish even a probable chronological arrangement of the individual revelations. In default of clear
allusions to well-known events, or events whose date can be
determined, we might indeed endeavour to trace the psycho-
logical development of the Prophet by means of the Koran,
and arrange its parts accordingly. But in such an undertaking one is always apt to take subjective assumptions or
mere fancies for established data. Good traditions about
the origin of the Meccan revelations are not very numerous.
In fact, the whole history of Mohammed previous to his
emigration is so imperfectly related that we are not even
sure in what year he appeared as a prophet. Probably it
was in A.D. 610; it may have been somewhat earlier, but
scarcely later. If, as one tradition says, xxx. 1 sq. (" The
Romans are overcome in the nearest neighbouring land ")
refers to the defeat of the Byzantines by the Persians, not
far from Damascus, about the spring of 614, it would follow
that the third group, to which this passage belongs, covers
the greater part of the Meccan period. And it is not in
itself unlikely that the passionate vehemence which characterises the first group was of short duration. Nor is the
assumption contradicted by the tolerably well - attested,
though far from incontestable statement, that when Omar
was converted (A.D. 615 or 616), xx., which belongs to the
second group, already existed in writing. But the reference
of xxx. 1 sq. to this particular battle is by no means so
certain that positive conclusions can be drawn from it. It
is the same with other allusions in the Meccan súras to
occurrences whose chronology can be partially ascertained.
It is better, therefore, to rest satisfied with a merely relative
determination of the order of even the three great clusters of
Meccan revelations.

In the pieces of the first period the convulsive excitement of the Prophet often expresses itself with the utmost vehemence. He is so carried away by his emotion that he cannot choose his words; they seem rather to burst from him. Many of these pieces remind us of the oracles of the old heathen soothsayers, whose style is known to us from imitations, although we have perhaps not a single genuine specimen. Like those other oracles, the súras of this period, which are never very long, are composed of short sentences with tolerably pure but rapidly-changing rhymes. The oaths, too, with which many of them begin, were largely used by the soothsayers. Some of these oaths are very uncouth and hard to understand, some of them perhaps were not meant to be understood, for indeed all sorts of strange things are met with in these chapters. Here and there Mohammed speaks of visions, and appears even to see angels before him in bodily form. There are some intensely vivid descriptions of the resurrection and the last day, which must have exercised a demonic power over men who were quite unfamiliar with such pictures. Other pieces paint in glowing colours the joys of heaven and the pains of hell. However, the súras of this period are not all so wild as these; and those which are conceived in a calmer mood appear to be the oldest. Yet, one must repeat, it is exceedingly difficult to make out any strict chronological sequence. For instance, it is by no means certain whether the beginning of xcvi. is really what a widely-circulated tradition calls it, the oldest part of the whole Koran. That tradition goes back to the Prophet's favourite wife Aïsha; but as she was not born at the time when the revelation is said to have been made, it can only contain at the best what Mohammed told her years afterwards, from his own not very clear recollection, with or without fictitious additions. Aïsha, moreover, is by no means very trustworthy. And, besides, there are other pieces mentioned by others as the oldest. In any case xcvi. 1 sqq. is certainly very early. According to the traditional view, which appears to be correct, it treats of a vision in which the Prophet receives an injunction to recite a revelation conveyed to him by the angel. It is interesting to observe that here already two things are brought forward as proofs of the omnipotence and care of God: one is the creation of man out of a seminal drop—an idea to which Mohammed often recurs; the other is the then recently introduced art of writing, which the Prophet instinctively seizes on as a means of propagating his doctrines. It was only after Mohammed encountered obstinate resistance that the tone of the revelations became thoroughly passionate. In such cases he was not slow to utter terrible threats against those who ridiculed the preaching of the unity of God, of the resurrection, and of the judgment. His own uncle, Abú Lahab, had somewhat brusquely repelled him, and in a brief special súra (cxi.) he and his wife are consigned to hell. The súras of this period form almost exclusively the concluding portions of the present text. One is disposed to assume, however, that they were at one time more numerous, and that many of them were lost at an early period.

Since Mohammed's strength lay in his enthusiastic and fiery imagination rather than in the wealth of ideas and clearness of abstract thought on which exact reasoning depends, it follows that the older súras, in which the former qualities have free scope, must be more attractive to us than the later. In the súras of the second period the imaginative glow perceptibly diminishes; there is still fire and animation, but the tone becomes gradually more prosaic. As the feverish restlessness subsides, the periods are drawn out, and the revelations as a whole become longer. The truth of the new doctrine is proved by accumulated instances of God's working in nature and in history; the objections of opponents, whether advanced in good faith or in jest, are controverted by arguments; but the demonstration is often confused or even weak. The histories of the earlier prophets, which had occasionally been briefly touched on in the first period, are now related, sometimes at great length. On the whole, the charm of the style is passing away.

There is one piece of the Koran, belonging to the beginning of this period, if not to the close of the former, which claims particular notice. This is i., the Lord's Prayer of the Moslems, and beyond dispute the gem of the Koran. The words of this súra, which is known as *al-fátiha* (" the opening one "), are as follows :—

" (1) In the name of God, the compassionate Compassioner. (2) Praise be [literally " is "] to God, the Lord of the worlds, (3) the compassionate Compassioner, (4) the Sovereign of the day of judgment. (5) Thee do we worship, and of Thee do we beg assistance. (6) Direct us in the right way; (7) in the way of those to whom Thou hast been gracious, on whom there is no wrath, and who go not astray."

The thoughts are so simple as to need no explanation; and yet the prayer is full of meaning. It is true that there is not a single original idea of Mohammed's in it. Several words and turns of expression are borrowed directly from the Jews, in particular the designation of God as the " Compassioner," *Rahmán*. This is simply the Jewish *Rahmáná*, which was a favourite name for God in the Talmudic period. Mohammed seems for a while to have entertained the thought of adopting *al-Rahmán* as a proper name of God, in place of *Alláh*, which was already used by the heathens.[1] This purpose he ultimately relinquished, but it is just in

[1] Since in Arabic also the root *RHM* signifies " to have pity," the Arabs must have at once perceived the force of the new name.

the súras of the second period that the use of *Rahmán* is specially frequent. It was probably in the first súra also that Mohammed first introduced the formula, " In the name of God," etc. It is to be regretted that this prayer must lose its effect through too frequent use, for every Moslem who says his five prayers regularly—as the most of them do—repeats it not less than twenty times a day.

The súras of the third Meccan period, which form a pretty large part of our present Koran, are almost entirely prosaic. Some of the revelations are of considerable extent, and the single verses also are much longer than in the older súras. Only now and then a gleam of poetic power flashes out. A sermonising tone predominates. The súras are very edifying for one who is already reconciled to their import, but to us, at least, they do not seem very well fitted to carry conviction to the minds of unbelievers. That impression, however, is not correct, for in reality the demonstrations of these longer Meccan súras appear to have been peculiarly influential for the propagation of Islam. Mohammed's mission was not to Europeans, but to a people who, though quick-witted and receptive, were not accustomed to logical thinking, while they had outgrown their ancient religion.

When we reach the Medina period it becomes, as has been indicated, much easier to understand the revelations in their historical relations, since our knowledge of the history of Mohammed in Medina is tolerable complete. In many cases the historical occasion is perfectly clear, in others we can at least recognise the general situation from which they arose, and thus approximately fix their time. There still remains, however, a remnant, of which we can only say that it belongs to Medina.

The style of this period bears a pretty close resemblance to that of the latest Meccan period. It is for the most part pure prose, enriched by occasional rhetorical embellish-

ments. Yet even here there are many bright and impressive
passages, especially in those sections which may be regarded
as proclamations to the army of the faithful.   For the
Moslems, Mohammed has many different messages.   At one
time it is a summons to do battle for the faith; at another,
a series of reflections on recently experienced success or
misfortune, or a rebuke for their weak faith; or an exhorta-
tion to virtue, and so on.   He often addresses himself to
the "doubters," some of whom vacillate between faith and
unbelief, others make a pretence of faith, while others
scarcely take the trouble even to do that.   They are no
consolidated party, but to Mohammed they are all equally
vexatious, because, as soon as danger has to be encountered,
or a contribution is levied, they all alike fall away.   There
are frequent outbursts, ever increasing in bitterness, against
the Jews, who were very numerous in Medina and its neighbourhood when Mohammed arrived.   He has much less to
say against the Christians, with whom he never came closely
in contact; and as for the idolaters, there was little occasion
in Medina to have many words with them.   A part of the
Medina pieces consists of formal laws belonging to the
ceremonial, civil, and criminal codes; or directions about
certain temporary complications.   The most objectionable
parts of the whole Koran are those which treat of Mohammed's relations with women.   The laws and regulations
were generally very concise revelations, but most of them
have been amalgamated with other pieces of similar or
dissimilar import, and are now found in very long súras.

   Such is an imperfect sketch of the composition and the
internal history of the Koran, but it is probably sufficient
to show that the book is a very heterogeneous collection.
If only those passages had been preserved which had a
permanent value for the theology, the ethics, or the jurisprudence of the Moslems, a few fragments would have been

amply sufficient. Fortunately for knowledge, respect for the sacredness of the letter has led to the collection of all the revelations that could possibly be collected,—the "abrogating" along with the "abrogated," passages referring to passing circumstances as well as those of lasting importance. Every one who takes up the book in the proper religious frame of mind, like most of the Moslems, reads pieces directed against long-obsolete absurd customs of Mecca just as devoutly as the weightiest moral precepts, — perhaps even more devoutly, because he does not understand them so well.

At the head of twenty-nine of the súras stand certain initial letters, from which no clear sense can be obtained. Thus, before ii. iii. xxxi. xxxii. we find *ALM* (*Alif Lám Mím*), before xl.–xlvi. *HM* (*Há Mím*). At one time I suggested that these initials did not belong to Mohammed's text, but might be the monograms of possessors of codices, which, through negligence on the part of the editors, were incorporated in the final form of the Koran; but I now deem it more probable that they are to be traced to the Prophet himself, as Sprenger and Loth suppose. One cannot indeed admit the truth of Loth's statement, that in the proper opening words of these súras we may generally find an allusion to the accompanying initials; but it can scarcely be accidental that the first verse of the great majority of them (in iii. it is the second verse) contains the word "book," "revelation," or some equivalent. They usually begin with : "This is the book," or "Revelation ('down sending') of the book," or something similar. Of súras which commence in this way only a few (xviii. xxiv. xxv. xxxix.) want the initials, while only xxix. and xxx. have the initials, and begin differently. These few exceptions may easily have proceeded from ancient corruptions; at all events, they cannot neutralise the evidence of the greater number.

Mohammed seems to have meant these letters for a mystic reference to the archetypal text in heaven. To a man who regarded the art of writing, of which at the best he had but a slight knowledge, as something supernatural, and who lived amongst illiterate people, an A B C may well have seemed more significant than to us who have been initiated into the mysteries of this art from our childhood. The Prophet himself can hardly have attached any particular meaning to these symbols: they served their purpose if they conveyed an impression of solemnity and enigmatical obscurity. In fact, the Koran admits that it contains many things which neither can be, nor were intended to be, understood (iii. 5). To regard these letters as ciphers is a precarious hypothesis, for the simple reason that cryptography is not to be looked for in the very infancy of Arabic writing. If they are actually ciphers, the multiplicity of possible explanations at once precludes the hope of a plausible interpretation. None of the efforts in this direction, whether by Moslem scholars or by Europeans, have led to convincing results. This remark applies even to the ingenious conjecture of Sprenger, that the letters *KHY'Ṣ* (*Káf Hé Yé 'Ain Sád*) before xix. (which treats of John and Jesus, and, according to tradition, was sent to the Christian king of Abyssinia) stand for *Jesus Nazarenus Rex Judæorum.* Sprenger arrives at this explanation by a very artificial method; and besides, Mohammed was not so simple as the Moslem traditionalists, who imagined that the Abyssinians could read a piece of the Arabic Koran. It need hardly be said that the Moslems have from of old applied themselves with great assiduity to the decipherment of these initials, and have sometimes found the deepest mysteries in them. Generally, however, they are content with the prudent conclusion, that God alone knows the meaning of these letters.

When Mohammed died, the separate pieces of the Koran, notwithstanding their theoretical sacredness, existed only in scattered copies; they were consequently in great danger of being partially or entirely destroyed. Many Moslems knew large portions by heart, but certainly no one knew the whole; and a merely oral propagation would have left the door open to all kinds of deliberate and inadvertent alterations. Mohammed himself had never thought of an authentic collection of his revelations; he was usually concerned only with the object of the moment, and the idea that the revelations would be destroyed unless he made provision for their safe preservation, did not enter his mind. A man destitute of literary culture has some difficulty in anticipating the fate of intellectual products. But now, after the death of the Prophet, most of the Arabs revolted against his successor, and had to be reduced to submission by force. Especially sanguinary was the contest against the prophet Maslama, an imitator of Mohammed, commonly known by the derisive diminutive Mosailima (*i.e.* "Little Maslama"). At that time (A.D. 633) many of the most devoted Moslems fell, the very men who knew most Koran pieces by heart. Omar then began to fear that the Koran might be entirely forgotten, and he induced the Caliph Abú Bekr to undertake the collection of all its parts. The Caliph laid the duty on Zaid, the son of Thábit, a native of Medina, then about twenty-two years of age, who had often acted as amanuensis to the Prophet, in whose service he is even said to have learned the Jewish letters. The account of this collection of the Koran has reached us in several substantially identical forms, and goes back to Zaid himself. According to it, he collected the revelations from copies written on flat stones, pieces of leather, ribs of palm-leaves (not palm-leaves themselves), and such-like material, but chiefly "from the breasts of men," *i.c.* from their memory. From these he wrote a

4

fair copy, which he gave to Abú Bekr, from whom it came
to his successor Omar, who again bequeathed it to his
daughter Hafsa, one of the widows of the Prophet. This
redaction, commonly called *al-sohof* (" the leaves "), had from
the first no canonical authority; and its internal arrangement can only be conjectured.

The Moslems were as far as ever from possessing a uniform
text of the Koran. The bravest of their warriors sometimes
knew deplorably little about it; distinction on *that* field
they cheerfully accorded to pious men like Ibn Mas'úd. It
was inevitable, however, that discrepancies should emerge
between the texts of professed scholars, and as these men in
their several localities were authorities on the reading of the
Koran, quarrels began to break out between the levies from
different districts about the true form of the sacred book.
During a campaign in A.H. 30 (A.D. 650–1), Hodhaifa, the
victor in the great and decisive battle of Neháwand—which
was to the empire of the Sásánians what Gaugamela was
to that of the Achæmenidæ—perceived that such disputes
might become dangerous, and therefore urged on the Caliph
Othmán the necessity for a universally binding text. The
matter was entrusted to Zaid, who had made the former
collection, with three leading Koraishites. These brought
together as many copies as they could lay their hands on,
and prepared an edition which was to be canonical for all
Moslems. To prevent any further disputes, they burned
all the other codices except that of Hafsa, which, however,
was soon afterwards destroyed by Marwán, the governor
of Medina. The destruction of the earlier codices was an
irreparable loss to criticism; but, for the essentially political
object of putting an end to controversies by admitting only
one form of the common book of religion and of law, this
measure was necessary.

The result of these labours is in our hands; as to how

they were conducted we have no trustworthy information, tradition being here too much under the influence of dogmatic presuppositions. The critical methods of a modern scientific commission will not be expected of an age when the highest literary education for an Arab consisted in ability to read and write. It now seems to me highly probable that this second redaction took this simple form: Zaid read off from the codex which he had previously written, and his associates, simultaneously or successively, wrote one copy each to his dictation. These, I suppose, were the three copies which, we are informed, were sent to the capitals Damascus, Basra, and Cufa, to be in the first instance standards for the soldiers of the respective provinces. A fourth copy would doubtless be retained at Medina. Be that as it may, it is impossible now to distinguish in the present form of the book what belongs to the first redaction from what is due to the second.

In the arrangement of the separate sections, a classification according to contents was impracticable because of the variety of subjects often dealt with in one súra. A chronological arrangement was out of the question, because the chronology of the older pieces must have been imperfectly known, and because in some cases passages of different dates had been joined together. Indeed, systematic principles of this kind were altogether disregarded at that period. The pieces were accordingly arranged in indiscriminate order, the only rule observed being to place the long súras first and the shorter towards the end, and even that was far from strictly adhered to. The short opening súra is so placed on account of its superiority to the rest, and two magical formulæ are kept for a sort of protection at the end; these are the only special traces of design. The combination of pieces of different origin may proceed partly from the possessors of the codices from which Zaid compiled his first

complete copy, partly from Zaid himself. The individual
súras are separated simply by the superscription, " In the
name of God, the compassionate Compassioner," which is
wanting only in the ninth. The additional headings found
in our texts (the name of the súra, the number of verses,
etc.) were not in the original codices, and form no integral
part of the Koran.

It is said that Othmán directed Zaid and his associates, in
cases of disagreement, to follow the Koraish dialect; but,
though well attested, this account can scarcely be correct.
The extremely primitive writing of those days was quite
incapable of rendering such minute differences as can have
existed between the pronunciation of Mecca and that of
Medina.

Othmán's Koran was not complete. Some passages are
evidently fragmentary; and a few detached pieces are still
extant which were originally parts of the Koran, although
they have been omitted by Zaid. Amongst these are some
which there is no reason to suppose Mohammed desired to
suppress. Zaid may easily have overlooked a few stray
fragments, but that he purposely omitted anything which
he believed to belong to the Koran is very unlikely. It has
been conjectured that in deference to his superiors he kept
out of the book the names of Mohammed's enemies, if they
or their families came afterwards to be respected. But it
must be remembered that it was never Mohammed's practice
to refer explicitly to contemporary persons and affairs in
the Koran. Only a single friend, his adopted son Zaid
(xxxiii. 37), and a single enemy, his uncle Abú Lahab
(cxi.)—and these for very special reasons—are mentioned by
name; and the name of the latter has been left in the
Koran with a fearful curse annexed to it, although his son
had embraced Islam before the death of Mohammed, and
although his descendants belonged to the high nobility. So,

on the other hand, there is no single verse or clause which can be plausibly made out to be an interpolation by Zaid at the instance of Abú Bekr, Omar, or Othmán. Slight clerical errors there may have been, but the Koran of Othmán contains none but genuine elements—though sometimes in very strange order.

It can still be pretty clearly shown in detail that the four codices of Othmán's Koran deviated from one another in points of orthography, in the insertion or omission of a *wa* ("and"), and such - like minutiæ; but these variations nowhere affect the sense. All later manuscripts are derived from these four originals.

At the same time, the other forms of the Koran did not at once become extinct. In particular we have some information about the codex of Obay. If the list which gives the order of its súras is correct, it must have contained substantially the same materials as our text; in that case Obay must have used the original collection of Zaid. The same is true of the codex of Ibn Mas'úd, of which we have also a catalogue. It appears that the principle of putting the longer súras before the shorter was more consistentl carried out by him than by Zaid. He omits i. and the magical formulæ of cxiii. cxiv. Obay, on the other hand, had embodied two additional short prayers, whose authenticity I do not now venture to question, as I formerly did. One can easily understand that differences of opinion may have existed as to whether and how far formularies of this kind belonged to the Koran. Some of the divergent readings of both these texts have been preserved, as well as a considerable number of other ancient variants. Most of them are decidedly inferior to the received readings, but some are quite as good, and a few deserve preference.

The only man who appears to have seriously opposed the general introduction of Othmán's text is Ibn Mas'úd. He

was one of the oldest disciples of the Prophet, and had often
rendered him personal service; but he was a man of con-
tracted views, although he is one of the pillars of Moslem
theology.   His opposition had no effect.   Now when we
consider that at that time there were many Moslems who
had heard the Koran from the mouth of the Prophet, that
other measures of the imbecile Othmán met with the most
vehement resistance on the part of the bigoted champions
of the faith, that these were still further incited against him
by some of his ambitious old comrades, until at last they
murdered him, and finally that in the civil wars after his
death the several parties were glad of any pretext for brand-
ing their opponents as infidels;—when we consider all this,
we must regard it as a strong testimony in favour of
Othmán's Koran that no party—that of Alí not excepted—
repudiated the text formed by Zaid, who was one of the
most devoted adherents of Othmán and his family, and that
even among the Shíites we detect but very few marks of
dissatisfaction with the Caliph's conduct in this matter.

But this redaction is not the close of the textual history
of the Koran.   The ancient Arabic alphabet was very
imperfect; it not only wanted marks for the short, and in
part even for the long vowels, but it often expressed several
consonants by the same sign, the forms of different letters,
formerly clearly distinct, having become by degrees identical.
So, for example, there was but one character to express B, T,
Th, and in the beginning and in the middle of words N and
Y (I) also.   Though the reader who was perfectly familiar
with the language felt no difficulty, as a rule, in discovering
which pronunciation the writer had in view, yet as there
were many words which admitted of being pronounced in
very different manners, instances were not infrequent in
which the pronunciation was dubious.   This variety of
possible readings was at first very great, and many readers

seem to have actually made it their object to discover pro-
nunciations which were new, provided they were at all
appropriate to the ambiguous text. There was also a dialectic licence in grammatical forms, which had not as yet
been greatly restricted. An effort was made by many to
establish a more refined pronunciation for the Koran than
was usual in common life or in secular literature. The
various schools of "readers" differed very widely from one
another; although for the most part there was no important
divergence as to the sense of words. A few of them
gradually rose to special authority, and the rest disappeared.
Seven readers are generally reckoned chief authorities, but
for practical purposes this number was continually reduced
in process of time; so that at present only two "reading
styles" are in actual use,—the common style of Ḥafṣ and that
of Náfi', which prevails in Africa to the west of Egypt.
There is, however, a very comprehensive massoretic literature in which a number of other styles are indicated. The
invention of vowel-signs, of diacritic points to distinguish
similarly formed consonants, and of other orthographic signs,
soon put a stop to arbitrary conjectures on the part of the
readers. Many zealots objected to the introduction of these
innovations in the sacred text, but theological consistency
had to yield to practical necessity. In accurate codices,
indeed, all such additions, as well as the titles of the súra,
etc., are written in coloured ink, while the black characters
profess to represent exactly the original of Othmán. But
there is probably no copy quite faithful in this respect.

The correct recitation of the Koran is an art difficult
of acquisition to the Arabs themselves. Besides the artificial
pronunciation mentioned above, a semi-musical modulation
has to be observed. In these things also there are great
differences between the various schools.

In European libraries, besides innumerable modern manuscripts of the Koran, there are also codices or fragments of high antiquity, some of them probably dating from the first century of the Flight. For the restoration of the text, however, the works of ancient scholars on its readings and modes of writing are more important than the manuscripts, which, however elegantly they may be written and ornamented, proceed from irresponsible copyists. The original, written by Othmán himself, has indeed been exhibited in various parts of the Mohammedan world. The library of the India Office contains one such manuscript, bearing the subscription: "Written by Othmán the son of Affán." These, of course, are barefaced forgeries, although of very ancient date; so are those which profess to be from the hand of Alí, one of which is preserved in the same library. In recent times the Koran has been often printed and lithographed both in the East and the West.

Shortly after Mohammed's death certain individuals applied themselves to the exposition of the Koran. Much of it was obscure from the beginning, other sections were unintelligible apart from a knowledge of the circumstances of their origin. Unfortunately those who took possession of this field were not very honourable. Ibn Abbás, a cousin of Mohammed's, and the chief source of the traditional exegesis of the Koran, has, on theological and other grounds, given currency to a number of falsehoods; and at least some of his pupils have emulated his example. These earliest expositions dealt more with the sense and connection of whole verses than with the separate words. Afterwards, as the knowledge of the old language declined, and the study of philology arose, more attention began to be paid to the explanation of vocables. A good many fragments of this older theological and philological exegesis have survived from the first two centuries of the Flight, although we have no complete commentary of this period. Most of the expository material will perhaps be found in the very large commentary of the celebrated Tabarí (A.D. 839–923), of which an almost complete copy is in the Viceregal library at Cairo. Another very famous commentary is that of Zamakhsharí (A.D. 1075–1144), edited by Nassau-Lees, Calcutta 1859; but this scholar, with his great insight and still greater subtlety, is too apt to read his own scholastic ideas into the Koran. The favourite commentary of Baidáwí (*ob.* A.D. 1286) is little more than an abridgment of Zamakhsharí's. Thousands of commentaries on the Koran, some of them of prodigious size,[1] have been written by Moslems; and even the number of those still extant in manuscript is by no means small. Although these works all contain much that is useless or false, yet they are invaluable aids to our understanding of the sacred book. An unbiassed European can no doubt see many things at a glance more clearly than a good Moslem who is under the influence of religious prejudice; but we should still be helpless without the exegetical literature of the Mohammedans.

Even the Arab Moslem of the present day can have but a very dim and imperfect understanding of the Koran, unless he has made a special study of its exegesis. For the great advantage, boasted by the holy book itself, of being perspicuous to every one, has in the course of thirteen centuries vanished. Moreover, the general belief is that in the ritual use of the Koran, if the correct recitation is observed, it is immaterial whether the meaning of the words be understood or not.

A great deal remains to be accomplished by European scholarship for the correct interpretation of the Koran. We want, for example, an exhaustive classification and discussion of all the Jewish elements in the Koran; a praiseworthy beginning has already been made in Geiger's

[1] See below, p. 206, on the commentary of Khalaf.

youthful essay, *Was hat Mahomet aus dem Judenthum aufgenommen?* We want especially a thorough commentary, executed with the methods and resources of modern science. No European language, it would seem, can even boast of a translation which completely satisfies modern requirements. The best are in English, where we have the extremely paraphrastic, but for its time admirable translation of Sale (repeatedly printed), that of Rodwell (1861), which seeks to give the pieces in chronological order, and that of Palmer (1880), who wisely follows the traditional arrangements. The introduction which accompanies Palmer's translation is not in all respects abreast of the most recent scholarship. Considerable extracts from the Koran are well translated in E. W. Lane's *Selections from the Kur-án.*

Besides commentaries on the whole Koran, or on special parts and topics, the Moslems possess a whole literature bearing on their sacred book. There are works on the spelling and right pronunciation of the Koran, works on the beauty of its language, on the number of its verses, words, and letters, etc.; nay, there are even works which would nowadays be called "historical and critical introductions." Moreover, the origin of Arabic philology is intimately connected with the recitation and exegesis of the Koran. To exhibit the importance of the sacred book for the whole mental life of the Moslems, would be simply to write the history of that life itself; for there is no department in which its all-pervading, but unfortunately not always salutary, influence has not been felt.

The unbounded reverence of the Moslems for the Koran reaches its climax in the dogma (which appeared at an early date through the influence of the Christian doctrine of the eternal Word of God) that this book, as the divine Word, *i.e.* thought, is immanent in God, and consequently *eternal* and *uncreated.* That dogma has been accepted by almost all

Mohammedans since the beginning of the third century. Some theologians did indeed protest against it with great energy; it was, in fact, too preposterous to declare that a book composed of unstable words and letters, and full of variants, was absolutely divine. But what were the distinctions and sophisms of the theologians for, if they could not remove such contradictions, and convict their opponents of heresy?

The following works may be specially consulted: Weil, *Einleitung in den Korán*, 2nd ed. 1878; Th. Nöldeke, *Geschichte des Qorán's*, Göttingen, 1860; and the Lives of Mohammed by Muir and Sprenger.

III.

ISLAM.[1]

On the 14th of September 629, the emperor Heraclius again set up the true Cross in Jerusalem. He had vanquished the Persians after a desperate struggle, and compelled them to restore this most sacred of relics, which they had carried off on their conquest of the Holy Land. It was a day of triumph for all Christendom, which is still marked in its calendars as the "Feast of the Elevation of the Cross." At the very moment of this striking celebration of the victory of Christendom over unbelievers, we may suppose tidings to have been brought to the emperor, that his Arabian troops beyond Jordan had been attacked by a small band from the interior, and had only with difficulty succeeded in repelling the violent onset. It is not likely that the news can have struck him as implying anything very serious. Nevertheless this was the first assault of the Moslems; it was quickly followed by others, and in a few years Palestine and many other provinces had been for ever torn away from the Roman empire, to which they had for seven centuries belonged, the empire of Persia had been destroyed, and in the native lands of Christianity and Zoroastrianism a new faith and a new people had attained an enduring ascendency. No overturn at once so great and so rapid is recorded in history.

The founder of this new religion, Mohammed, son of Abdallàh, was no martial hero. It was under the pressure of circumstances, and by the necessities of thoughts which

[1] Originally published in *Deutsche Rundschau,* ix. (1883) p. 378 sqq.

carried him much farther than he could possibly have divined, that he became a prince and a conqueror. The hysterical enthusiast, conscious of a vocation to make known the Oneness of God, was forced into a career of battle by the opposition of his kinsfolk and neighbours. The conviction that his light came from God gave him strength and confidence, and raised him above every prejudice and scruple. The character of the new religion was very powerfully influenced by the manly spirit of some of its first confessors and champions; both the good and the bad qualities of the Arabs, among whom it arose, and for whom it was in the first instance promulgated, have stamped their unmistakable impress upon it.

It may be doubted if the original teaching of any other founder of a new religion is known to us so exactly as Mohammed's. For the sacred book of Mohammedanism, the Koran, consists entirely of his own revelations, given in the name of God; and among his spoken utterances which have been handed down by tradition there is, mixed up with a great deal that is spurious, so much of what is genuine, that by its aid we are able at many points to supplement the Koran. And Koran and *Sunna*, that is, "the rule," given by the tradition of the Prophet's words and deeds, have ever been regarded by Mohammedans as the sources of their religion.

In the several heads of Mohammed's doctrine there is practically nothing original. The Arabs of that time had outgrown their crude heathenism, and it was only by force of habit, without real attachment, that, a highly conservative people as they were, they held firmly by the ancient practices. In particular, isolated ideas originating in Christianity had become widely diffused through the agency of wandering bards. Very many Arabs were already Christians. Their Christianity, it is true, sat but loosely on them; for the finest elements of that religion they had no organ. Moreover, there were in Arabia many Jews who here also occasionally, as in Abyssinia, made numerous proselytes; but the rigid and irksome ordinances of Judaism were suited to the nature of the proud and untamed inhabitants of the Arabian desert as little as were the mystical doctrines and the too ideal ethics of Christianity. Mohammed borrowed from both religions, but especially from Judaism, those elements which instinct rather than reflection taught him to be suited to his countrymen. The main lines of his doctrine are a further development of Judaism, only simpler and coarser; speaking generally, it stands much nearer to the religion of the Old Testament than the Christianity of the Church does.

Mohammed's idea of God is essentially that of the Old Testament, only he gives greater prominence to the divine omnipotence and arbitrary sovereignty, and less to the divine holiness. He attributes to God many human features, but these no longer have the naive and poetic charm possessed by so many of the Old Testament anthropomorphisms. Everything is done and determined by God; man must submit himself blindly; whence the religion is called *Islám* (" surrender "), and its professor *Muslim* (" one who surrenders himself "). Mohammed had the strongest antipathy for the doctrines of the Trinity and the divine Sonship of Christ. True, his acquaintance with these dogmas was superficial, and even the clauses of the Creed that referred to them were not exactly known to him; but he rightly felt that it was quite impossible to bring them into harmony with simple genuine Semitic monotheism, and probably it was this consideration alone that hindered him from embracing Christianity.

According to the Koran, God makes known His will through prophets, of whom, in the course of time, He has sent many into the world. From Jesus down to the time of Mohammed, it was the duty of men to follow the former and His gospel; the Jews incurred grave sin by rejecting Him. Jesus was greater than all the prophets before Him; but the final revelation was first made known through Mohammed. The earlier sacred writings taught the same doctrine as the Koran, and bear witness to Mohammed; but they had been falsified by the Jews and the Christians. The laws which God laid down through the prophets are not necessarily in harmony with each other, for God changes His ordinances at will; even in the Koran itself He sometimes cancels commandments which He had previously laid down in that very book. Mohammed is but a frail mortal, only chosen of God. He is subject to sin, and without the gift of miracles bestowed on former prophets. This last limitation, which is clearly expressed in the Koran, was, as was to be expected, very soon explained away by his followers, and numerous miracles are accordingly related of him.

God rewards good and punishes evil deeds; only, He is merciful, and is easily propitiated by repentance. But the punishment of the impenitent wicked will be fearful. The horrors of hell are vividly presented; we can see how grievously the thought of them afflicted the Prophet himself. In accordance with Christian precedent, he conceives of hell as fire. In his description of the heavenly paradise, or "garden," also, Mohammed appropriates representations from the Old and New Testaments, yet depicts its joys according to his own fancy. His picture of the glory of the saints above can be properly understood only when the reader remembers the barrenness of Mohammed's native land and the exceedingly simple manner of life of his countrymen. The bright - eyed maidens who give their society to the righteous in paradise are the innovation of a sensual nature. The crude representations of hell and heaven took powerful hold of the Arab imagination, and

unquestionably contributed much to the diffusion and establishment of Islam. Other eschatological imaginings, about
the resurrection and the last judgment, have an important
rôle in the Koran. All of them attach to older ideas, and
particularly to such as had already been borrowed from the
Persians by Judaism, and partly also by Christianity. Awe
of the judgment day was perhaps the most important cause
of Mohammed's becoming a visionary and a prophet. The
Koran has, of course, much to say of angels and devils.
Alongside of these figure also demons or *jinn*, taken from
Arab popular belief, but connected also with late Jewish
notions. The minor contradictions that naturally occur in
such myths and fancies have caused little difficulty to the
ingenuity of interpreters, and still less to the simple faith of
the masses.

The ethics of Islam are not so strict or earnest as those of
Judaism. Mohammed, it is true, insists on virtuous disposition and action, and is energetic in his denunciations of vice :
he urges honourable dealing, benevolence, placability, and so
forth, and requires men ever to be mindful of God and of
the retribution beyond the grave. But he is no rigorist.
His very crass doctrine of retribution, which governs the
rules of conduct, admits the application of commercial
principles : the consequences of sins can be averted by
certain penances ; under certain circumstances one can rid
oneself of the duty of fulfilling an obligation, and even
perjury can be made up for by good works. In dire
necessity even the faith may be denied in words (contrast
Matt. x. 32, 33) ; against making a free use of this permission, Mohammedans have, it is true, been protected by
their pride and the strength of their conviction. Islam is
a thoroughly practical religion, which does not make it
necessary to explain away too high demands (such as those
of Matt. v. 33–41) by artificial interpretations. The Koran

also has comfort for the persecuted and the suffering; but it is too Arab—or, shall we say, too natural and too manly?— to declare the poor and oppressed to be in themselves happy. The Koran, further, pronounces all earthly things to be indeed vain; yet it takes much account of human wants and desires, and lays down definite regulations about property and goods. If the Prophet had immediately met with recognition in his native town, he might perhaps have founded a contemplative monkish community; but, driven by necessity to become the ruler of a warrior State, he had to follow another course. After some hesitation he finally preached war against unbelievers as such; they have no choice but between acceptance of Islam and extermination. Only to the professors of old religions of revelation, that is to say, in the first instance, to Jews and Christians, does it remain lawful to live on as subjects on payment of tribute. The Moslem's vocation, alike in this and in the future life, is to rule the world.

Islam has no mystical sacraments, although it has a number of external observances. Originally Mohammed himself had attached the greatest value to severe exercises of penance, such as watching and fasting; gradually he relaxed much both to himself and to his followers, but an Oriental religion wholly without mortifications of this kind is quite unthinkable. Accordingly he made fasting in the month of Ramadán obligatory in the sense that throughout the entire month, as long as the sun is above the horizon, both eating and drinking are absolutely forbidden. In Oriental heat this is a severe burden, and one can readily believe that in the month of the fast, towards the end of the day, the majority of the faithful are thinking much more about the enjoyments of the coming night than about God and the hereafter. Still more important than fasting is the *salát*. As with all Oriental Christians a certain number of daily prayers are prescribed to the clergy, and partly also to

5

the laity, so Mohammed again, after some hesitation, finally fixed for all believers that there should be five daily "prayers." This *salát* is essentially different from what we call prayer. It consists in a fixed series of bowings, prostrations, and other attitudes, accompanied by the recitation of certain religious formulæ. Of course the worshipper is not forbidden at other times or in other ways to call upon God in words of his own; but to do so is not the official and obligatory action. Prayer is preceded by an ablution; when water, a commodity of such rarity in Arabia, is wanting, rubbing with sand can be substituted.[1] It is more meritorious to take part in the public *salát* of the community, conducted by a leader (*Imám*), than to discharge the *salát* by oneself. Public attendance ought to be given, in particular, on Friday, which is especially set apart for public worship, but in other respects is regarded as a working day : the Sabbath rest is unknown to Islam. The common prayer and its formalities have done much to give stability to Islam. The multitudes, while doing what was indispensable for the salvation of their souls, became trained to the habit of strictly following a leader. As Von Kremer has pointed out, the mosque was the drill ground for the warlike believers of early Islam.

A noteworthy survival of Arab heathenism is the pilgrimage to Mecca. In Mohammed's native town there was a temple called the Caaba ("the die"), with an object of ancient veneration, "the black stone." This sanctuary had gradually come to be the centre of pilgrimage for the greater part of Arabia. In connection with this a lively trade was developed, which must have been very advantageous to the inhabitants of Mecca, the Koraish. Still more important for these was the circumstance that their whole territory

---

[1] This substitution was also known among the Jews. From them also were borrowed certain mitigations of the task in time of travel or circumstances of danger.

was held to be holy and inviolable, and that they had the most favourable opportunities for entering into friendly relations with the various Bedouin tribes. They were thus able to maintain a caravan traffic with the old lands of civilisation beyond the desert and its predatory nomads. In this way they not only became prosperous, but also gained a great intellectual superiority over the other Arabs. As a man of Koraish, Mohammed himself had grown up in pious reverence for the Caaba and the black stone. Properly speaking, indeed, this reverence was at variance with the principles of his religion; but he managed to adjust matters by his theory that these holy things had been established by Abraham, and only abused by the heathen. Possibly in this view he was but following some Meccan predecessor whom Jews or Christians had told about Abraham and Ishmael. The heathen of Mecca, of course, knew nothing about these or any other characters of the Old Testament. That the retention of this sanctuary on Mohammed's part was due less to calculation than to deeply-rooted religious habit, seems to be shown by this, among other things, that between his emigration and the capture of Mecca, he frequently expressed his sorrow at being excluded from free participation in the ceremonies there. When at last he made his entry as a conqueror, he did away with all the open signs of idolatry, and in his last Pilgrimage, shortly before his death, he finally fixed the observances—some of them very peculiar—to be followed. Everything heathenish was to disappear; or, if various things of that nature remained, they were uncomprehended, and therefore inoffensive. Yet one rock of offence was unremoved—the veneration of the old fetish—the black stone, a veneration to which some consistent Moslems could only reluctantly bring themselves, and which in later times is occasionally even scoffed at by less steadfast believers. In strictness it is the duty of every

Moslem to take part in the yearly pilgrimage as often as he can; but it is not contrary to the intention of Mohammed (who was always ready to take account of practical difficulties), if the proviso "as he can" is strongly accentuated in practice, and thus comparatively few join in the expedition from the more distant lands of Mohammedanism. With all this the pilgrimage has been a chief pillar of Islam. In Mecca the most pious Moslems still meet from year to year out of regions so remote as Turkestan, British and Dutch India, the Turkish dominions, Morocco, and Nigritia, and exchange ideas and prejudices; a custom which naturally helps to maintain the unity of the faith. What is of particular importance is that many of the most zealous and learned pilgrims stay permanently in Mecca, and from this centre labour to promote the pure faith, and hostility against all idolaters (Europeans in particular).

Another relic of rude heathenism handed down from hoary antiquity is circumcision. It is not specially enjoined in the Koran, but is taken for granted as being the custom with all Arabs. It is not, however, theoretically at least, an integral part of religion, as it is in Judaism.

Like the Jews, Mohammed puts a high value upon alms. Gradually, however, he changed the freewill offering of love into a formal and somewhat heavy tax, out of which not only were the poor supported, but also the expenses of government were met.

Mohammed's laws relating to food are not nearly so complicated as those of the Jews. The animals of which the Moslem, whether by Mohammed's injunction or by some later rule, may not eat are mostly such as men are naturally averse to (*e.g.* carnivora). Only the pig and the dog are wholly unclean. Moreover, it is lawful to eat only of such animals as have been duly slaughtered with the formula: " In the name of God, the compassionate Compassioner." The Moslem, like

the Jew, and, strictly speaking, the Christian also (Acts xv.
20, 29, xxi. 25), is enjoined to abstain from blood. But, in
danger of death by starvation, he is permitted the use of
any food. Wine is interdicted; and under this name the
legislature meant to include all intoxicating drinks. No
impartial observer will deny that this regulation, much as it
has been broken, has proved a real blessing to all the lands
of Islam. It is not certain whether the prohibition of a
favourite Arab game of chance (*meisir*), in which pointless
arrows were used as lots, is intended to include all forms
of gambling; perhaps Mohammed had in view only the
heathenish practices, or the wastefulness, that used to be
associated with the *meisir*.

On the whole the ritual commands and prohibitions of
Islam do not bear with excessive hardness on the life of
the Oriental, which in any case moves somewhat monoton-
ously in fixed forms. Of the anxious scrupulosity with which
Judaism discusses "clean" and "unclean," "lawful" and
"unlawful," there are but few traces, even in the writings of
the later theologians of Islam, not to speak of Mohammed
himself, or the life of his followers until now.

Religion and the law of the State are not separated in
Islam. Here, accordingly, properly speaking, would be the
place for considering the whole system of civil and criminal
law which Mohammed gave in the Koran or in his spoken
utterances. In his decisions, which were usually occasioned
by some particular case definitely before him at the moment,
he follows partly Arabian partly Jewish custom, but very
often also the promptings of his own mind. Completely to
abolish blood revenge would have been impossible, and probably was never in his thoughts; he only bound it to the
observance of certain forms. It is not the executive, but the
nearest relative of the slain that decides whether the mur-
derer shall die, or whether he shall buy himself off.

The anomalies that can result when an individual man essays permanently to fix the order of Church and State according to his own discretion on the spur of the moment, are exemplified with singular clearness in the Moslem calendar. The Arabs, like the majority of ancient peoples, had a year of twelve true (lunar) months; and this, as often as seemed to be required, they brought roughly into accordance with the solar year by the intercalation of a thirteenth month. The intercalation was not very skilful, it is true; still any trifling derangements of the calendar which may have resulted were not such as could produce any practical inconveniences in the simple relations of life in those days. But Mohammed, who objected either to the inequality of the year, now of twelve now of thirteen months, or to the connection that subsisted between this arrangement of the calendar and the heathen system, shortly before his death unfortunately took it into his head to ordain that Moslems should have a movable lunar year of twelve lunar months, without any intercalations whatever. Every Mohammedan year is thus some ten days shorter than the solar year which governs the course of nature; so that the Mohammedan festivals move in succession through all the seasons.[1] The husbandman must accordingly everywhere provide himself with a second (Christian or Persian) calendar, based upon the solar year, in addition to the ecclesiastical one. A Mohammedan at thirty-three is no older than a Christian at thirty-two. The conversion of Mohammedan into Julian or (what is worse) Gregorian dates, is for the student who has not the requisite tables at hand a very laborious task.

The position of women was left by Mohammed essentially where it had been among the Arabs. He limited polygamy

---

[1] One can see how hard is the precept of fasting for the Tartars in Kasan when Ramadán falls in summer with a day of eighteen hours, as contrasted with its lightness when it falls at the time of the winter solstice.

somewhat, and made the separation of women from men rather more strict. But Islam changed for the worse the lot of women in those countries where polygamy had already disappeared, and divorce was not so easy or so common as among the Arabs. That the husband can dismiss the wife at any time, a moment of ill-temper thus very often resulting in a divorce, is, moreover, a far worse evil for Moslem society than its polygamy (which in practice is not very extensive), or the permission it gives to take female slaves as concubines. The Bedouins, who then, as they still do, showed the most chivalrous respect for a defenceless woman, nevertheless placed the weaker sex so low that they had no scruple in burying new-born girls alive. This barbarity, which perhaps never occurred in the more prosperous towns, was opposed by Mohammed at the very outset of his career, and he afterwards completely suppressed it. The Arabs, further, in their wars were accustomed to carry off the wives and children of their enemies as prisoners or slaves; between Moslems this totally ceased. On the other hand, by giving up the holy month's "truce of God," Mohammed inflicted a serious injury on his country. His wish was to put an end to all wars among his followers, but in this he was least successful of all in Arabia, where to this day the feuds never cease from year's end to year's end.

The thought of abolishing slavery never so much as occurred to Mohammed any more that it did to the apostles; but he declared manumission of slaves to be a meritorious deed, and he gave to slaves a certain security in the eye of the law.

Islam in its original form as a whole ranks far below primitive Christianity. In many respects it is not to be compared even with such Christianity as prevailed, and still prevails, in the East; but in other points, again, the new faith, simple, robust, in the vigour of its youth, far surpassed the religion of the Syrian and Egyptian Christians,

which was in a stagnating condition, and steadily sinking
lower and lower into barbarism. Above all things, Islam
gave, and gives, to those who profess it a feeling of confidence
such as is imparted by hardly any other faith. The Moslem
is proud of being a Moslem; he is convinced that he is
preferred by God before all other men, whom accordingly
he despises as fuel appointed for hell-fire. The Christian is
bidden enter into his closet to pray; the Moslem takes his
stand, and especially when unbelievers are near, in as conspicuous a place as possible for the performance of his
ceremonies of prayer. His heart has little part in these,
but he nevertheless feels himself raised by them, and equally
so whether he rightly understands the Arabic formulæ he
repeats or not. Islam is not very well fitted to produce
purity and delicacy of feeling; we shall be justified if we
assume that during the first centuries of its existence many
a deep and finely-touched spirit had to pass through severe
inward struggles because his religious needs were not satisfied
by it. But all such struggles fully fought themselves out
long ago, and deep peace now fills every Moslem's heart.
All those who make faith and assurance of salvation the
chief heads of religion, ought to work for Islam. A religion
amongst the followers of which suicide is almost absolutely
unknown, has surely some claim on our respect.

After Mohammed's death (8th June 632) the most prominent of his companions united to elect as his successor
Abú Bekr, who had been his most trusted friend. At first,
indeed, it had cost some trouble to get the Medinites, the
old "helpers" of Mohammed, off the idea that one of themselves ought to become the leader. But no attention was
paid to the sulking of Alí, whose wife, Fatima, was the only
surviving child of his cousin Mohammed. There was no
doubt that the choice of Abú Bekr was what the Prophet
himself would have desired. But hardly had the Arabs

heard of Mohammed's death when they rebelled *en masse*.
Many renounced Islam entirely; many attached themselves
to new prophets who arose here and there after the pattern
of the Prophet of Mecca; others were willing to retain
Moslem prayer indeed, but not to pay taxes; in a word,
Mohammed's whole work was brought into question. Then
it was that the strength of Islam, and of a firm will, was
shown. Abú Bekr, assured as he was in his own faith,
scorned, even in the hour of most pressing need, to make
any concession whatever to the insurgents; he insisted on
absolute submission to the commands of Islam. The insurrections, which were unconnected with each other, were
for the most part easily quelled by the Moslems, led as they
were by a single will; but in some instances torrents of
blood had first to be shed. The military merit of these
deeds belongs chiefly to Khálid, " the sword of God," a man
of Koraish, like almost all the prominent warriors and
statesmen of that time, the same who nine years before had
turned the battle in favour of the unbelieving Meccans
against Mohammed at Mount Ohod.

As soon as all Arabia had been again brought into subjection, the great wars of conquest began. It was certainly
good policy to turn the recently subdued tribes of the
wilderness towards an external aim in which they might
at once satisfy their lust for booty on a grand scale, maintain their warlike feeling, and strengthen themselves in
their attachment to the new faith. But I do not believe
those undertakings to have been mainly the result of cool
political calculation. Mohammed himself had already sent
expeditions across the Roman frontier, and thereby had
pointed out the way to his successors. To follow in his
footsteps was in accordance with the innermost being of
the youthful Islam, already grown great amid the tumult
arms. The Bedouins knew uncommonly little Koran, but

on such children of nature it is success that makes the deepest impression. That faith which had subdued themselves, and which was now leading them on to victory and plunder, must be true; very soon there was no one to doubt this. Though the nomads among the Arabs have naturally few religious needs, they yet possess as the purest of all Semites a deeply - seated religious disposition; and this simple religion, which corresponded to their inclinations and flattered their self-esteem, soon took entire possession of them. Under the sagacious, clear-headed, and strong-handed Omar (634–644), the fresh force of the new faith, and the warlike disposition of the Arab people, now united for the first time, and led by great generals, speedily achieved successes against the Romans and the Persians of which Mohammed had never so much as dreamed. This astonishing overturn is, when all has been said, not easy of explanation. It is indeed true that both empires were in a state of decay. Both were at the moment terribly weakened by the wars they had waged with each other during the first three decades of the century. The Persian empire, which had finally been vanquished after long years of victory, had, moreover, been shaken both before and after the conclusion of the peace by bloody struggles about the succession to the throne. On the other hand, both Byzantium and Persia had at their command genuine soldiers regularly armed and disciplined. The traditions of Roman warfare were not yet entirely lost, and the Persians still possessed their dreaded cuirassiers, before whom, in better times, even the armies of Rome had often fled. The reduction of the fortified towns must in any case have been at least as severe a task to the Arabs as it was to the Goths and Huns, who were by nature much more warlike peoples. Moreover, Persia, when the chief attack upon its territory was made, happened to have come once more under the rule of a firm hand. Its king,

indeed, Yezdegerd III., was a boy; but the royal power and
the command of the army were held by a man of energy
and bravery—Rustem, the head of one of the first princely
houses of the empire. Yet these wretchedly armed Arabs,
fighting, not in regularly organised military divisions, but by
families and clans, and under leaders who never before had
faced disciplined troops, after long struggle overcame Rustem
and his mighty hosts (636); soon afterwards took the fortified capital, Ctesiphon (637); and, a few years later, by the
decisive battle of Neháwend (640, 641, or 642), brought the
empire itself to the ground. How was such a thing possible ?
The Arabs' own explanation indeed was very simple : " God
took away the courage of the uncircumcised ;" " God smote
the Persians ;" " God slew Rustem." In such words, so
thoroughly like those of the Old Testament, we can only
recognise how great a force lies in the rudest religious conviction. Almost more marvellous are the conquests they
gained on Roman territory. The emperor Heraclius was
certainly the greatest man who had held the empire since
Constantine and Julian. He was an astute diplomatist, a
very competent general, and, as a soldier, bold even to
rashness. How could it come about that he of all men
was compelled to yield up to the sons of the desert the
territories he had wrested back from the Persians ? We
certainly are aware of one or two circumstances which made
their conquests easier to the Arabs. Most of the inhabitants
of Syria, and almost all the Egyptians, were Monophysite
heretics, and as such had experienced great oppression at
the hands of the Orthodox Byzantines; they accordingly
aided and abetted the Arabs as occasion offered, especially
as they might promise themselves some relief of the burden
of taxation through the latter. The Syrian Nestorians also,
who formed the majority of the inhabitants of the richest
lands of the Persian empire (those on the Tigris and on the

lower Euphrates), we may believe to have been more favourably inclined to the Arabs than to the Persians. But in connection with conquests like these, much weight is hardly to be assigned to the sympathies and antipathies of unwarlike peasants and townsmen. More important, perhaps, is the circumstance that the numerous Arab tribes, which had been subject to the Roman and Persian rule, although for the most part nominally Christian, appear to have gone over to the Moslems almost unanimously soon after the first victories. It would be possible to multiply explanations still further, yet the phenomenon continues mysterious as before. Rhetorical expressions about the decaying condition of both empires, and the youthful energy of the Moslems, are unsatisfying to the inquirer who keeps the concrete facts before him.

Omar, who became Mohammed's successor or "substitute" (*Khalífa*) after Abú Bekr's brief rule of two years, and who was the first to assume the title of "Commander of the Faithful" (*Emír almúminín*), organised a complete military-religious commonwealth. The Arabs, the people of God, became a nation of warriors and rulers. The precepts of the religion were strictly maintained; the Caliph lived as simply as the meanest of his subjects. But the enormous booty and the taxes levied on the vanquished supplied the means of giving adequate pay to every Arab. This pay, the amount of which was graduated according to a definite scale, and in which women and children also participated, was raised as the revenues increased. For the leading principle was that everything won from enemies and subjects belonged to Moslems collectively, and therefore all that remained over after payment of common expenses had to be divided. But in the conquered territories the Arabs were not allowed to hold landed property; they were only to set up camps. It was bad for Islam, but good for the world, that this military communist constitution did not last long. It was contrary to human nature; aƞd, besides, the receipts did not permanently continue to come in on such a scale as afforded adequate pay to every one. The principle also, that new converts of foreign nationality must be placed on a level with the Arabs, was not yet capable of being fully carried out; the aristocratic feeling of the Arabs long stood out against making a reality of that equality among its professors which Islam demanded.

Under Omar's successor, Othmán (644–656), the field of conquest was still further and greatly extended; but the purely warlike character of the State was nevertheless already somewhat abated, permission being now given to Arabs to hold landed property in the newly-acquired regions. The landed proprietor and the peasant are naturally less inclined for expeditions of distant conquest than is the mere soldier. The principle of at least relative equality in profit-sharing was violently broken through by the bestowal of crown domains on persons of prominence. The conversion of the religious into a secular State followed rapidly and inevitably. The secular State, it is true, still remained in relations of the closest kind with religion,—much closer than those of the so-called Christian State anywhere in modern times,—but the attempts to set up the empire of Islam again upon a purely religious basis ended in failure.

In the supreme command there was no hereditary succession. Abú Bekr was, as we have seen, chosen to be Caliph by the most influential Meccan Companions of the Prophet. Abú Bekr himself had finally nominated as his successor Omar, his right-hand man, and the second most intimate friend and counsellor of the Prophet. Omar, himself the ideal of a Moslem ruler, clearly thought none of his own companions quite worthy of the command. He arranged accordingly that after his death five of the most distinguished of the old friends of Mohammed should decide as to who among themselves ought to succeed. After long deliberation they united upon Othmán. Now Othmán had been, it is true, one of the very first to acknowledge Mohammed as a prophet, and he had successively married two daughters of the latter; but he belonged to the Omayyads, one of the most prominent families of pre-Islamite Mecca, the head of which, Abú Sufyán, had for years been leader in the struggle against Mohammed and the Medinites. Preference for kinsmen is deeply seated in the blood of every genuine Arab, and the Prophet himself was not free from it. Omar, who in many respects was a more consistent exponent of Islam than Mohammed, never laid himself open to the smallest charge of nepotism, but Othmán was a weak man; he showed exorbitant favour to his relatives, and in a short time a number of the most important and profitable posts were in the hands of Omayyads—able men for the most part, but of an intensely worldly disposition. The good Othmán was not himself conscious of anything wrong in this; but many of his subjects saw the matter in another light. The righteous indignation of some strict Moslems, the tumultuary disposition of the mass of the people, and very specially also the instigations of three of the five men who had formed the electoral college after Omar's death,—Alí, Talha, and Zubair, —as also of Aïsha, daughter of Abú Bekr, and the intriguing favourite of the Prophet, resulted in a rebellion, in which the grey-headed Othmán was put to death (17th June 656). This deed of violence was an evil precedent for many subsequent scenes of terror, the beginning of bloody civil wars, and eventual schisms. The slayers of Othmán called Alí to the caliphate; Talha and Zubair also acknowledged him, but soon broke their word, and united with Aïsha against him. Alí's bravery was soon a match for these enemies; but already another and more formidable opponent had

arisen in the person of the astute Moáwiya, son of the Abú
Sufyán mentioned above, who had long been governor of
Syria, and held sway there like a prince. The struggle was
carried on with animosity for years. Moáwiya came forward
as avenger of his kinsman Othmán. As the powerful head
of the family, he was, according to old Arab ideas, well
entitled, and indeed bound to do this, and Islam had not
abolished this view of his duty. But, as successor of Mohammed, the son of the man who had led the heathen
against him at Ohod and in the battle of the Fosse, could,
of course, set up no other claim than the unconditional
attachment of his troops and the superiority of his own
genius. Alí also was without hereditary right, and the proclamation by Othmán's slayers was a very doubtful title in
law; but as kinsman, favourite, pupil, son-in-law of Mohammed, he might well seem better suited to represent the
interests of religion than Moáwiya, who also, however,
appears to have been an acceptable person with the Prophet
in his declining years. The Moslems who were faithful to
their convictions accordingly went over for the most part to
Alí's side, especially the Medinites, who (or their fathers)
had once fought Mohammed's battles, but were now being
more and more thrust into the background by the lukewarm
Moslems of Mecca. In the heat of controversy the view for
the first time germinated that Alí had a divine right to the
supreme power, and that even Abú Bekr, Omar, and Othmán
had been usurpers. Those who hold this view are the
Shíites proper, the partisans (*shía*) of Alí. The great majority of the Moslems, on the other hand, recognise, indeed,
Alí's right as against Moáwiya, but also hold the first three
caliphs for legitimate. And, indeed, many good Moslems
stood by Moáwiya in this struggle, and by other sovereigns
of his family thereafter, though since the fall of the Omayyads few Moslems would justify Moáwiya's appearance

against Alí. In the disorders of this time there now arose
also a new extreme radical party, who denied the right of all
claimants, and awarded the command to "the best." These
people, the Kharijites (*Khawárij*, "dissenters"), certainly had
hold of a fundamental idea of Moslem, which they developed
to the utmost; they were in a certain sense in the right, but
on such principles as theirs it would be impossible to establish any State, and least of all in the East. They were
fanatics who sought to carry out their ideas with the wildest
energy and the most desperate bravery, and to a certain
extent they maintained a loyalty to conviction worthy of
all admiration; but they only caused a great deal of
suffering, and produced nothing. The controversy about
the caliphate has long ago ceased to have any concrete
bearings, but it still continues to divide the Mohammedan
world. Historical tradition on the subject is very rich,
but greatly coloured by party feeling. It is much too
favourable to Alí, and fails to show Moáwiya quite in his
full historical importance. Naturally it does not allow us
to see, except dimly, that at bottom the struggles really had
reference merely to the plunder, and were only the expression
in another direction of the same wild warrior spirit which
shortly before had gained the mastery over Persians and
Romans. In the older time, however, people were sometimes
able to see rather more clearly how much of human passion
—very often passion of the lowest kind—was at work in
these civil wars in spite of all the religious party cries. To
a truly pious Moslem it must often have caused the gravest
reflections to see how unworthily such persons as Talha,
Zubair, Aïsha, and, essentially, Alí also had conducted themselves, while yet the Prophet had long before promised a
place in heaven to them all.

Alí was a thoroughly brave man, but could hardly be
called a general, was certainly wanting in true insight, and

in no sense whatever born to be a leader. He fell (22nd January 661) by the dagger of one of three Kharijites who had brought themselves under an oath to remove both the rivals, and also Amr, the powerful governor of Egypt, so as to make a free choice possible; but the attempts on Moáwiya and on Amr failed. By this deed of blood Alí was delivered from the humiliation of living to see everything fall to the clever Omayyad. The death of the rival left the road clear; Moáwiya assumed the title of Caliph. Alí's incapable son, Hasan, gave in his submission without much difficulty, in consideration of a handsome pension. The governor of Syria, now universally recognised as chief of the Believers, paid every regard to the stricter Moslems; his outward demeanour was entirely that of a spiritual prince (he preached, for example, every Friday in the mosque, as the Prophet and previous Caliphs had done, and as was also the practice of provincial governors and of generals), but he was none the less a secular ruler. The support of himself and of his house were "the people of Syria,"—that is to say, not, of course, the old inhabitants of the country, but the Arab troops that had settled there. The Omayyads, accordingly, were compelled to retain Damascus, the most important town in Syria, as their capital, although it had no such religious nimbus as invested Medina, the residence of the Prophet and his first successors, and although it lay too far to the west to be a good point from which to keep watch over the numerous subject countries in the east. The Omayyad rule set up by Moáwiya had to encounter many storms. The unchurchly and even frivolous demeanour of some members of the dynasty embittered the Faithful and encouraged a variety of pretenders, as well as the wild Kharijites, to repeated outbreaks, which were not suppressed without much bloodshed. Twice was the holy city of Mecca desecrated by troops of the Omayyad Caliphs (683 and 692);

and the unruly sons and grandsons of Mohammed's most faithful champions, the Medinites, were cut down by the soldiers of Yezíd, Moáwiya's son, in their native place, the city of the Prophet (28th August 683). It was against this same Caliph, a man pretty much without religion, that Alí's second son Husain also rose in rebellion. The rising, like most others that proceeded from the family of Alí, was begun and carried on in a headless way, and was suppressed with little trouble. To all appearance it was an affair of absolutely no consequence; but the way in which men regard a matter is often more important than the matter itself. Even contemporaries were deeply impressed to see the grandson of the Prophet put to death by the satellites of the profane Caliph, and his bloody head set up to open show after the common fashion of the East. Husain, the thoughtless rebel, was in the eyes of pious Moslems metamorphosed into a martyr, and his glory grew with time. The cry of "vengeance for Husain" contributed much to the downfall of the Omayyad throne. To this day the Shíites observe the anniversary of Husain's death as a day of mourning, which never fails to stir up deep emotion and wild rage in their bosoms; and with them Kerbelá, where he perished on 12th October 681, is a site almost as holy as Mecca and Medina. The non-Shíite Mohammedans also acknowledge Husain to have been a holy martyr, and hold in the deepest abhorrence the light-living but by no means wicked Yezíd.—If the dynasty of the Omayyad Caliphs was imperilled by the hostility of the stricter Moslems, it received injury from another quarter through the religious zeal of the only really pious man among them, the honest but narrow idealist Omar II. (717–720), who sought with all his might to bring the Koran into practice, and to restore once more the constitution of Omar, but of course brought about dire disorganisation as the sole result.

Although the Omayyads produced great rulers, they failed,

for various reasons, to establish an enduring empire. Their fall was inevitable when they themselves, and with them the Syrian troops on whose support they were wholly dependent, began to quarrel; and a rival family came upon the scene, that of the Abbásids. The descendants of Mohammed's uncle Abbás, who became a convert to Islam only on the capture of Mecca, and who never had any conspicuous *rôle*, lived for a long time in obscurity. But now they had the wit to turn to account the powerful apparatus which the descendants of Alí had prepared for the undermining of the empire. Much was made of ambiguous expressions, such as " the right of the house of Háshim " (which included Abbás as well as Alí) and " the right of the family of the Prophet " (which might suggest his uncle quite as readily as his cousin and son-in-law); there was word also of an alleged transfer of the hereditary right by one of the descendants of Alí to the Abbásids. The chiefs of the latter family succeeded in winning over to their side a large portion of the troops in the remoter part of Eastern Persia (Khorásán), which could not be kept under firm control from Damascus. These troops consisted for the most part of Persians who had accepted Islam, but were anything but friendly to the Arabs. After severe struggles the Abbásids were victorious (750). Few members of the fallen house escaped the terrible massacre.

The triumph of the Abbásids made an end of the purely Arab, and at the same time of the purely Semitic, State ; in it we see, in a great measure, a reaction of the Persian element, and a repristination of the old Asiatic world-empires, the structure of which had been at least a little more stable. It was not a mere casual circumstance that forthwith and from the first the seat of government was transferred to where it had been held successively by Achemenids, Arsacids, and Sásánians,—the plains of the lower Euphrates and Tigris. There arose the proud city of the

Caliphs, Bagdad. The Abbásids paid more external respect to religion than the Omayyads had done, but they were in reality quite as worldly-minded. Over and above this, there showed itself in them a very unpleasing strain of insincerity. The first two Caliphs of the family were nevertheless very considerable men. The second in particular, Mansúr (754–775), was one of the greatest princes, one of the most unscrupulous also, that ever have guided a mighty empire. He it was who established the Mohammedan empire on a firm basis.[1] Under his grandson Hárún ar-Rashíd (786–809) the caliphate unquestionably enjoyed its period of greatest splendour, although Hárún himself was very far from being a great ruler. In his day almost all the lands from the Jaxartes and the Indus to near the Pillars of Hercules obeyed the Caliph. The Arabs had ceased to be the props of the empire, but the Arabic language had spread far and wide; it was the language of religion, of government, of poetry, and of the science that was just rising. On the banks of the Tigris there flourished a civilisation more brilliant than under the best of the Sásánians. A fair measure of quiet prevailed in most of the provinces, and thus the enormous prodigality of the court did not press upon the subjects beyond endurance. Syria and the adjoining lands found themselves in better circumstances than they had for a long time experienced. True, the administration was very defective if judged according to modern ideas; but good government in the East must be measured by a very modest standard. The Christian population had gone over to Islam *en masse*. The desire to stand on an equality with the conquerors in the eye of the law, and to pay diminished taxes, was, of course, a powerful motive to this; but no less strong an influence was the suitability of Islam

[1] For a fuller treatment of Mansúr and the establishment of the Abbásid empire, see next essay.

to Oriental peasants and townsfolk of the humbler class, especially as God Himself had by the event declared Himself in its favour. The Christian Churches of the East have never been very persevering in their zeal to educate and elevate their adherents on the spiritual side; they have always attached the principal importance to the externalities of worship, confessional formulas, and the condemnation of heretics. A fact specially worthy of note is that Islam was accepted by a majority of the East-Syrian Christians even,—the Nestorians of the lands watered by the Tigris, whose ancestors could not be brought to apostasy by all the fierce persecutions of the Persian kings. In explaining this result, perhaps some weight ought to be assigned also to the consideration that, in adopting the priestless religion of Islam, the Christians got rid of the tutelage and oppression of their own clergy. Speaking generally, the civilisation of the Syrians, Copts, and other Oriental Christians lost but little by their change of faith. Islam, of course, severed many old associations that made for culture, but in compensation for these it called many new germs into life. Conversions were seldom due to direct compulsion. The pious rejoiced when Christians accepted Islam in crowds; but to the rulers these conversions were, for the most part, positively unwelcome, as the converts were thereby relieved from the heaviest of the taxes, and their change of faith thus meant a serious decrease of revenue. Nor were Christians systematically maltreated. They had indeed to suffer much repression and scorn, and to make up their minds to a position of inferiority; for, apart from the legal inferiority of non-Moslems as merely protected aliens, Islam gives to its followers a tone of haughty contempt for all outsiders.[1]

[1] It is not inconsistent with this that individual Christians and Jews, whether by princely favour or by their own talents, occasionally rose to positions of power and dignity, especially as physicians; still less is it so that Coptic clerks were regularly employed in the administration of Egypt.

Moreover, the lords, great and small, whose exactions pressed
so hard even on their Moslem subjects, saw still less reason
to spare unbelievers. But this is the Oriental way in everything. The different Christian Churches might keep up
their controversies as before, if they chose, but they could
no longer actually persecute one another. It was certainly
easier for a man to live as a Christian under the rule of the
Caliphs than as a Christian heretic within the Byzantine
empire. The situation of the adherents of the old Persian
religion in the East was similar to that of the Christians in
the West, save that their legal position was not so firmly
secured by unambiguous passages of the Koran. In some
parts of the old Persian empire conversion to Islam on a
large scale took place very early; but in others, and particularly in Persia proper, the national faith long persisted
with great tenacity.

.The decline of the Abbásid caliphate begins with the
celebrated Mámún (813–833). Hárún by his last will had
foolishly divided the empire between his sons Amín and
Mámún, but reserving for the former the suzerainty and
title of Caliph. The natural consequence was civil war.
After desperate struggles the incapable Amín, who both on
the father's and on the mother's side was a descendant of
Mansúr, lost his throne and life through the Khorásán
troops of Mámún, whose mother had been a Persian slave.
It was a fresh victory of the Persian over the Arabian
interest. Through these occurrences, which were followed
by further confusions, the governors who headed the troops
of their respective provinces, and also the commanders of
the mercenaries, in many cases reached a dangerous degree
of power. Táhir, to whom Mámún was mainly indebted
for his successes, established for himself, and handed on
to his descendants, in the important province of Khorásán,
a principality which was but loosely dependent on the

caliphate. Mámún knew neither how to keep his victorious generals in their proper places, nor how to destroy them, as Mansúr had done. That he was hindered by scruples of conscience, no one will believe who duly considers his conduct towards Músá, the descendant of Alí. In order to win over the still powerful Shíite party, Mámún had made it great concessions, and had taken steps, which can hardly have been sincere, to secure the succession to Músá. But when he came to encounter the energetic opposition of his own house and its immediate dependants, he secretly made away with that unfortunate prince. Mámún had great interest in art and science, and favoured the translation into Arabic of Greek scientific works. But along with this he had an unfortunate liking for theological controversy.

The Caliphs from this time leaned for support on great bands of foreign mercenaries, chiefly Turks, and their captains became the real lords of the empire as soon as they realised their own strength. How thoroughly the Abbásid caliphate had been undermined was shown all at once in a shocking manner, when the Caliph Mutawakkil was murdered by his own servants at the command of his son, and the parricide Muntasir set upon the throne in his stead (Dec. 861). The power of the Caliphs was now at an end; they became the mere playthings of their own savage warriors. The remoter, sometimes even the nearer, provinces were practically independent. The princes formally recognished the Caliph as their sovereign, stamped his name upon their coins, and gave it precedence in public prayer, but these were honours without any solid value. Some Caliphs, indeed, recovered a measure of real power, but only as rulers of a much diminished State. Theoretically the fiction of an undivided empire of Islam was maintained, but it had long ceased to be a reality. The

names of Caliph, Commander of the Faithful, Imám, continued still to inspire some reverence; the theological
doctors of law insisted that the Caliph, in spiritual things
at least, must everywhere bear rule, and control all judicial
posts; but even theoretically his position was far behind
that of a pope, and in practice was not for a moment to
be compared to it. The Caliph never was the head of a
true hierarchy; Islam, in fact, knows no priesthood on
which such a system could have rested. In the tenth
century the Búids, three brothers who had left the hardly
converted Gílán (the mountainous district at the south-
west angle of the Caspian Sea) as poor adventurers,
succeeded in conquering for themselves the sovereign
command over wide domains, and over Bagdad itself.
They even proposed to themselves to displace the Abbásids
and set descendants of Alí upon the throne, and abandoned
the idea only because they feared that a Caliph of the
house of Alí might exercise too great an authority over
their Shíite soldiers, and so become independent; while, on
the other hand, they could make use of these troops for
any violence they chose against the Abbásid puppet who
sat in Mansúr's seat.

It was this period that for the first time witnessed any
great successes of the Shíites. Out of what had originally
been a political party a sect, or rather a number of sects, had
gradually grown. The doctrine of the divine right of Alí
and his descendants had under foreign influences, Christian
and Persian, gradually developed into a complete or partial
deification. At the beginning of the Abbásid period there
were some who taught the divinity of Alí without qualifica-
tion, and if the majority of Shíites energetically repudiated
this, they nevertheless believed in a supernatural, divine
illumination of Alí and his descendants the Imáms, or even
that the Spirit of God passed from the one to the other of

these. As early as 750, dreams were cherished of the Messianic return of "a hidden Imám;" and the names of Abú Bekr, Omar, and Aïsha were cursed more fervently than those of the Omayyads. Here, as in other things, the ground of Islam was entirely abandoned; but men, of course, concealed this from themselves, by putting allegorical interpretations upon the sacred book, and by setting up against the (certainly much falsified) tradition or "sunna" of the orthodox ("Sunnites") a still more falsified sunna of their own. Moreover, from the simple Shíitism that is still essentially Islamitic, many intermediate connecting links lead over to strange heathenish sects, as offshoots of which we still have (for example) the Druses and the Nosairians. The first actually Shíite empire on a large scale was that of the Fatimid Caliphs, founded (about 910) by Obaidalláh, a real or alleged descendant of Alí. He thoroughly understood how to utilise the credulity of the Berbers so as to become master over large territories in North Africa. But his connections reached also far into Asia. He and his successors allowed themselves to be regarded by their intimate dependants as supernatural beings. A court poet says (about 970) of the Fatimid, in whose service he is, things which the genuine Moslem could at most allow to be said of the Prophet himself. Thus in some measure we are able to understand how it has come to pass that one of them, and he the crazy Hákim (996–1021), is worshipped by the Druses as God. But while the Fatimids imposed some reserve upon themselves in their own proper kingdom, where the Shíites were certainly in the minority, they gave a free hand to their partisans elsewhere. The Karmatians in Arabia utilised the plundering zeal of the Bedouins for their own ends, threatened the capital of the Abbásids, fell upon the pilgrim caravans, and finally, during the pilgrim festival, forced their way on one occasion into

Mecca, perpetrated a horrible massacre, and carried off the black stone of the Caaba (930). This was an open breach with Islam. The Fatimid Caliph disavowed the Karmatians, but we know that they had acted on his suggestion, and they subsequently (951), at the command of his successor, again restored the holy stone for a heavy payment. After their conquest of Egypt (969) the Fatimids were the most powerful princes of Islam, and it seemed at times as if even the form of power had passed from the Abbásids. The Fatimids, moreover, governed excellently as a rule, and brought Egypt to a high pitch of prosperity. But at last they, too, shared the usual fate of Oriental dynasties; the Abbásids lived to see the utter downfall (1171) of their worst rivals, and continued to enjoy for nearly a century longer the empty satisfaction of being named in public prayer in Egypt as Commanders of the Faithful. Since then there has never been another Shíite Caliph.

In the history of Islamite peoples the politico-religious controversies which turned upon the right to the caliphate are by far the most important. But alongside of these there were a multitude of purely dogmatic disputes. Above all, Islam was agitated with the old and ever new question as to whether, and how far, man is a free or a determined agent in his purposes and actions. The Koran, generally speaking, teaches a rather crass determinism. According to the Koran, God is the author of everything, including the dispositions of men; He guides whom He wills, and leads into error whom He wills. But at a very early period some pious souls began to take offence at the horrible thought that God should thus have foreordained multitudes of men to sin and to the everlasting pains of hell. They could recognise a divine righteousness only if God leaves men free to choose between good and evil, and determines the retribution according to the character of the choice. They found points of support for this doctrine of theirs in the Koran itself; for Mohammed, who was anything but a consistent thinker, has in his revelations often treated man as free. A popular teacher of religion will, it is clear, whatever be his inclination to determinism, inevitably find himself ever and anon addressing himself to his hearers, in his exhortations to faith and virtue, as if they were in possession of freedom of will. The people who taught in this strain were called Kadarites. Possibly they were not wholly exempt from Christian influences. The procedure of their successors, the Mutazila ("Dissidents"), was more systematic. They constituted a school of a strongly rational-istic tendency, and with the aid of Greek dialectic, with which the Arabs became acquainted first in a limited degree, and afterwards much more fully, through the Syrians, reduced their orthodox opponents to desperation. They also opposed with special zeal the proposition that the Koran is uncreated.[1] This dogma was certainly in flagrant contradiction to the fundamental position of the Koran itself. On this point the Mutazila were in reality the orthodox; but it could hardly fail to happen that in the heat of debate some went further, and thought of the Koran altogether more lightly than befits a Moslem. The fair beginning of a truly progressive movement which was in-volved in this was inevitably checked within Islam at a very early stage. The school of the Mutazila could hardly have attained to any significance at all had it not been favoured by some of the earlier Abbásids. Mámún especially took sides with great zeal for the doctrine that the Koran is created. But that he is not on this account to be designated as in any sense a "friend of free thought," is evident from the fact that he imposed severe punishments on those theologians who publicly avowed their adherence

[1] See above, p. 58 sq.

to the opposite doctrine then generally prevalent. So also
his successors, down to Mutawakkil, who reversed the condition of matters, and caused it to be taught that the
Koran is increate.—Another controversy had reference to
the divine attributes. The Koran in its unsophisticated
anthropomorphism attributes human qualities to God
throughout, speaks also of His hands, of the throne on
which He sits, and so forth. The original Moslems took
this up simply as it was written; but, later, many were
stumbled by it, and sought to put such a construction on
the passages as would secure for the Koran a purer conception of God. Some denied all divine attributes whatever,
inasmuch as, being eternal equally with Himself, they would,
if granted, necessarily destroy the divine unity, and establish
a real polytheism. Many conceded only certain abstract
qualities. On the other hand, some positively maintained
the corporeity of God, — in other words, an anthropomorphism of the crassest kind, which even Mohammed would
have rejected. The Mutazila maintained their dialectical
superiority until Ash'ari (in the first third of the tenth
century), who had been educated in their schools, took the
dialectic method into the service of orthodoxy. It was he
who created the system of orthodox dogmatic. Of course
the later dogmatists did not in all points agree with him,
and by some of them, on account of some remains of
rationalism in his teaching, he was even regarded as
heterodox. Since Ash'ari's time the commonly accepted
doctrine on the three controverted points just mentioned
has been:—(1) God produces the good as well as the evil
deeds of man, although the latter has a certain measure of
independence in his appropriation of them. (2) The Koran
is eternal and increate. Some maintain this, indeed, only
with regard to the original of the sacred book in heaven, but
others hold it also of the words and letters of the book as it

exists on earth. (3) God really has the attributes which are attributed to Him in the Koran; it is a matter of faith that He has hands and feet, sits on His throne, and so on, but it is profane curiosity to inquire as to how these things can be. Whatever be the exceptions that a man may take to any of these doctrines, the first and the third at least are in entire accord with the Koran—even in respect of their illogicality. The Mutazilite, like other rationalistic movements which make their appearance here and there in Islam, may awaken our sympathy, but they are too plainly in contradiction with the essence of a crassly supranaturalistic religion; and this explains how it is that at a later date only a few isolated after-effects of the Mutazila continue to be met with. We must be particularly careful not to attach undue importance to these controversies of the school. The Mohammedan people as a mass was hardly touched by them. The same holds good of other dogmatic differences, unless, perhaps, when they happened to have a political side also; as, for example, the dispute between the rigorists, who regarded every grave sin as "unbelief," of which the punishment is hell; and those who, on the other side, gave prominence to the divine mercy. The former was the doctrine of the Kharijites, who declared Othmán, Alí, Aïsha, Moáwiya, and many other "Companions" of Mohammed to have been unbelievers; while their opponents, more in the spirit of the Prophet, left it with God to pronounce judgment on these as well as on others who might have fallen into sin.

The theologico-juristical schools are of much greater practical importance than the dogmatic. In Islam "law" embraces ritual also in the widest sense of the word; for example, the rules of prayer (*salát*), purification, pilgrimage. Law, like dogma, rests upon the Koran and upon tradition. But this tradition is a very heterogeneous composition. All of it is alleged to come from the Prophet, and much of it can, in fact, be traced back to him; but a great deal has another origin. Mohammed's doctrine and example could not in reality suffice as rules of life for highly-developed peoples. The law and custom of the Arabs, and still more of the lands of ancient civilisation which accepted Islam, opinions of the school, political tendencies, and many other such things, are the real sources of much that is given out as precept or practice of the Prophet. It is only recently that scholars have begun to see on how great a scale traditions were fabricated. In many cases it was believed in good faith that one was justified in ascribing immediately to the Prophet whatever one held to be right in itself and worthy of him; but other falsifications arose from baser motives. In this mass of traditions, which claim to be binding on all true believers, many contradictions, of course, occur. Hence there arose, from the eighth century onwards, a variety of schools whose masters determined for their disciples the rules of law, in the widest sense of that word, on the basis of those traditions which they themselves regarded as correct. The impulse to reconcile internal differences, which is exceedingly strong in Islam, was not successful indeed in removing the discrepancies of the schools of law, but it was able to extend recognition to four of them (which had very soon thrown all the others into the shade) as equally orthodox. These orthodox schools differed from one another in a number of juristic and ritual particulars, but were practically at one on all the most important principles. Every Sunnite is under obligation to hold by the prescriptions of one or other of the four schools. These go deeply into the affairs of daily life, especially in what relates to forms of worship and to the regulation of the family; but on another side, again, they are exceedingly doctrinaire, often presupposing as they do an ideal State, such as never existed even under Omar, and by no means the actual conditions of greedy Oriental despotism. Of these the Hanbalite school has now almost entirely disappeared, and the Hanefites, Shafiites, and Malikites are distributed over the countries of Sunnite Islam.—Shiite law is something different from that of any of these four schools.

The supreme authority in law, as in other things, is the consensus of the whole Mohammedan world—that is to say, the generally accepted opinion. It decides upon the validity of traditions, and also upon the interpretation of the Koran. For in Islam, as in other Churches, it is only the accepted interpretation of the sacred book that is of consequence to believers, however violent may be the disagreement between this interpretation and the original sense. The consensus of the entire body of Mohammedanism is, of course, an ideal that is never actually realised, but nevertheless it has great practical importance. By its means gradual recognition came to be accorded to things which were foreign, and even opposed, to the teaching of Mohammed—as, for example, the worship of saints. It silently tolerates all kinds of local variations, but exercises a steady pressure towards an ever-extending realisation of its binding prescriptions.

From the prosperous period of the Abbásids onwards, freethinking spread to a considerable extent among the more highly-cultivated classes. Some poets ventured to ridicule or gainsay, more or less openly, fundamental doctrines of Islam, and even the faith itself. Persian writers expressed, in prose and verse, their detestation of Arabism; and the reflecting reader noted that the detestation extended to the Arab religion. One may imagine what expressions were used in conversation in such circles. The scholastic philosophers contrived for the most part to accommodate themselves outwardly to Islamite dogma, and often, we may be sure, in good faith; but the theologians nevertheless, and with reason, held them in deep suspicion; the old pagan Aristotle, on whom they leaned, fits in with Islam even less than with Christianity. All sorts of ideas—some of them very fantastic, of Persian and other foreign origin, and distinctly non-Islamite—also from time to time met with acceptance in the cultivated world. Once and again, indeed, a quite too audacious freethinker or heretic was executed; but in general people were allowed to speak and write freely, if only they put on a touch of Mohammedan varnish. Islam has no inquisition, and accepts as a Moslem the man who externally professes it, however doubtful his real sentiments may be. Accordingly, in some instances individuals whose thinking and teaching was quite un-Islamite, such as the famous mystic poet Abul-Alá al Maarrí (973–1057), were regarded by the people as devout, and even as saintly. But even from this very fact we can see that the danger for Islam was by no means very great. Such ideas were confined to very narrow circles of thinkers and poets, or of profligates, and were never long in dying out again. Nothing of it all penetrated to the great mass of the people, and it is in this that the strength of Islam lies.

The mysticism of the Súfis was a greater danger to the dominant religion. The impulse to self-mortification and introspection, which in Mohammed's own case was very active at only one period of his life, found new nourishment after his followers had become masters of the neighbouring Christian countries, in which this type of piety was only too flourishing. It was all genuinely Semitic; and during the ascendency of the youthfully energetic element in Islam there was no danger of its exercising an enervating influence on the latter. But subsequently Persian and Indian ideas became associated with this mysticism. The Súfis sought to submerge themselves in God, and arrived at the Indian conception of the All-One, which is irreconcilable with Islam.

In Indian fashion, systematic rules were devised for attaining the mystic victory over earthly limitations. He who believed himself to have succeeded in this might venture to break away from the precepts of positive religion, and often enough he allowed the moral law to go in the same way. The enthusiast, essentially a supernaturalist, who had merged himself in the All and One, readily held himself to be a worker of wonders; and still more easily was he so regarded by his adherents. What are the limits of the laws of nature (which Orientals, in fact, never recognise) to one who has effected the leap from the finite to the infinite? The finest and the coarsest attributes of the human spirit often worked together here. Amongst the Súfis we find deep souls, magnificent enthusiasts, fantastic dreamers, sensual poets, many fools, and many rogues. The systematic character of their procedure, which had to be learned, and the impression produced by the personality of leading Súfis, led to the formation of schools and orders. We have here a sort of monasticism, though without celibacy and without permanent vows. The fakírs or dervishes (*i.e.* " poor ") live on pious gifts or foundations, but often also carry on some civil calling. They keep up regular ascetic exercises, often of a very extraordinary character, in order to attain to the supersensuous. By these means they over-stimulate the nerves, exhaust body and spirit, and fall into a temporary insanity. However fine may be the blossoms which Súfic mysticism has produced, and however quickening its influence upon Persian poetry, the existence of dervishism, which plays a great part in almost all Mohammedan countries, is on the whole a mischief. For the rest, most Súfis believed themselves to be good Moslems. By allegorical interpretation they also were able to come to an understanding with the Koran. Not many can have clearly seen how fundamentally opposed is the pantheistic conception of God in mysticism

to the rigid monotheism of the Koran. The great mass of
dervishes are, of course, much too unthinking and superficial
to follow in the fanciful footsteps of the old masters. They
dance and howl for the glory of God, as other men pray.
The people regard the dervishes as the props of Islam, and
in fact hostility against all unbelievers is fomented in a
quite special way by some of these brotherhoods. There is
no suspicion how un-Islamic are the fundamental ideas on
which these orders rest. The simple axioms of Islam itself
meanwhile remain unshaken.

About the year 1000, Islam was in a very bad way. The
Abbásid caliphate had long ceased to be of any importance,
the power of the Arabs had long ago been broken. There
was a multitude of Islamite States, great and small; but even
the most powerful of these, that of the Fatimids, was very
far from being able to give solidity to the whole, especially
as it was Shíite. In fact, large regions which had been
conquered by the first Caliphs were again lost to the Byzantines, who repeatedly penetrated far into Mohammedan
territory. At this point a new element came to the aid
of the religion, namely, the Turks. Warriors from Turkestan
had long played a part in the history of Moslem kingdoms,
but now there came a wholesale migration. The Turks
pressed forward in great masses from their seats in upper
Asia, and, newly converted to Islam, threw themselves in the
first instance upon the lands of Persia. These nomads
caused dreadful devastation, trampled to the ground the
flourishing civilisation of vast territories, and contributed
almost nothing to the culture of the human race; but they
mightily strengthened the religion of Mohammed. The rude
Turks took up with zeal the faith which was just within the
reach of their intellectual powers, and they became its true,
often fanatical, champions against the outside world. They
founded the powerful empire of the Seljuks, and conquered

new regions for Islam in the north-west. After the downfall of the Seljuk empire they still continued to be the ruling people in all its older portions. Had not the warlike character of Islam been revived by the Turks, the Crusaders perhaps might have had some prospect of more enduring success.

But this Turkish influx was followed by another of evil augury for Islam. Jenghiz Khan led his Mongols and Turks into Mohammedan territory in 1220, and his grandson Hulagu (January 1258) took Bagdad, the Mohammedan capital, and brought the Abbásid caliphate to an end. The loathly heathens were masters of Asia. But Islam, with its simple dogmas, its imposing ceremonial, and its practical character, soon won over these barbarians. Fifty years after the capture of Bagdad, those Mongols who had Moslem subjects had themselves accepted Islam. The frightful injuries they had inflicted on the lands of Islam were, however, not to be repaired. Babylonia, the home of primeval civilisation, was till then still the chief seat of Mohammedan culture; but since the Mongols set foot on it, it has been a desolation.

Through the dynasty of the Ottoman Turks, Islam once more became the terror of Christendom. The old dream of the conquest of Constantinople, and of the complete destruction of the Roman empire, was realised (1453). On his occupation of Egypt in 1517, Selím I. even proclaimed himself Caliph. The sultans of Egypt had, after the destruction of Bagdad, given their protection to a scion of the Abbásid family, to whom they gave the title of Caliph (1261), and similar nominal Caliphs, without any trace of power, " reigned " there till the Ottoman conquest. But how little the Moslem world troubled itself about them may be judged from the fact that the great philosophical historian Ibn Khaldún (of Tunis, 1332-1405), in the introduction to his History of the World, where he speaks very exhaustively about the caliphate, the spiritual and the secular State, never once alludes to this make-believe.   But, armed with the enormous power of the then Turkish empire, the caliphate now once more bore another aspect.   Although the sultan of Stamboul was wanting in one attribute which almost all orthodox teachers had regarded as essential in Caliphs, namely, descent from the Prophet's tribe of Koraish, his claims found wide recognition, for his successes filled every Moslem heart with pride and joy, and the holy cities of Mecca, Medina, and Jerusalem did homage to him as their lord.   The caliphate, let it be added, did not bring any actual increase of strength to the Ottoman sultans, who on the whole have not themselves attached much value to it ; on their coins they do not assert the title either of " Caliph," or " Imám," or " Commander of the Faithful."   They have never actually possessed spiritual authority over Moslems who were not their own subjects. At the same time, it might be a serious thing for the Ottoman empire if the sultan should cease to be mentioned in public prayer at Mecca and Medina as overlord and Caliph, a thing which might very well happen if besides Egypt he were to lose Syria.   For a kingdom that is slowly but steadily collapsing, the removal of even a weak pillar may be of disastrous consequence.   It would appear that in the last confusions in Egypt prior to the English occupation, this idea was actually made use of, and alarm thereby excited in Constantinople. The Sherífs of Mecca as Caliphs (a suggestion that has been made) would, it must be said, play but a poor part.   They are descended, indeed, from Alí, and thus theoretically have a vastly greater claim to the dignity than the Ottomans have ; but their territory is small and excessively poor, and they of necessity could live only by the favour of other princes.   Moreover, the heads of the different branches of this numerous family are constantly in conflict with each other in true Arabic fashion. Lastly, the sultans of Morocco have for a long time been also in the habit of calling themselves "Commanders of the Faithful," and thus, for their own kingdom at least, they expressly lay claim to the supreme spiritual authority.

In the later Middle Ages the opposition between Sunnites and Shíites seemed to be dying down. The Sunnites had at an early period accepted certain Shíite views, particularly the exaggerated respect in which Alí was held, and on the other hand, all Shíites did not go so far as to declare Abú Bekr and Omar infidels. The Sherífs of Mecca, just spoken of, from being moderate Shíites had imperceptibly become Sunnites. But the enmity of the two parties received a new lease of life when, just about the time when the Sunnite Ottomans were attaining their highest power, a great empire arose also for the Shía. In Persia the doctrine of the divine right of Alí had of old fallen on specially fruitful soil; it is to Persian influences that the Shíite dogmas chiefly owe their development. In Persian lands smaller or greater Shíite States have also arisen at various times, but it was through the founding of the Sefid [1] empire (about 1500) that Persia first became in a strict sense the land of the Shíite faith, whilst formerly (what is often overlooked) it had been in great part Sunnite. This Shíite empire constituted a weighty counterpoise to the Ottomans, and through it many a diversion was created in favour of Europe when most distressed by the pressure of the Turks. Since the fall of the Sefids in last century, Persia has continued to sink deeper and deeper; the State and the nation are far feebler than even in Turkey; but Shíitism has taken Persia into its exclusive possession. So full of life is it, that even in our own time it was able to throw out a vigorous offshoot—the strange enthusiastic sect of the Bábís, which has profoundly agitated

[1] In Old English the kingdom of the Sophy.

the entire country, and has not yet been definitively eradi-
cated.   The antithesis between Shía and Sunna is very sharp
to this day.   The Orientals, who have extraordinarily little
feeling of patriotism, have all the more zeal for religion.
Bitter hatred still separates the Persians from their Moslem
neighbours,—Ottomans, Arabs, Uzbegs, Afghans, and so on,
—because, forsooth, the Companions of Mohammed were
not able to agree as to who should be the successor of the
murdered Othmán.

Islam has, on the whole, undergone but little change
during the last thousand years.   The spread of mysticism
and dervishism, as we have seen, did not affect the faith
of the multitude.   These things, of course, gave fresh
stimulus to the business in saints and miracles.   The
mystic submerges himself in God, and ignores earthly
things; the masses, accordingly, are only too much inclined
to take for a saint the rogue who imitates him without
scruple and seemingly surpasses him, and the madman
who can make nothing of the world at all.   Belief in
miracles is deep-seated in the blood of the Oriental; religious
impostors, themselves often the victims of imposition, have
never been wanting there.   That saints are able to work
miracles, has been faintly questioned only by a few
theologians.   Of long time, accordingly, the real or alleged
sepulchres of saints have been venerated as fountains of
grace.   They give rise to local cults, and often are hotbeds
of fanaticism.   It is no accident that in the last troubles
in Egypt atrocities were perpetrated upon Europeans at
the sepulchre of the most highly venerated of the Egyptian
saints, es-Seyyid el Bedawí, at Tantá.   Of holy places of
this class many are of ancient Christian origin, and some
even date from heathen times.   All sorts of chicanery,
crass superstition, and much that is totally un-Islamite
easily connect themselves with such places.   No Moslem,

it is true, is under obligation to believe in any of these things; there is no such thing as an authoritative list of saints; and some Mohammedan scholars have even disputed the legitimacy of saint - worship altogether, but without success.

Towards the middle of last century there arose in the native land of Islam a violent storm of puritanism against the prevailing apostasy. The Wahhabites, or followers of Abdal-wahháb, brought forward no new doctrine; they were thoroughly orthodox Moslems; but they broke with tradition thus far, that they sought to abolish certain abuses which had been tolerated or even approved by general consent. In this they proceeded with a strictness which reminds more of Omar than of the Prophet. They were far from denying Mohammed to have been the Apostle of God, but they held in detestation the exaggerated honour which was paid to his name, his dwelling-places, and his grave. The worship of saints they condemned as idolatry, and wherever they went they destroyed the saints' tombs and places of martyrdom. They wanted to restore the original Islam; for example, they took in serious earnest the legal prohibition against the wearing of silk, and, in agreement with many learned theologians, interdicted tobacco as an innovation. The kingdom which they founded was a copy of the original Islamitic one; it once more reunited by force almost all the inhabitants of Arabia, but could not succeed in infusing a real spirit of religion into the great mass of the Bedouins. Their strict spiritual discipline was particularly irksome to the inhabitants of Mecca—on the whole a very secularly disposed people. The armies of Mohammed Ali of Egypt at length broke the power of the Wahhabites, not without great exertions, took back the sacred cities, Mecca and Medina, which had fallen into their hands in 1803, and penetrated into the heart of their kingdom (1814, 1815). They again took another start at a later period, but neither was this permanent; a purely Arab State, and that, too, founded upon religion, can be kept together for any length of time only by rulers of uncommon efficiency. At present the Wahhabite kingdom, properly so called, is powerless; it is subject to that of the Shammar, which lies to the north of it, and the prince of which, Ibn Rashíd, a ruler of extensive tracts, is also a professor of Wahhabitism, though with none of the fiery zeal of earlier times. The Wahhabites are no longer a menace to Damascus and Bagdad. Their reform of Islam has remained confined to Arabia, and even there is hardly likely to operate long. But it has rightly been remarked as noteworthy, that this purely Semitic religious movement with all its energy has produced nothing new; it has been directed exclusively towards the repristination of pure monotheism.

For a considerable time Islam has seemed to be in a state of deep humiliation. Even the great Moslem kingdoms are without strength. By far the larger portion of the Moslem world is ruled by Christian powers. But let us not deceive ourselves as to the vitality of this religion. How many catastrophes has it not already survived! Immediately on the death of its founder the revolt of the Arabs threatened it with extinction. Soon afterwards, from being a spiritual State (as corresponded with its essential nature), it was changed into a secular one, and it survived the transformation. Its united empire was broken up and fell into fragments. The Moslems tore one another to pieces in fierce party warfare. The Karmatians carried off the black stone, the palladium of Islam, and for years made impossible the pilgrimage, one of the most important expressions of Mohammedan life. The heathen Mongols destroyed the caliphate, and long ruled over half of the lands of Islam.

Instead of being able to carry on the holy war against the unbeliever, one Moslem State after another is in these days either directly or indirectly falling under infidel control. But the faith that there is no God but Allàh, and that Mohammed is his Prophet, and all that is involved in this faith, remain unshattered. It would seem as if Islam were now in course of being driven out from the Balkan peninsula, even as it was long ago compelled to quit Sicily and Spain; whether it shall be able to maintain its hold everywhere in Asia and North Africa may be questioned; but in the Indian Archipelago it is steadily advancing, among the nomads of Central Asia it has gained strength just as the Russian sway has extended, and in Central Africa it is achieving conquest upon conquest. Precisely because the consolidation of European power in the lands of Nigritia brings with it greater security of intercourse, it may be presumed that the spread of Islam will be powerfully promoted there. But in the dark continent, which offers no favourable soil for Christianity, the acceptance even of Islam means progress from the deepest savagery to a certain culture, however limited and limiting, and to association with peoples who in the Middle Ages were higher in civilisation than the people of Europe. Perhaps slave-hunting and kidnapping will come to an end only when practically all the negro peoples shall have become Moslem.

If religion among the higher classes in Turkey is, undeniably, sometimes a matter of doubt or even of ridicule, more as the result of frivolity than as a consequence of serious thinking, and if similar phenomena manifest themselves still more frequently among the light-minded, bright, and unconscientious Persians, the firmness of the faith nevertheless remains unshaken with the vast mass of the people, even with those who are remiss in the discharge of ritual duties. Without any qualms of doubt, peacefully resigned to the will of God, the Moslem sees his kingdoms go down. But we must also be prepared to find the strength of this faith continuing to maintain itself in frightful outbursts of fanaticism. If the occurrences in Egypt during the last rebellion showed little of death-defying courage and energy, that is to be attributed to the languid temper of the Egyptians; a great rising in Syria or Asia Minor might conceivably give Europeans a good deal more trouble. The best strength of the great Indian Mutiny of 1856 lay with the Moslems. The Moslem subjects of Britain and other European States sigh for the moment when they shall be able to shake off the yoke of the infidel. The successes of the "dervishes" in the Soudan may serve to warn Europeans of the strength that still resides in the warrior zeal of Islam.

CALIPH MANSÚR.

THE Arabs had established a vast empire with great rapidity, but to keep it together was hardly possible so long as its purely Arab character was retained. The reigning house of the Omayyads had to contend with very dangerous political and religious antipathies; and, perhaps a greater danger, the Arabs, who now controlled a world-empire, kept up without abatement the old untractableness and exaggerated zeal for the honour of family and tribe which they had developed in their desert life. The only difference now was, that their tribal patriotism had reference not so much to the small subdivisions in which the Bedouin lives, as to large tribal groups, the unity of which was in part no more than a fiction. If a governor leaned upon the Yemenites, the Modarites forthwith became his open or secret foes; any prominent official who belonged to the Kais group was hated by the Kelb. And almost every one in authority was ready to overlook in his tribesmen even those offences which, in members of another tribe, he severely, and rightly, punished. The Omayyad Caliphs accordingly found the utmost difficulty in keeping down the private feuds even of the Arabs of Syria, who were generally loyal; and their troubles were much greater in the remoter provinces, where there was little or no sympathy with the reigning house. The kingdom of the Omayyads was never in a state of tolerable order and prosperity unless there was an eminently astute and energetic governor in Babylonia (Irák) as well as a capable

sovereign in Syria. For the seat of supreme power was tied
to Syria by the circumstances under which the dynasty had
arisen; while the eastern provinces, too remote to be controlled from Damascus, were necessarily administered from
Irák. All steady order ceased with the reign of the talented
but utterly profligate Walíd II. (743–744). The struggles of
various Omayyads with one another did the rest.

The ground had long before been undermined by the
efforts of a religious party hostile to the Omayyads. The
descendants of Alí, who, as blood-relations, in fact descendants, of the Prophet (through his daughter Fátima), considered themselves to have the nearest right to the throne,
alienated from the Omayyads the hearts of many of their
subjects. There was an expectation that the house of
Mohammed, should it once attain to the supreme authority,
would fill the earth as full of righteousness as it was now
full of iniquity. The pious professors and followers of the
divine law had little liking for the rule of the reigning
house, which, for all its forms of religion, was purely secular.
And though the risings of the Alids were unsuccessful
through the bungling of their leaders, the very failure cost
the Omayyads dear; for the incapable grandchildren of the
Apostle of God, who had fallen or been put to death, in
the eyes of the people became martyrs, whose blood cried
to heaven for vengeance.

In perfect quietness, meanwhile, another family was
setting itself to work to gather in the fruits of the efforts of
the Alids for its own behalf,—their cousins, the Abbásids.
Abbás, from whom they traced their descent, had held a somewhat ambiguous attitude towards his nephew the Prophet.
His son Abdalláh passes for one of the strongest pillars of
religious tradition; but, in the eyes of unprejudiced European
research, he is only a crafty liar. Abdalláh's grandson
Mohammed, and the sons of the latter, so far as they are

known to us, combined considerable practical vigour with their hereditary cunning and duplicity. They lived in deep retirement in Humaima, a little place to the south of the Dead Sea, seemingly far withdrawn from the world, but which, on account of its proximity to the route by which Syrian pilgrims went to Mecca, afforded opportunities for communication with the remotest lands of Islam. From this centre they carried on the propaganda in their own behalf with the utmost skill. They had genius enough to see that the best soil for their efforts was the distant Khorásán,[1]—that is, the extensive north-eastern provinces of the old Persian empire. The majority of the people there had already gone over to Islam; many had embraced the new faith with ardour, and had even fought bravely on its behalf against the unbelieving populations to the north and east. But the converted Persians were held in little esteem by the dominant Arabs, who looked on them as " clients,"[2] and refused to accord to them the full rights to which they had a claim as Moslems. The internal wars of the Arabs, moreover, raged in those parts with exceptional violence. To the Persians it was a matter of indifference whether the Yemenites or Modarites or Rabía were victorious; but they keenly felt the devastation of their country, and their own subordinate position; and thus a great proportion of the newly-converted Persians were filled with hatred towards their Arab " brethren in the faith." This hatred was easily turned against the reigning house, which was named as the source of all unrighteousness, and whose secular disposition

[1] By the Khorásán of that period we are to understand, not merely the modern Persian province of this name, but also extensive tracts to the east and north. Its capital was Merv, now in the hands of Russia.

[2] At that time even the noblest non-Arabian convert, on his acceptance of Islam, had to attach himself as "client" to some Arab tribe ; whereupon he was entitled to add to his own name another, which designated him as belonging to this tribe.

must certainly have been very offensive to the truly pious.
The Persians, moreover, were naturally inclined to legitimism, and to enthusiastic attachments to spiritual leaders.
Accordingly they were drawn over in multitudes to the
doctrine that "the house of the Prophet" alone is called to
dominion over his kingdom and his Church. Well-chosen
emissaries of the Abbásids canvassed for the family of the
Prophet, for the Háshimids, by which expression were
understood, in the first instance, the descendants of Alí.
Other watchwords and fictitious sayings of Mohammed
were also successfully put in circulation. Gradually and
furtively the place of the Alids was taken by the Abbásids,
who undoubtedly also were descendants of Háshim, and
who, since descent from Mohammed in the female line was
represented as unimportant, could claim to be just as nearly
related to the Prophet as the others.[1] The main point was,
that the adherents secured for the cause became entirely
attached to the persons of the emissaries, so that the latter
were able in the end to direct their followers as they
pleased. To secure adherents there seems to have been no
scruple about favouring all sorts of objectionable opinions
(partly due to a mixing up of the old with the new religion)
inconsistent with the fundamental laws of Islam. Of details
of the progress of the agitation we know little; but so much
is certain: that it was very active, that the emissaries had
a regular organisation, and that frequent communication
was maintained between Khorásán and the centres from

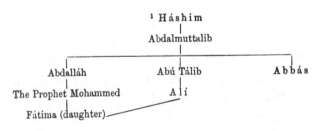

[1] Háshim
|
Abdalmuttalib
|
Abdalláh   Abú Tálib   A b b á s
| |
The Prophet Mohammed   A l í
|
Fátima (daughter)

which the wires were pulled—Cufa, the residence of the
supreme agent, and Humaima, the home of the Abbásids.
The yearly pilgrimages gave special opportunities for meeting
without arousing suspicion; many important consultations
may possibly have taken place in Mecca itself. Operations
had long been carried on in this way, when the head of the
Abbásids—either Mohammed, who died in 743, or his son
Ibráhím, it is not quite certain which—discovered the man
who was destined to bring the movement to a successful
issue. This was Abú Moslim, a freedman whose country
and descent are unknown, but who in any case was not of
Arabian blood. This quondam slave united with an agita-
tor's adroitness and perfect unscrupulosity in the choice of
his means the energy and clear outlook of a general and
statesman, and even of a monarch. Within a few years he
brought it about that the black banner of the Abbásids was
openly unfurled (in the beginning of summer, 747). In a
perfidious but masterly manner he contrived still further to
foment the mutual antipathies of the Arab parties which
were openly at war with each other, although Nasr, the
governor, was not the only one who clearly saw that nothing
less was at stake than the supremacy, and even the very
life, of the Arabs. Ibráhím is even said to have given
orders to Abú Moslim that, so far as possible, no Arab
should be left alive in Khorásán. Soon the brave Nasr was
compelled to quit the country; and immediately afterwards
he died (November 748). The Khorásánians pressed steadily
forwards. The chief control was in the hands of Abú
Moslim, although he remained in Khorásán; not only the
Persians, but also the Arab leaders, put themselves under
the command of the freedman, a thing unheard-of for Arab
pride. It should be added, that the Arabs of Khorásán
undoubtedly had a strong strain of Persian blood, and that
they had taken on much that was Persian.

A large portion of Southern Persia had not long before been seized by another of the Háshimids, Abdalláh, son of Moáwiya, a descendant of Alí's brother Jaafar. He had had the support of the Abbásids. But this thoroughly unworthy person (for such he seems to have been) was overcome by the generals of the Omayyad Merwán II., and betook himself in flight to Abú Moslim. He had served his turn, in so far as he had thrown the empire into wilder confusion, and called the attention of the people to the family of the Prophet; now as a rival he might prove inconvenient. Abú Moslim therefore first cast him into prison, and afterwards took his life.

Babylonia, the most important province of the empire, was occupied by the troops of the Abbásids. Once more a great battle took place close to the field where Alexander had gained his final victory over Darius (middle of January 750). The men belonging to Yemenite tribes, who formed the majority of the Omayyad troops, were disinclined to stake their lives on behalf of Merwán, who was not favourably disposed towards them; and accordingly the battle was lost. Over and above this, there now arose internal struggles in Syria and Egypt, which facilitated the work of the Abbásid troops. Merwán, a tried warrior, had to flee from place to place, and soon afterwards fell, almost deserted, at the village of Búsír,[1] in Middle Egypt (August 750).

The head of the Abbásids was now no longer Ibráhím; he had been thrown into prison by Merwán when his complicity with Abú Moslim was discovered, and, shortly before the triumph of his party, had either died or been murdered in captivity. His brothers had fled to Cufa, and kept themselves in hiding there. Here, immediately after the occupation of the city by the Khorásánians, and before the last blow had been struck against Merwán, Abul-Abbás,

[1] Probably on the right bank of the Nile, opposite Eshmúnein.

now the head of the house, was proclaimed Caliph (November or December 749). In his inaugural sermon in the principal mosque, Abul-Abbás designated himself as Saffáh, *i.e.* "the bloodshedder;" and to this dreadful name, which has since been his standing title, he did ample justice. All Omayyads were ruthlessly struck down. The watchword was: "Vengeance for the Háshimids slain by the Omayyads." It is, of course, possible that the Abbásids, themselves Arabs, may really have had Arab feelings in the matter, and required vengeance for the blood of their relations as such. But the actual motives were nevertheless other than these; their object was to excite the mob against the Omayyads, as being impious men and worthy of death, and to make their whole house absolutely harmless. To this end no violence or treachery was spared. Even those members of the house who had fled for mercy to the conquerors, and had been received by them, nay more, even those who had yielded only on the solemn promise that no harm should befall them, were put to death; and the Abbásids, the Caliph himself, as well as his uncles, and particularly Abdalláh, who led the pursuit of the defeated Merwán, personally gloated over the murder of their adversaries. And yet Abdalláh had only a short time before experienced an act of clemency when, while taking part in the rebellion of the Jaafarids, he had fallen into the hands of Merwán's general. Notwithstanding the fierceness of the massacre, a few members of this very numerous Omayyad family managed to escape. Some kept themselves in hiding, and by and by were ignored or forgiven; others made their escape into the far west, where the Caliph's power did not extend. Nor was it only Omayyad ·blood that was freely shed at the establishment of the Abbásid rule, whether to excite terror among its subjects, or because the new ruler was hardly able to control the lust for slaughter in his victorious troops. Syria, however, did not accommodate itself to the new dynasty without trouble. Various disturbances gave the conquerors a great deal to do from the very first. In particular, it proved an arduous task to suppress those insurgents who had placed at their head Abú Mohammed, a descendant of the first two Omayyad Caliphs.

Shortly after the death of Merwán, his last powerful supporter, Ibn Hobaira, who had taken possession of the important town of Wásit, on the lower Tigris, made his peace after he had been blockaded for a long time by Mansúr, the brother of the Caliph. By both these princely brothers he had been promised not only life, but continuance in his high office. But so lofty a personage, with a large body of adherents, who had already asserted a very independent position as governor of Babylon, harmonised ill with the new condition of affairs. Mansúr accordingly, in concert with his brother, caused him to be put to death; solemn promises and oaths had no meaning for these men. This was done, it is said, on the advice of Abú Moslim. It is more probable that Abú Moslim had a hand in making away with Abú Salama, "the vizier of the Háshimids," who from Babylonia had directed the movement in Khorásán, and who had rendered great services in connection with the change of dynasty. It is alleged that—perhaps in full consistency with his original orders—he had, after the death of Ibráhím, shown more inclination to the Alids than to the Abbásids. In any case he stood in the way of Abú Moslim.

Saffáh appears to have been a strong ruler, who, had he lived longer, might perhaps himself have done for the empire what it was left for his follower to achieve. Great differences between the caliphate of the Abbásids and that of the Omayyads immediately emerged, due in part to the manner in which it had been set up, and in part to the personal character of the rulers. The seat of empire was transferred to Babylonia, the true centre. The power of the sovereign rested primarily on Persian troops, which were more amenable to discipline than Arabian. The Caliph no longer needed to take much account of the tribal jealousies of the Arabs, although he occasionally utilised them for his own ends. Hence he could act much more autocratically than his predecessors; the lands of the caliphate now formed much more of a political unity than before. In short, on the old soil of the great Asiatic empires, another was once more set up, which at the most was only half Arab in its character, the rest being Persian.

Even in Saffáh's lifetime Mansúr took a prominent place as an influential counsellor, and as governor of great provinces, but it is hardly likely that the Caliph allowed himself to be led entirely by his brother.

Abú Moslim, whose people were blindly devoted to him, and who held sway like a prince in Khorásán, in 754 desired to be the leader of the pilgrimage, that is, to represent the Caliph himself before the entire Islamite world. Saffáh, however, quickly instigated Mansúr to seek this dignity for himself, so that he had to express his regret that the office had been already bestowed, and that Abú Moslim could only go as a companion to Mansúr. It seems that in the course of the pilgrimage friction arose between the parvenu who had founded the new empire and the no less self-conscious brother of the Caliph; in any case, Abú Moslim did not by any means overdo the part of a devoted servant. By his liberality he so won over the Bedouins that they declared it a pure slander to call this man an enemy of the Arabs. The two were already on their return journey when news arrived that Saffáh had died (on Sunday, 9th June 754)[1] at Anbár (north of Cufa), and that Mansúr had been proclaimed Caliph on the same day.

Abú Jaafar Abdalláh al Mansúr (*i.e.* "the victorious") was

[1] According to others, on Saturday, 8th June.

at that time a man of over forty. Of his outward appearance we learn that he was tall and thin, and that he had a narrow face, lank hair, thin beard, and brownish complexion. What his inward character was is shown by his deeds. His mother, the Berber slave Sallám2, during her pregnancy dreamed, it is said, that she had brought forth a lion, to which other lions came from all quarters to render homage.[1] A lion, truly, who tore in pieces all who came within his reach, unless they acknowledged him as their master !

Mansúr can hardly have reached the neighbourhood of the Euphrates when he learned that he had a very dangerous rival. His uncle Abdalláh,[2] then posted in the far north of Syria ready to march against the Byzantines, laid claim to the throne. His pretensions, perhaps, were not altogether unfounded, for it is not so certain as is usually asserted that Saffáh nominated Mansúr as his successor. It was indeed unfortunate that the dynasty was hardly established before it was torn asunder by disputes about the succession. As Abú Moslim with the Khorásánians held by Mansúr, Abdalláh was compelled to rely upon the Arab troops of Syria and Mesopotamia, and on this account caused thousands of Khorásánians who were with him to be massacred. Humaid, son of the Arabian general Kahtaba, who five years previously had led the Khorásánian troops from victory to

[1] Compare the dream of Pericles' mother, Herod. vi. 131.

[2]

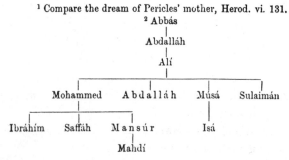

victory, suddenly went over from Abdalláh to Mansúr, and rendered to the latter conspicuous service both in this and in many subsequent wars. Abú Moslim brought an end to the war which had been going on for some months in Mesopotamia by a victory gained on 26th (or 27th) November 754. Abdalláh fled to his brother Sulaimán, Mansúr's governor in Basra (near the mouth of the Tigris), and remained here in hiding for some time.

Abú Moslim thus had not only set up the Abbásid dynasty, but also had saved the throne for Mansúr. A man who had done so much could do still more, and was a danger to his master. Mansúr resolved to get rid of Abú Moslim, a course which is said to have suggested itself even to Saffáh. How they first fell out is told in various ways. It is probable that the Caliph nominated Abú Moslim to be the governor of the western provinces of Syria and Egypt in order to keep him at a distance from Khorásán, where his power had its root, but that the latter did not agree to this. In any case he had noted that Mansúr wished to deprive him of influence, and he resolved accordingly, without reference to Mansúr, to return to Khorásán. Of his own soldiers he was perfectly sure, even in a campaign against the Caliph. At this stage a correspondence took place between the two. Abú Moslim in the end suffered himself to be befooled by the sworn assurances of Mansúr (with a slight admixture of threats), and came with but a small following to the Caliph at the "city of the Romans," a decayed place that had belonged to the Seleucia-Ctesiphon group of Persian royal cities. Mansúr received him graciously, but after having made sure of him, caused him to be slain before his eyes, and the body to be cast into the Tigris (February 755).

The removal of the powerful individuality, of whom we hear that his followers would have sacrificed their lives and their very souls for him, but upon whose fidelity the Caliph could hardly rely, was a political necessity. An intimate of Mansúr's is said to have quoted to him against Abú Moslim the verse of the Koran in which it is said that if the world held other gods besides Alláh it would go to ruin (súra 21, 22). Such a prince as Mansúr could tolerate no rival in the kingdom. Nor can any great claim upon our pity be made for Abú Moslim, who shrank from no resource of violence or treachery, whether against enemies or against inconvenient friends, and of whom it is said (no doubt with huge exaggeration), that he caused as many as 600,000 prisoners to be slain. Mansúr gave proof of admirable astuteness when he overreached the cunningest of the cunning. But that his conduct was abominable goes without saying.

The murder was by no means without danger for its perpetrator. The soldiers indeed whom Abú Moslim had brought with him were restrained from making any disturbance, partly by their dismay at the accomplished fact, and partly by a lavish distribution of money. But mutterings were heard in Khorásán. There the dead man had thousands who clung to him with religious attachment. In fact, there were many who could not believe in his death, and who expected him to return once more as a Messiah. A Persian named Sampádh excited in that very year a great revolt in Khorásán to avenge Abú Moslim. What is reported of him, that he was a professor of the old Persian religion, is improbable; he may have belonged to one of the half Persian sects, which the majority certainly could not regard as Mohammedan. In any case the revolt was a popular movement. Sampádh advanced far towards Media, but thereupon was defeated by Jahwar, whom Mansúr had despatched against him, and slain somewhere near the spot where the last of the Dariuses met his end. The victorious general had made himself master of the treasures of Abú Moslim, and now in turn himself rebelled, but was quickly overcome, and put to death (755 or 756). Khorásán was once more securely in the hands of the Caliph.

In other directions also disturbances of various kinds occurred. The Kharijites,[1] who had no reason for regarding the rule of the Prophet's kinsmen as juster or more in accordance with the laws of God than that of the Omayyads, fought on for their ideals in various parts of the empire, with few followers indeed, but with a courage that defied death. Thus a certain Kharijite, Mulabbid, in Mesopotamia gave much trouble to the armies of the Caliph, and was only at last overcome in 756 by Házim, perhaps the ablest of Mansúr's generals.

A handful of strange mortals brought the Caliph into a very difficult position, probably in 757–8. The Ráwendí, who are guessed to have been connected with Abú Moslim, not only believed in the transmigration of souls, but had also taken into their heads that Mansúr was God Himself. They accordingly betook themselves to his capital, and set themselves in an attitude of worship around his palace. Mansúr, indeed, was quite of the mind that it was better to have people obey him and go to hell in consequence, than earn heaven by rebellion against him; but the Commander of the Faithful durst not tolerate such conduct as this of the Ráwendí, unless he wished to provoke a universal rising of all Moslems against him. He accordingly caused a number of the fanatics to be imprisoned. But they did not take this well; they freed their comrades and now assailed the life of the Caliph, who only had a limited guard at hand. In mastering them, which he did only with difficulty, he displayed great courage. In the struggle

[1] See above, p. 80.

there came to the front one who had been a conspicuous general under the Omayyads, afterwards had kept himself in concealment, and now seized this opportunity to gain favour with the Caliph. This was Maan, son of Záida, famed for his bravery, and still more for his liberality, but at the same time stern and pitiless towards his foes. Mansúr, whom it thoroughly suited to intermingle pure Arabs with his Khorásán generals of mixed Arabian and Persian origin, willingly took the fire-eater into his grace. Shortly afterwards he sent him into Yemen, where, during his nine years' governorship, he subdued all opponents with much bloodshed. Subsequently he sent him to south-eastern Persia, where he was surprised and slain by the Kharijites.

The dynasty of the Omayyads once overthrown, the Alids saw that they had not gained much. It made no difference to them whether their nearer cousins, the descendants of Abbás,[1] or whether their slightly more distant kinsmen, those of Omayya, possessed the sovereignty; the name of Háshim was not enough. When the house of the Prophet had been canvassed for, every one in the first instance had thought of his actual descendants; these last now deemed, not unrightly, that they had been defrauded of their birthright. It is probable that even the Abbásids, in the secret negotiations, at an early stage had at one time freely acknowledged the Alid Mohammed,

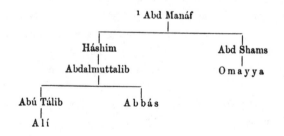

[1] Abd Manáf

son of Abdalláh, as head of the entire house, and as the future Caliph. Why this particular man should have been selected from among the very numerous descendants of Alí, we are unable to say. One advantage, which fell into the scale when a legitimist claim was being urged, he undoubtedly had—namely, that the females also who came into his genealogy were all free Arabs of good family, and that the Hasanid Mohammed was through his grandmother a descendant also of Husain, and thus in a twofold way descended from the Prophet.[1] His father, who might have advanced still stronger claims, was perhaps over-timid or too little ambitious.

The Abbásids knew too well how it was that they themselves had reached the throne to be other than exceedingly jealous of the hereditary advantages of their cousins. One and another Alid now and again expressed tolerably openly his opinion of the situation. And the Mohammed just mentioned, as well as his brother Ibráhím, had betrayed themselves by refraining to come to pay their respects to Mansúr when he made the pilgrimage during the lifetime of his brother. If Mansúr actually had at one time acknowledged Mohammed's right to the caliphate, this would be to him a further motive for effort to have them in his power. But neither promises nor threats availed; they hid themselves in various quarters of Arabia, and are

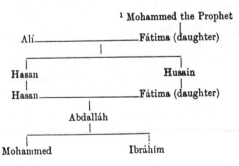

[1] Mohammed the Prophet

Alí————————Fátima (daughter)

Hasan   Husain

Hasan————————Fátima (daughter)

Abdalláh

Mohammed   Ibráhím

said to have wandered about in even remoter lands. As
their father when closely questioned persisted in declaring
that he had no idea where his sons were living, Mansúr,
when he came on pilgrimage once more to Mecca in April
758, caused him to be imprisoned. But even this did not
avail. The governors in Medina either could not or would
not find the fugitives. The inhabitants were attached to
the Alids as being children of the Prophet and children
of their city, and the majority of the officials even would
doubtless have felt it to be a crime to deliver them up to
destruction. Riyáh, however, of the tribe of Morra, who
entered upon the governorship of Medina on 27th December
761, was free from any such weakness. He threatened the
inhabitants with the same fate with which, sixty-eight years
before, his fellow tribesman Moslim, son of Okba, had visited
their rebellion against authority.[1] He caused all the nearer
kinsmen of Mohammed's family, and many of his adherents,
to be imprisoned, and also a number of the Juhaina Bedouins,
among whose mountains, to the west of Medina,[2] it was
supposed that the claimant was in hiding. When, at the
close of another pilgrimage (March 762), Mansúr visited
Medina, he took these captive Alids, including the father
of the two brothers, and various other persons of consideration, and carried them with him in chains into Babylonia.
Amongst these exiles was the step-brother of Abdalláh, who
secretly, and in violation of his plighted word, had given
his daughter in marriage to his nephew, the claimant,
and is said also to have himself seemed formidable by
reason of his personal distinction as a descendant of Caliph
Othmán. A son of Mohammed's fell into the hands of the
governor of Egypt, and was sent to the Caliph. We can
readily believe what we read, that the treatment of these

[1] See above, p. 81.
[1] The Juhaina (Jchéne) have their home there to this day.

hostages was by no means indulgent;[1] several were put to death, many died in prison. But popular imagination, or personal hatred, has raised the colours of the picture; the story goes that the Caliph kept the bodies of all the murdered Alids in a great chamber to which no one had access but himself; in the ear of each was a label with his name and genealogy neatly written. Mansúr's son Mahdí ventured to use the key after his father's death, and, horrified at the discovery, caused them all to be buried.

Riyáh's diligent search seems at length to have led Mohammed to attempt a premature revolt, which towards the end of 762 broke out in Medina. Mohammed was proclaimed Caliph, the captives set free, the governor and other adherents of Mansúr thrown into prison. The famous doctor of Islam, Málik, son of Anas, gave his decision that the oath of allegiance to the Abbásids, having been obtained by force, was of no binding obligation. This is characteristic at once for the ethics of Islam and for the view of the rule of the Abbásids which was taken by those persons who were, properly speaking, the guardians of religion and of the sacred law.[2] At Málik's dictum everybody went over to Mohammed. Even the descendants of Abú Bekr and other men of Koraish, who had formerly distinguished themselves at the founding of the empire of Islam, for the most part joined him. So also did the poet Abú Adí al Ablí, who belonged to a side branch of the house of Omayya. These

---

[1] During the journey Abdalláh is reported to have shouted to Mansúr: " We did not so treat the prisoners we took from you at Badr ! " This was a bitter allusion to the fact that Abdalláh's ancestor Alí had been a champion of Islam in the Prophet's very first battle, while the ancestor of the Abbásids, who now wished to be taken as representing the rights of the Prophet's house, took at that period the side of the heathen, and with many of his comrades had been taken prisoner, but had been mercifully treated.

[2] Historical tradition, on the whole, is not indeed against the Abbásids, but it is at the same time very favourable to the Alids. This is shown even by the great fulness of detail with which it records all Alid rebellions.

individuals, however, seem to have inherited but little of the statesmanlike and warlike ability of their ancestors. From the very first many clear-headed men saw that the enterprise had small prospect of success. When a volunteer courier, in the extraordinarily short space of nine days, brought news of the insurrection to Mansúr at Cufa, he was far from dissatisfied with this clearing of the situation. "Now, at last," said he, "I have the fox out of his hole!" Medina was of all places least suited for the foundation of an anti-caliphate,—for this, among other reasons, that the whole region was dependent on imports from Egypt, the supply of which was now at once cut off. Mansúr sent his cousin Isá, son of Músá, with a small but tried army against Medina. Mohammed proved no more equal to his task than the other Alid pretenders had done. Instead of taking the advice of persons skilled in war, and assuming the offensive, he remained within the city of the Prophet, the sanctity of which he took to be his best defence : once, in a dream, it had appeared to the Prophet under the figure of a breastplate. By way of fortification he çaused the fosse of the Prophet to be restored; a work which indeed had filled with astonishment the Arabs combined against Mohammed, —men who had had no experience of war on a large scale, or indeed of any kind of strenuous united action,—but which was mere child's play for the veterans of Khorásán. Isá had already, by letters, won over from Mohammed various important persons. The great bulk of his followers quietly melted away as the foe drew near. Isá paused for three days before Medina, to obtain, if possible, an amicable settlement by negotiation, and operations then began. The fosse was bridged with some house-doors. A woman of the family of Abbás secretly caused a large black cloth to be hoisted on the tallest minaret; upon this all the pious townsmen immediately rushed to the conclusion that the Khorásánians had entered the city by the rear, and there had planted the black banner of the Abbásids. Only a few, including a company of Juhaina Bedouins, stood by Mohammed. Mohammed, a tall and handsome man, fell after a heroic struggle late on the afternoon of Monday, 6th December 762. He had caused the captive Riyáh to be put to death immediately before. One more addition was thus now made to the roll of Alid "martyrs," who had inherited from their ancestors courage and bravery, but with these also an incapacity for generalship and supreme command. The supporters of the house surnamed Mohammed as "the pure soul."

Isá, obeying orders, showed comparative clemency. It was of importance to the descendants of Abbás that the sanctity of the city of the Prophet, to whom they traced back their rights, should not be violated too grossly. Some prominent participators in the rebellion, indeed, were put to death, or else imprisoned or subjected to severe corporal chastisement. The goods of that branch of the Alid family to which the pretender had belonged were confiscated. According to the custom of the time, his head was brought to the Caliph, who sent it by courier-post round the provinces as an awful example. It arrived in Egypt in the spring of 763, just in time to check a rising of the Alid party there.

While affairs in Medina were still undecided, the Caliph learned that Ibráhím had risen in the interests of his brother Mohammed at Basra (Monday, 22nd November 762). Mansúr had previously come to know that Ibráhím was in hiding there, and had taken some precautionary measures accordingly; but he nevertheless seems to have been greatly taken aback by this new insurrection. Basra was not merely a wealthy trading city, but also, from a military point of view, very different in importance from Medina.

To a man of enterprise it offered great opportunities; from it as a basis, the Tigris and Euphrates could be blockaded, and the maritime provinces to the east comparatively easily mastered. Nor was this all; the very important city, in the immediate neighbourhood of which Mansúr had his residence, the turbulent Cufa, was thoroughly Alid in its sympathies. Should an Alid make his appearance in the neighbourhood with an army, an outbreak might be expected within it at any moment. In addition to this, the whole central province was in a state of ferment. But Mansúr had at the moment only a very few troops at hand. He afterwards confessed that it had been a great mistake to leave himself so bare, and declared that in future he would always retain at least 30,000 men beside him. He managed, however, to arrange them so that the Cufans considerably overestimated the number of his forces. The Cufans were, moreover, always much more heroic in words than in deeds. Mansúr, however, was not yet able to take the offensive against Ibráhím; but was constrained to suffer the latter, into whose hands the treasure of the rich province of Basra had fallen, to become master of Susiana and Persis also. Wásit also received the troops of Ibráhím. In the neighbourhood of this city, indeed, he was encountered by an officer of Mansúr's; and here the two armies stood, facing one another, until the whole struggle was ended.

Ibráhím deemed himself already a sovereign, and spent his time with a wife whom he had just married. Mansúr, on the other hand, never looked on the face of woman till the conflict was over. A contemporary praises, in eloquent words, the courage and determination which he maintained in his critical position. The advice to incite Cufa to revolt was set aside by Ibráhím because such a step would cause much harm to children, women, and other non-combatants. In the same spirit he forbade pursuit of fugitives, and so forth. All this sounds very well, but is out of place in one who, for his own interests, is carrying on a rebellion which, under any circumstances, must involve much bloodshed, and can ultimately achieve success only by concentration of every energy. In such tenderness there is more of weakness than of humanity. " Thou desirest the sovereignty, yet darest not to slay !" some one said to him. *Pour faire des omelettes il faut casser les œufs.*

Soon after the middle of December 762, Ibráhím received the crushing intelligence of his brother's death. Yet if even now he had advanced immediately, he would still have been able to put Mansúr to great straits. But when he finally marched towards Cufa with barely 10,000 men, a sixth or a tenth of his strength on paper, Isá had already arrived at the head of a superior army. The Caliph had ordered troops from Media against Susiana, which soon captured the capital Ahwáz. In Bákhamrá, only sixteen hours south of Cufa, the army of Ibráhím, who had now assumed the title of Caliph, encountered the advancing host of Isá (Monday, 14th February 763). Mansúr's vanguard was driven back; but Isá held his ground, and the fugitives soon rallied. Mansúr's cousins, the sons of Sulaimán, fell upon Ibráhím's rear. After a fierce battle he fell, mortally wounded with an arrow. The Caliph caused his head also to be publicly exhibited, but would not suffer a bystander to treat the dead with contumely. He punished with frightful cruelty a coarse person who had spat on Ibráhím's head in his presence.

A victory for Ibráhím seems to have been widely counted upon. The famous blind poet, Basshár, no sectary, but an enlightened freethinker, had sent him a poem, in which he was praised, and Mansúr violently attacked; after the battle he so altered the poem, that he was able to give it out as an earlier production directed against Abú Moslim.

Ibráhím's death was a much greater relief to Mansúr than

that of Mohammed. He could now feel pretty sure that henceforth no Alid claimant could be of danger to him. True, he caused the whole family of those kinsmen of his to be strictly watched, but he was particularly willing to receive into his service any members of it whom he thought he could venture to trust. Perhaps in this the old Arab feeling for family ties had still some part; however that may be, it produced a good effect, as showing to subjects that both the main branches of the Háshimids still held by one another.

In Medina these struggles were followed by a little after-piece. Persian soldiers behaved with violence towards peaceful inhabitants. The people complained to the chief authority, but received no attention. Then active resistance began. The town butchers (black freedmen, it would seem) killed a soldier; from this it grew to a general *melée*. The negroes, who were numerous, both slaves and freedmen, drew together, and killed part of the little garrison. The governor fled. They even seized on the stores that had been set apart for the troops. The higher classes trembled before the wrath of Mansúr. It is noteworthy that two who specially exerted themselves for the restoration of order were a member of the Omayyad family and an official who had been imprisoned for his participation in the rising of Mohammed. The loyalty of the population towards the sovereign was strongly insisted on. The stores that had been plundered were given back or made good. The blacks suffered themselves to be persuaded by the representations of the most prominent citizens, and returned home. It was now seen to have been only a momentary outburst of temper, no social revolution. The governor returned at the earnest invitation of the notables. Four ringleaders had a hand chopped off — the punishment of thieves. The chief mis-chiefmaker perished in prison.

The rebellion of the Alids had interrupted Mansúr in a

great undertaking—the building of Bagdad. With the fall
of the Omayyads it had become quite a matter of course
that the rulers of the enormous empire, which extended from
what is now Russian Turkestan and the Indus to Aden,
Algeria, and Eastern Asia Minor,[1] should have their seat in
Babylonia; but they had not as yet any definite capital.
Mansúr lived a great deal in Háshimíya, founded by his
predecessor, in the immediate neigbourhood of Cufa. But
the Cufans, little attached as they were to the Abbásids,
were no desirable neighbours. After the death of Ibráhím,
Mansúr had preached them as sharp a sermon against their
sins as any Omayyad governor could have delivered, and
expressed in it his astonishment that the Omayyads had not
long ago depopulated the accursed place as an abode of unbelievers. Moreover, nothing but a creation of his own could
have satisfied Mansúr's haughty nature. After long deliberation he determined to build the new capital on a site on the
west bank of the Tigris, then occupied by a little place named
Baghdád.[2] So far as we can judge, the district had already
before this time been brought into communication with the
Euphrates by means of canals. Mansúr caused the connection to be notably extended and improved. The official
name of the city here planted was Madínat-as-Salám ("the
city of welfare"), but in practical use the old name Bagdad
maintained exclusive currency. Mansúr's keen vision in
the selection of this site may well be compared with that
shown by Alexander when he founded the Egyptian Alexandria. At any rate, the situation of this city, which he

[1] In area Mansúr's empire was much greater than that of Rome at its
greatest, in population much poorer, and, on that account, as well as for
geographical reasons, much more difficult to govern.

[2] In this choice of site one element that came into consideration was the
comparative absence of mosquitoes. Any one who has made acquaintance
with the gnats of the Rhine or of Venice can form some faint conception of
what the inhabitants of those hot countries, with their many pools and
marshes, have to suffer from these little bloodsuckers.

called into being out of nothing, is so favourable that it
soon became a world-city, with all the lights and shadows of
such ; a place which, Constantinople apart, had no rival, and
which, even in the deep decline of all these countries since
that time, and notwithstanding the irreparable injury suffered
by Bagdad itself when it was destroyed by the Mongols in
1258, still remains a considerable city, by far the most
important in the whole region of the Euphrates and Tigris.
The work of building had been begun in early summer of
762. When news came of Mohammed's revolt, the walls
were hardly six feet high. When Ibráhím approached, the
rumour spread that he had gained a great victory. Hereupon the freedman who had been left in charge of the vast
accumulations of building materials set fire to the stores of
timber, that they might not fall into the hand of the enemy.
As soon as the empire was once more pacified, Mansúr caused
operations to be resumed. The building was carried out on a
magnificent scale. Vast sums were expended by the Caliph
in building residences for himself, his dependants, kinsfolk,
and freedmen, as well as his officers and troops, and also in
constructing mosques, government offices, aqueducts, canal
bridges, and fortifications. He assigned allotments to the
members of the reigning house and the grandees on which
to build their houses. Troops of handicraftsmen, traders,
and other settlers flocked to the spot. Houses of sun-dried
brick cost but little, and it is possible that even directly,
certainly indirectly, the trifling outlay of the builders was
in many cases made good out of the public exchequer.
Traders had, moreover, to pay a duty upon their shops. In
766 the great city was practically finished; its walls were
completed in 768. Mansúr's city, as already mentioned, lay
on the west bank of the river. Yet even he caused the
opposite side, where now the main part of Bagdad lies, to
be built on. "The camp" of his son Mahdí was there. It

seemed expedient to place a portion of the garrison on the
other side of the river, so that, in case of necessity, the two
divisions of the army might be able to hold one another in
check. A peculiar police regulation was introduced later
by Mansúr; he caused the markets, which were frequented
by an excessive number of strangers, whose supervision was
not easy, to be removed outside the city proper. Bagdad
was strongly fortified. Mansúr caused other important
inland cities also to be fortified in such a way that the
garrisons might be able to cope with casual insurrections.
This he did also in the case of the city of Ráfika, founded
by him in 772 in the neighbourhood of Rakka (Callinicus),
on the east bank of the middle Euphrates, in which he
placed a garrison of Khorásánians.

The active superintendence which Mansúr gave to the
building of his capital is only an instance of the whole
system of his government, which was, as far as possible,
personal. Posts were still conferred on a certain number
of Arab nobles, who still sometimes showed the insubordi-
nation and tribal patriotism of their race, but he took care
that they never overgrew himself. At the same time, he
conferred the most important governorships upon various
members of his own family, and made ample provision for
all of them; but he kept them in strict subjection, and
on occasion chastised them severely. He had absolutely
trustworthy tools in his freedmen and clients of foreign
extraction, to whom, to the horror of the aristocratic Arabs,
he sometimes gave even the most important administrative
offices. The governors and other high officials of the
provinces were strictly overseen by special officers, entirely
independent of them, who sent an uninterrupted series of
couriers with their reports to the Caliph.[1] When, for

---

[1] The imperial posts were, as in the ancient Persian empire, well managed,
—not, however, for general use, but only for that of government.

example, Mansúr on one occasion learned through this channel that the governor of Hadramaut (in the extreme south of Arabia) was more attentive to the pleasures of the chase than to the duties of his office, he deposed him at once. Even the actions of Mahdí, the heir-apparent, in his capacity as governor of the lands of the east were subjected to this kind of control. Thus, the Caliph having on one occasion learned that Mahdí had given to a certain poet much too great a reward for a laudatory copy of verses, he compelled the recipient to repay the greater part of the sum.[1] These officers, in addition to their special duties, reported all the more important law cases, and all occurrences of any particular interest; they further apprised the Caliph of the price of provisions; for, with a view to public peace and security, it was judged necessary to take prompt measures for the prevention of dearths.[2] So well was Mansúr informed as to the state of the provinces, that it was whispered he had a magic mirror in which he could see all his enemies. Still better is he characterised by his own words to his son: "Sleep not, for thy father has not slept since he came to the caliphate; when sleep fell upon his eyes, his spirit remained awake." He was an excellent financier. He is frequently reproached with avarice even; he was surnamed "the father of farthings," — a reproach which presumably came chiefly from those whose interests would have been served by that prodigality to favourites which has procured a very undeserved reputation for many Oriental sovereigns. In the same way other eminently good

[1] As Caliph, Mahdí afterwards restored the whole sum once more to the poet.

[2] It is much to be regretted that none of these reports have come down to us. Altogether, we have extremely few original documents for the history of the Arabian empire; nor are those very numerous even which have been preserved for us, either wholly, or in substance, in extant works. On the other hand, the narrative of the history of the caliphate is copious.

rulers, such as the Omayyads Abdalmelik and Hishám, have the reputation of avarice. Mansúr was certainly strict in money matters. The vast expenditures on the building of Bagdad he caused to be accounted for down to the last farthing, and he compelled his officials to refund little profits which they had made for themselves. He looked sharply after his tax collectors. In payment of the land tax he commanded that only certain kinds of the gold coins of the Omayyads which were quite of full weight should be received. Of course he followed also the old established principle of Oriental princes, according to which high officers who had gorged themselves were compelled to give back their accumulations.[1] Even one of such exalted position, and of such conspicuous service in the establishment and support of the Abbásid dynasty, as was the Persian [2] Khálid, son of Barmek, the founder of the Barmecide power, was subjected to an operation of this kind. He was called upon within a very short time to pay 3,000,000 dirhems (about £57,000); the Caliph in the end was satisfied with 2,700,000. Nay, even Mansúr's own brother Abbás was compelled to give up the money which he had squeezed from the people when governor of Mesopotamia, and was imprisoned besides. An Oriental State can never altogether prevent the abuse by which officials, small and great, enrich

---

[1] "At a time when no conception of any such thing as operation on the credit of the State had been thought of, whenever receipts fell short of expenditure, there was no other way of raising money but that of taking it where it was to be had. The State, that is, the Caliph, did this in the form of money fines, by taking from people of notorious wealth a portion, or the whole, of their generally ill-gotten gains. . . . The people, as a whole, found themselves under this system much better off than if ever-increasing burdens had been accumulated upon them by a universal raising of customs and dues, and for this reason, doubtless, I find no word of complaint on the subject in any of the historians of the period." A. von Kremer, in his exceedingly instructive dissertation, *Ueber das Einnahme budget des Abbasiden-Reiches vom Jahre* 306 H. (Vienna 1887) p. 11.

[2] More correctly, Bactrian.

themselves in illicit ways.   On the occasion of a land survey
at Basra it was discovered that a family of consideration,
the descendants of the Prophet's freedman Abú Bekra, had
increased their estate to a prodigious extent; the Caliph
cut it down to a tenth.   Here is a piece of the higher
finance:[1] Mansúr ordered every inhabitant of Cufa to pay
five dirhems (nearly two shillings); all, of course, complied.
Having in this way ascertained their exact number, he
imposed on all a poll-tax[2] of forty dirhems (fifteen shillings),
and applied the money to the fortifications of the city.
Whether this story is exact we will not undertake to say;
in any case, it is probable that he sought by stringent
measures to raise the revenue as much as possible, especially
as he left to his successor an overflowing-exchequer.   It
must, however, be considered that the comparative measure
of quiet which he secured for most of the countries of his
empire more than compensated for high taxation.   How far
the Christians' complaints of special fiscal oppression under
Mansúr were justified, is a point we can hardly clear up
now; perhaps they arose chiefly from the circumstance that
he taxed churches and monasteries, which was not so very
unreasonable.   If he again reduced the tribute of the
Cyprians to the sum originally fixed by treaty, this was
probably due, not so much to a sense of justice as to policy;
it was expedient that so exposed a possession should be
considerately treated.

We are safe in saying that the rule of Mansúr, however
hard, treacherous, or ruthless it may often have been, was
on the whole a blessing to the empire.   He could say of
himself with truth, that he had done for the mass of the
people the one thing which the masses needed; he had
insisted on righteousness (in the administrative and judicial

---

[1] It recalls the anecdotes in the pseudo-Aristotelic *Oeconomica*, Bk. ii.

[2] So we read ; but we may be sure that only heads of families are meant.

acts of his officials), had protected them against external attack, and had secured internal peace and quiet. The fruits of his exertions were reaped by his successors, who were by no means on a level with himself. The great prosperity of the empire under his grandson Hárún ar Rashíd is mainly due to Mansúr. It must be borne in mind, of course, that when we speak of an Oriental State, justice and internal peace must always be taken with large qualifications. Even the best of Oriental governments is extremely defective from our point of view.[1]

The personal requirements of Mansúr were few. Born and bred in the deserts of Edom, he had no turn for such luxury as prevailed in the court of his son, and which afterwards often passed into extravagant profligacy. Like his predecessor, he seems to have been no slave of women. He drank no wine, and did not tolerate at his court music and song, which at that time were only too often the handmaids of debauchery. On the other hand, he was a friend of literature; he particularly admired the fine heroic histories of old Arabia. Himself a man of high mental endowments, he liked to associate with people of culture and intellect. He found pleasure also in the verses and drollery of the talented bibulous and frivolous negro Abú Duláma, who seems to have been more of a court fool than of a court poet. By natural gift and by cultivation, he became one of the most famous of Arabic orators. He it was, moreover, who first caused Greek scientific works to be translated into Arabic. He had at least a share in the rise of Arabic science which took place in his time.

The sovereign before whose wrath all the world bowed in shrinking fear, and of whose bloody severity frightful things were told, was under his own roof a kindly father and master. He knew how to appreciate frank, dignified

[1] In saying this, I do not mean that we Europeans live in a political Paradise.

demeanour in cases where this did not appear to carry
danger. Thus he pardoned a Kharijite who was to have
been beheaded in his presence, and whom he had assailed
with insulting language, when the latter pointed out to
him how unseemly such conduct was. And he fully
appreciated the Omayyad sovereigns Moáwiya, Abdalmelik,
and Hishám, as also that brave and unselfish servant of the
Omayyads, the great Hajjáj.

The most devoted followers of the Alids were in the
habit of asserting that they had derived from the Prophet
a hereditary wisdom; this was one, or even the sole ground
on which the sovereignty was claimed for them. Among
the Persians, in particular, views of this kind had great
currency. The first Abbásid claimants and sovereigns also
made similar pretensions. It was the part of the good
subject to believe that the heads of this house enjoyed a
special divine illumination. But, apart from the individuals
who had been won over by their emissaries at the beginning, this faith did not spread. Even the Arab Moslems
were much more inclined to attribute such an advantage
to the Alids than to the reigning family. Mansúr himself
doubtless viewed this doctrine of his own special enlightenment much as an intelligent Roman emperor regarded the
divine honours paid him by poets and subservient provincials.
At any rate, his nature was cool, and religious zeal will be
imputed to him by no one. So long as heterodox persons
were not dangerous to the State he left them unmolested.
Under his reign there were no persecutions of sectaries,
such as his son Mahdí so soon afterwards instituted, and still
less of the supporters of unpopular school opinions, such as
occurred frequently at a later date. In his time, moreover,
the unanimity of a later age as to orthodox doctrine or
orthodox practice in Islam had not yet been attained;
much leaven was still at work which was afterwards cast

out. His Christian physician was accustomed to wine; Mansúr in his own palace caused the obnoxious liquor to be supplied to him. On the other hand, he praised this functionary for his fidelity to the now aged wife whom he had left behind at home, when he sent back the beautiful female slaves presented to him by the Caliph because Christianity enjoined monogamy. But, of course, Mansúr's edicts and letters, according to the fashion of the time, overflowed with pious phrases and texts from the Koran ; and this was most of all conspicuous in the religious political discourses which, after the example of the earlier Caliphs, he delivered on Fridays from the pulpit of some great mosque. Mansúr was further led by the traditions of his family to assume to some extent the part of a theologian, especially in giving forth alleged sayings of the Prophet. Some characteristic specimens of such oral traditions communicated by him to others have come down to us. Thus he declared the Prophet to have said, that if he had appointed to a governor a definite revenue, then everything which the latter took in excess of this was unlawful spoliation. Unfortunately, not many of Mansúr's governors were so tender of conscience as to take seriously to heart a word of the Prophet guaranteed on such authority. At the same time, all things considered, I do not venture to maintain that Mansúr was at heart an utter unbeliever. In the East, still less than in the West, does one expect to find absolute consistency in matters of religion. The man who in cold blood violated his most sacred oaths may yet have argued with himself that Alláh the All-merciful would at last forgive him, good Moslem as he was, all his sins. Perhaps he hoped even that God would impute it to him for righteousness that he was the cousin of the Apostle of God; that would have been a truly Arab thought. In the same way it is also possible that his repeated pilgrimages, over and above their political purpose, which is obvious, may have been designed also to satisfy a personal need. It is conceivable, too, that the old sinner may have counted on the divine favour because he had vigorously carried on the holy war against unbelievers.[1]

The baneful frontier war, carried on for centuries between the caliphate and the Byzantine empire, and interrupted only by short truces, pursued its course under Mansúr, though mostly only in the form of plundering forays, devastation of the open country, and destruction of single fortresses and cities. Mansúr sought to make his frontier against the Byzantines as secure as possible by freshly fortifying a number of cities and supplying them with adequate garrisons. In this respect his restorations of the ruined fortresses of Melatia in Lesser Armenia, and of that of Massísa (Mopsuhestia) in Cilicia,—a town which he almost founded anew, — were of special importance. These frontier fortresses naturally served also as bases of operations against the enemy's territory. The maritime towns on the Syrian coast were in like manner placed by Mansúr in a state of defence.

The other frontiers also gave enough to do. In 764 the wild Khazars (in what is now Southern Russia) invaded the territory south of the Caucasus, took Tiflis, devastated the country far and wide, and defeated more than one army. Before a sufficient force could be sent against them, they had again disappeared. But Mansúr now took precautions, by defensive works, to check as much as possible the inroads of these and other northern barbarians, at whose hands these lands had long suffered severely. He took firm possession of the whole territory

---

[1] "Tantum relligio potuit suadere malorum," wrote Lucretius, without any inkling of the misery yet destined to come upon the world through the aggressiveness of Semitic religious zeal.

up to the great mountain chain, and even levied a tax upon the naphtha-springs of Baku.

The mountainous districts on the southern margin of the Caspian, on the other hand, remained unsubdued. The Dílemites (in Gílán) made frequent plundering attacks on the adjoining country, as had been their immemorial habit. The war against them was continual. We learn incidentally that in 760–61 the Caliph summoned expressly the richer inhabitants of Cufa to take arms against the Dílemites. Now, theoretically, every Moslem capable of bearing arms is under constant obligation to fight against unbelievers; but we may conjecture that what Mansúr had chiefly in view was the money which those not very warlike people would have to pay for exemption from service.—Tabaristán (Mázenderán), which borders Gílán on the east, where a family of high functionaries of the Sásánian empire had maintained themselves as an independent dynasty and still kept up the religion of Zoroaster, was almost entirely annexed for the first time under Mansúr.[1] A former butcher of Rai (Rhagae, near the modern Teheran), who, on his own responsibility, had collected a body of men, and at its head had fought bravely against Sampádh,[2] received the appointment of governor. But this conquest of Tabaristán was not yet final.

The struggle continued to be carried on—with many interruptions, it is true—against the unbelievers (Turks and others) beyond the Oxus; so also on the Indian frontier, where during Mansúr's reign Kandahár, among other places, was taken. But the extension of the Mohammedan empire in these frontier regions was nowhere great. We do not know whether the fleet which Mansúr despatched from Basra in 770 to chastise a tribe of pirates in the delta of the Indus was successful. Two years before members of

---

[1] The exact year is unknown.　　　　[2] See above, p. 118.

this tribe had ventured up the Red Sea, and had plundered Jiddah, the port of Mecca.[1]

In the repression of the Alid rebellion Isá, son of Músá, had, as we have seen, specially distinguished himself, and, by a binding arrangement, the succession to the sovereignty had been secured to him. But Mansúr wished to be succeeded by his own son Mahdí. He according wrote to his cousin a letter full of unction, in which he represented the troops as having taken Madhí to their heart to such a degree that the former must of necessity yield to him. The claim had even a stronger foundation, for the unscrupulous poet Mutí had produced before the assembled court a prediction of the Prophet which clearly pointed to Mahdí as the future pattern prince, and had even had the audacity to call in Abbás, the Caliph's brother, as a witness to the genuineness of the announcement,—a testimony in which the latter had, against his will, to concur. In spite of all this Isá held his own, and maintained, certainly with good reason, not only that the Caliph and his officials were obliged by the oath which they had tendered to him to protect him in his rights, but that he had also bound himself by his oath, and dared not abandon his claim. At last, by threats and all sorts of importunities, he was rendered pliable, and renounced on condition that he was to be the successor of Mahdí. Officials and people were in this way released from the terms of their oath to Isá (764). The condition attached was from the first rather illusory, for Mansúr's son was much younger than Isá, and actually survived him; but before Isá's death Mahdí as Caliph had already compelled him definitely to resign his claims in favour of Mahdí's son Hádí.

·At this time also (764) Mansúr's quondam rival, his uncle

[1] At sea the great Arab dynasties, like the Roman, have seldom done anything considerable.

Abdalláh, died. Abdalláh, as already related, had after his
defeat taken refuge with his brother Sulaimán at Basra (end
of 754). When Mansúr came to know that he was in hiding
there, he demanded his surrender; but this was not granted
until after he had pledged himself in the most solemn way
that no harm should befall Abdalláh. In the deed in which
this security was promised,—a deed accepted by the Caliph,
—it was specified, among other things, that Mansúr, should
he break the agreement, would be held as renouncing the
sovereignty, and as releasing his subjects from their oath of
allegiance. These clauses were little to Mansúr's taste;
people might, perhaps, one day think of taking him at his
word! The author of the document, Ibn Mokaffa, famous
as a stylist and as a poet, and particularly meritorious as
translator of older Persian works, was accordingly, on
account of the words in question, put to death with cruelty
on a hint from the Caliph. And when Abdalláh (12th May
759) came to his nephew, in spite of every promise he was
seized, and his companions slain. Abdalláh himself also,
according to accounts, died a violent death. Yet it is difficult to see why Mansúr should have spared his uncle for so
long a time if imprisonment was not a sufficient measure of
security; a seven years' imprisonment was of itself enough
to account for the death of a man no longer young. Still
less can we rely on the various rumours according to which
the death of Mohammed, son of Saffáh (beginning of 767),
was due to violence; for Mansúr had no occasion to be
afraid of this dissolute nephew. The fantastic stories that
are told in connection with these things show us, at all
events, what the Commander of the Faithful was deemed
capable of. On the other hand, I am bound to point out
that Mansúr, if he never shrank from an atrocity that he
deemed serviceable, hardly can have found his pleasure in
mere murder and bloodshed. Accordingly, he disapproved

of Isá's having put to death a son of Nasr; for, bravely as Nasr had fought on behalf of the Omayyad, his son was now no source of danger.

Though, after the defeat of the Alids, Mansúr had the empire as a whole well in hand, yet in the remoter provinces all sorts of trouble still arose, some of them very serious. For example, the Armeniän nobles, who had always been restless, had once more to be put down by force. In 767 there was another violent outbreak in Khorásán. Its leader[1] is said to have claimed to possess the gift of prophecy; however this may be, the movement undoubtedly was of a religious, strongly heretical character. The histories do not recognise the insurgents as Moslems at all. Kházim himself born or bred in Khorásán, was sent against them; but could effect nothing until he got it arranged that the vizier of Madhí, the heir-apparent, who governed the eastern provinces from Rai as viceroy, should no longer be allowed to interfere with the unity of the command by giving separate orders to the subordinate officers. This done, he brought the insurrection to an end by a brilliant victory and a terrible massacre (768). He is said to have caused 14,000 prisoners to be beheaded. If we consider that Charlemagne, fourteen years afterwards, caused 4,000 captive Saxons to be massacred,[2] and that by command of prince (afterwards Caliph) Hárún, who certainly was a man of much higher culture than either Mansúr's general or the Frankish king, 2,900 Byzantine prisoners were put to death in the year 765, the number just given will not appear much too great. From other facts, also, we know Kházim to have been a man of great severity. The wars with unbelievers, especially with Turks and Byzantines, and the civil wars, had trained

[1] His name is now, owing to the ambiguity of the Arabic characters and the mistakes of copyists, quite uncertain.

[2] The objections that have recently been urged against this statement are hardly strong enough to invalidate it.

a race of brave but pitiless fighters. The leader of the insurrection was brought a prisoner before Mansúr, and executed.

Another great rebellion broke out soon afterwards in the province of "Africa" (corresponding nearly to the modern Tripoli and Tunis), where, indeed, matters had never been thoroughly quiet. It, too, had a religious and also a national origin ; the rebels were Berbers and Kharijites. The Caliph's governor, who shortly before had been transferred to Africa from the Indian frontier,—a distance of about sixty degrees of longitude,—fell in battle against them. Mansúr now sent Yezíd, son of Hátim, with a great army upon the scene, and, to show how important the matter was in his eyes, accompanied him in person as far as to Jerusalem (770). In the following year Yezíd gained a decisive victory, and triumphantly entered the capital, Kairawán, where he remained as governor till long after Mansúr's death. The Caliph's territory did not extend much farther than this. The regions more to the west had been separated from the caliphate since the fall of the Omayyads. In Spain the Omayyad Abderrahmán, a grandson of Caliph Hishám, after surmounting innumerable dangers, and landing in the country without resources and without allies, at the age of twenty-five, in the spring of 756, had rapidly established an independent empire. All efforts of Mansúr to shatter his power proved vain. Like Mansúr himself, he was the son of a Berber slave-girl. The Caliph, who, as we have seen, knew how to recognise valour and greatness even in enemies of his house, called him " the falcon of the Koraish " (the tribe to which the Omayyads, Abbásids, and many other families of consideration belonged).

Much less important than either of those just spoken of were the risings in northern Arabia, which were quelled by Okba in 768 or 769. In doing so Okba, a Yemenite Arab,

out of tribal hostility shed an inordinate quantity of blood.
Wishing to give a handsome present to an official whom the
Caliph had sent to him, he handed over to him fifty
prisoners, whom he was to take with him to Basra, making
as if he was about to decapitate them and hang up their
bodies; their tribesmen in that city would then be ready to
redeem them at 10,000 dirhems (nearly £200) a piece. The
pretty plan was unfortunately spoiled by the temper of the
populace and the interference of an intelligent Cadi. On
the report of the latter to the Caliph, he was thanked, and
the prisoners let go.

It was while returning from a pilgrimage to Mecca that
Mansúr had become Caliph; on a similar journey to Mecca
he was destined to die. In 775 he once more set out; on
the way he was seized with a disease of the bowels
(dysentery ?), which was probably connected with troubles
of the digestive system from which he had formerly suffered.
The heat of the Arabian late summer, and the fatigues and
privations of the journey (on which even the Caliph must
often have had to content himself with very indifferent
drinking water), can only have aggravated the malady in a
man now somewhat advanced in years, if they did not even
occasion it. He succeeded in reaching the holy territory,
but not the sanctuary itself. His death took place on
Saturday, 7th October 775,—according to other authorities,
on the Wednesday before,—at Bír Maimún, about one hour's
journey from Mecca, after a reign of twenty-one years and
some months; his age was over sixty, the authorities vacil-
lating between sixty-three and sixty-eight lunar (sixty-one
and sixty-six solar) years.[1] The only persons present were
the freedman Rabí, an influential confidant, and some servants. Rabí kept the death secret for some little time, with

---

[1] Compare above, p. 70. Probably Mansúr himself did not know exactly
his own birth year, not to speak of his birthday.

a view to the arrangements necessary to secure the throne for Mahdí. Mansúr lies buried near the holy city, the cradle of his family. Later generations believed they knew his grave; but the statement is not improbably correct that at the time a number of graves ("a hundred," it is said) were dug, in order that his true resting-place might remain unknown. At this meeting-place of all restless spirits, where the power of the central government was never able to assert itself so firmly as in the lands of ancient civilisation, some embittered enemy of the dynasty might easily one day gain the upper hand, in which case it was not inconceivable that he might disinter and insult the body of its most powerful and most hated member, as Mansúr's own uncle Abdalláh had done with the bodies of the Omayyads.

The East has seen many sovereigns who came near, or even surpassed, Mansúr in duplicity and absolutely unscrupulous egoism, but hardly one who was at the same time endowed with such commanding intellect, or who (speaking generally and on the whole) had so strong an influence for good on the development of his empire.

V.

A SERVILE WAR IN THE EAST.

IMMEDIATELY after the tragic night in which the Caliph
Mutawakkil was murdered at the instigation of his own son
(11th or 12th December 861), the proud fabric of the Abbásid
empire—already greatly shaken—began to collapse. The
troops, Turkish and others, raised and deposed the Caliphs;
the generals, for the most part quondam slaves, like those
whom they commanded, strove for a mastery which in turn
was often dependent on the humours of the soldiery. In
the provinces new rulers arose, who did not always think
it necessary to acknowledge the Caliph as lord, even in name.
Claimants belonging to the house of Alí had success in some
places. In the great towns of the Tigris region there were
serious popular tumults. Peace and security were enjoyed
only in those districts where a governor, practically independent, held firm and strict rule.

This circumstance alone makes it in some degree intelligible how a clever and unscrupulous adventurer, leaning
for support on the most despised class of the population,
should have been able, not far from the heart of the empire,
to set up a rule which for a long time was the terror of the
surrounding regions, and only yielded at last, after nearly
fourteen years of effort on the part of the caliphate, which
had in the meanwhile recovered a little of its former strength.

Alí, son of Mohammed, a native of the large village of
Verzenín, not far from the modern Teherán, gave himself out
to be a descendant of Alí and of his wife Fátima, the daughter

of the Prophet. The claim may have been just; the descendants of Alí by that time were reckoned by thousands, and were very far from being, all of them, persons of distinction. It is, of course, equally possible that his alleged descent was a mere invention. According to some authorities his family belonged to Bahrein, a district of north-eastern Arabia, and was a branch of the tribe of Abdalkais, which had its seat there. In any case, he passed for a man of Arab blood. Before he became known to the world, Alí is said, among other adventures, to have gone about for a while in Bahrein, seeking a following there. This statement is made extremely probable by the fact that several of his principal followers belonged to that district, though it is far removed from the world's highways, and but seldom mentioned in history; among these was the black freedman, Sulaimán, son of Jámi, one of his most capable generals. The ambitious Alí, utilising the prevailing anarchy, next sought to secure a footing in Basra. This great commercial city, next to Bagdad the most important place in the central provinces, was suffering much at that time from the conflicts of two parties, to all appearance the inhabitants of two different quarters of the town.[1] Yet Alí gained little here; some of his followers, and even the members of his own family, were thrown into prison, a lot which he himself escaped only by flight to Bagdad. But soon afterwards, in connection with a change of governor, new disturbances broke out in Basra, the prisons were broken, and Alí was soon again on the spot. He had already thoroughly surveyed the ground for his plans.

We are very imperfectly acquainted with the scene of the occurrences which I am about to relate. Even if the modern condition of these parts admitted of being represented on maps much more closely than defective surveys allow, and

---

[1] Enmity of this kind between two quarters or guilds is nothing unusual in Arab towns.

were the surveys better, they would not help us very much,
for the whole face of the land has greatly changed since the
times we write of.   At that time the Euphrates in the lowest
part of its course discharged itself into a region of lake
and marsh, connected with the sea by a number of tidal
channels. The most important of these waters was near Basra,
which lay farther to the west than the modern much smaller
city of the same name (Bussorah).   That place and its
immediate neighbourhood was intersected by innumerable
canals (more than 120,000, it is asserted). The chief arm
of the Tigris was at that time the southward flowing, now
called Shatt al Hai, upon which stood the city of Wásit.
Farther down, the stream must have turned towards the
south-east. The present main arm, whose main course is to
the south-east, was at that time dry, or had a very limited
volume of water. The lowest part of the Tigris was connected with the stream on which Basra stood by numerous
canals, some of them navigable to large sea-going ships.
All these waters were reached by the tide. Floods and
broken embankments had even by that time converted much
arable land into marshes; while, on the other hand, by drainage and embanking, many pieces of land had been reclaimed.
Since that time, in common with all the rest of Irák (Babylonia), this southern portion, in a very conspicuous degree,
has been so grievously wasted and neglected, that the forces
of nature have entirely gained the upper hand. What was
a smiling country has been turned into a wilderness by the
spread of the marshes, or by the silting up and stoppage
of the drainage channels. The rivers have in part quite
changed their beds. On this account we can follow only
in a vague way the very precise topographical details which
our sources give in describing the campaigns against Alí and
his bands.

At no great distance eastward from Basra there were

extensive flats, traversed by ditches, in which great numbers of black slaves, mostly from the east coast of Africa, the land of the Zenj,[1] were employed by rich *entrepreneurs* of the city in digging away the nitrous surface soil, so as to lay bare the fruitful ground underneath, and at the same time to obtain the saltpetre that occurred in the upper stratum. An industry of such magnitude in the open country is seldom met with in the East. The work in such a case is very hard, and the supervision must be strict. The feeling of affection which in the East binds the slave very closely to the family in which he lives and has grown up, is here altogether wanting. On the other hand, among such masses of slaves working together there easily springs up a certain community of feeling, a common sense of embitterment against their masters, and, under favourable circumstances, a consciousness of their own strength; thus are combined the conditions of a powerful insurrection. So it was in the servile wars of the last century of the Roman republic, and so it was here. Alí recognised the strength latent in those black slaves. The fact that he was able to set this strength in motion, and that he developed it into a terrible power which required long time and the very greatest exertions to overcome it, conclusively shows that he was a man of genius. The " leader of the Zenj," the " Alid," or the " false Alid," plays a very great part in the annals of his time —such a part, indeed, that it is easy to understand why our main informant, Tabarí, should by preference call him " the abominable one," " the wicked one," or " the traitor."

Once before in Babylonia a talented and unscrupulous Arab had utilised a time of internal confusion to raise a sovereignty on religious pretexts by the aid of a despised class; the cunning Mokhtár had appealed to the Persian or half-Persian population of the great cities, particularly

[1] Properly Zeng, hence Zangebar (corrupted into Zanzibar).

Cufa, upon whom the dominant Arabs in those early days of Islam looked down with supreme contempt (685–687 A.D.). But our hero went much deeper, and maintained himself much longer, than Mokhtár.

Before openly declaring himself, Alí had sought out from among the lowest strata of the population, and the freedmen in particular, suitable tools for the execution of his plans. In the beginning of September 869 he betook himself, at first under the guise of business agent for a princely family, to the saltpetre district, and began at once to rouse the slaves. Saturday, 10th September 869, is reckoned as the date at which he openly declared himself. He represented to the negro slaves how badly they were being treated, and promised them, if they joined him, freedom, wealth, and— slaves. In other words, he did not preach universal equality and well-being, but reserved the supremacy for the particular class to which he addressed himself. All this, of course, was clothed in religious forms. He proclaimed the restoration of true legality. None but those who followed himself were believers, or entitled to claim the heavenly and earthly rights of the true Moslem. Alí thus appealed at once to the nobler and to the more vulgar feelings of the rudest masses, and with complete success. We may accept the statement that he gave himself out for inspired ; at any rate to the blacks he seemed to be a messenger of God. That he himself believed in his own heavenly vocation is hardly to be assumed ; all that we know of him bespeaks a very cool understanding. We learn much more, it is true, about his warlike deeds than about his true character ; religious fancy has often great influence even upon coolly calculating natures, and in the East especially it is very difficult to draw the line between self-deception and im- position upon others. That Alí was sincere when he betook himself to astrology in important crises need not be doubted, for this superstition at that time held sway over even the clearest heads with hardly an exception.

Since the rebel leader claimed, as we have seen, to be descended from Alí, Mohammed's son-in-law, we should naturally have expected to find him, like other Alids, appealing to the divine right of his house, and coming forward as founder of a sect of Shíites. But instead of this he declared himself for the doctrine of those most decided enemies of Shíite legitimism, the Kharijites or Zealots, who held the first two Caliphs alone to have been lawful, and rejected Othmán and Alí alike, because they had adopted worldly views; who demanded that none but "the best man" should wield the sovereignty, "though he were an Abyssinian slave;" [1] who, moreover, in their ethical rigorism regarded as idolatry every grave sin, and most of all, of course, opposition to their own doctrine as the true Islam; and who accordingly regarded all their Moslem enemies, with their wives and families, as lawfully given over to the sword or to slavery. One of the most prominent officers of the negro leader preached in this sense in Basra when it was taken; the same idea lent fury to his black troops; and even his banner bore the text of the Koran [2] which had been one of the chief watchwords of the old death-defying Kharijites. It was certainly also with a purpose that he called himself upon this banner simply, "Alí, son of Mohammed," without allusion to his high descent. With this it agrees that an original document of the period shortly after his death designates him as a Kharijite. His choice of party was in the highest degree

[1] See above, p. 80.

[2] "God has bought from the faithful their life and their goods with this price—that Paradise is to be their portion, and they are to fight, slay, and be slain in the path of God;" and so on (súra 9, 112). In accordance with this word "bought," the Kharijites called themselves by preference "sellers" (*Shurát*); for heaven as their price they gave God their souls.

appropriate. The slaves were easily gained by a strong personality who could condescend to them, but they were not to be inspired with enthusiasm for a mystical hereditary claim. But that they themselves were the true believers and the lawful destroyers or masters of all others, the blacks were ready to believe; and they acted accordingly. Perhaps their leader took this also into account, that in Basra (on the lower classes of which place he seems at first to have reckoned), the Shíite doctrine was at that time very unpopular, quite the opposite of what it was in Cufa, the old rival of Basra. From what has been said it will be abundantly clear why Karmat, one of the founders of the Karmatians, an extreme Shíite sect which was destined soon after this to fill the whole Mohammedan world with fear and dismay, should, on religious grounds, have decided not to connect himself with the negro leader, however useful this association might otherwise have been to him.

The nature of the ground was highly favourable to a rising of the kind. Indeed, some forty years before this, in the marshes between Wásit and Basra, the Gypsies (Zutt) settled there had, augmented by offscourings of humanity brought together from all quarters, lived the life, first of robbers, and afterwards of declared rebels, and were only after the greatest exertion compelled to capitulate; yet these were people who neither in courage nor in numbers could be compared to the East Africans, and that, too, at a time when the caliphate was still in reality a world-empire.[1]

Of the beginning of the negro insurrection we have exceptionally minute details from the accounts of eye-witnesses. We learn how one band of slaves after another

[1] An Arab rebel at that time mockingly said of Caliph Mámún that he was not able to catch "four hundred frogs" that were within arm's-length of him.

—a troop of fifty, a troop of five hundred, and so forth—obeyed the call of the new Messiah. We even know the names of those slaves who incited their companions to join the rebel leader. As was natural, their wrath was directed, not merely against their masters, who were mostly absent, but even more against the taskmasters, all of them, we may suppose, themselves slaves or at most freedmen. Yet the leader spared their lives and let them go, after they had first been soundly beaten by their former subordinates. The owners more than once begged him to let them have their slaves back again, promising him amnesty and five gold pieces per head; but he refused all offers; and when the blacks began to show uneasiness about such negotiations, he solemnly pledged himself never to betray them, and to further their best interests. This oath he kept.

The most numerous class of these negroes—the Zenj, properly so called—were almost all of them ignorant of Arabic; for during their common labours in the open air they had had no occasion to learn this language, though the Oriental black, for the most part, very readily drops his mother-tongue to take up that of his master. With these, accordingly, Alí had to use an interpreter. But others of the negroes—those from more northern countries (Nubia and the like)—already spoke Arabic. With the saltpetre workers were undoubtedly associated many fugitive slaves from the villages and towns, and probably all sorts of fair-skinned people as well, but apparently few representatives of the urban proletariat. A valuable accession to their strength was contributed by the black soldiers who, especially after defeats, went over to the Zenj from the government troops. So, for example, at the very outset a division of the army fell upon the almost unarmed rebels, but was beaten; whereupon three hundred blacks at once went over to the latter.

Unfortunately we possess practically no particulars as to the internal arrangements of this singular State, composed of fanatical warriors or robbers who once had been, for the most part, negro slaves. With regard to their great achievements in war, it is to be remembered that they were excellently led; that they fought upon a favourable and familiar soil, full of marshes and canals, of which they thoroughly knew how to take advantage, while the enemy was equipped for an altogether different kind of fighting; and, finally, that the East African blacks, as a rule, are brave. It was not without reason that many negroes were at that time enrolled in the troops of the empire; even at present the black regiments of the Khedive are much more serviceable than those raised in Egypt. We know, too, that the negro leader maintained strict discipline.

It would seem that he had exerted himself to win over the villagers also, who for the most part, if not altogether, were dependent on aristocratic or wealthy masters. Perhaps he was more successful in this than our authorities say. He sometimes gave up hostile villages to plunder; but the provisioning of his large masses of men was probably, to a considerable extent, made easier for him through the connivance of the peasants. And when, at the very outset, he allowed a band of Mecca pilgrims to pass unharmed, this action was not only sagacious, but also in accordance with the doctrine which he professed.

Hardly had the slaves' revolt declared itself when troops upon troops were sent for its suppression; but within a few weeks the Zenj had gained several victories. The imperial armies were, it may be presumed, not large enough, and were badly led; the enemy, as was natural, was underrated. Here, at the outset, we find the Zenj's peculiar mode of fighting,—namely, out of concealed side-channels, heavily overgrown with reeds, to fall suddenly upon the rear of the enemy's troops as they rowed along. In this war it is the regular thing that a number of the vanquished are drowned. The leader of the Zenj was always well served by his scouts.

Of the booty taken in the first encounters, the most important part consisted of arms. Prisoners were remorselessly put to death. In fact, according to Kharijite doctrine, they were unbelievers, and worthy of death; while the women and the children, as non-Moslems, were made slaves. When at last the negro chief had defeated an army consisting principally of inhabitants of Basra, he marched in person against that town; he calculated, it would seem, that one of the two town parties, with which he had frequently had dealings, would declare itself for him; but in this he was deceived. The people, high and low, stood together. They faced him on Sunday, 23rd October 869 (full six weeks only after the date of his first rising), and completely shattered his army; he himself barely escaped death, fighting bravely. But the citizen-army, though it had manfully defended hearth and home, was hardly fit to take the offensive, and certainly had no leader who could be matched with Alí, who quickly rallied his followers. When, on the second day, the first division of the Basrans was advancing by water, bodies of Zenj posted in ambush on both sides of the canal fell upon their rear. Some vessels capsized. The negroes fought with fury; their women threw bricks. Those also who were advancing by land were involved in the disaster; many were killed or drowned. The defeat of the townspeople was complete. A large number of members of the ruling family even, descendants of Sulaimán,[1] the brother of the first two Abbásid Caliphs, perished. Alí caused a whole ship to be laden with heads of the slain and sent along a canal to Basra. His associates now urged him immediately to fall upon the town; but his reply was,

[1] See above, p. 116, note.

that they ought to be glad that they might now count upon peace for some time, so far as the Basrans were concerned. He had in the meanwhile no doubt satisfied himself that he had no substantial following in Basra, and still felt himself too weak to make himself master of the great city.

After these events the Zenj chief caused to be established, on a suitable dry spot, impregnated with salt and thus without vegetation, a settlement of his blacks, which he exchanged for another in the following year. His people reared huts of palm branches, we may suppose, or perhaps of mud. The "palaces" of the chief and of his principal officers, the prisons for the numerous captives, the mosques, and some other public buildings which were gradually added, may in some cases have been relatively handsome and internally adorned with the spoils of the enemy, but their material was certainly, at best, sun-dried brick. In the broader sense, the city finally founded, called Mokhtára ("the elect city"), covered a large area, and included extensive fields and palm groves. It lay somewhat below Basra, abutted on the west bank of the Tigris, and was intersected by the canal Nahr Abilkhasíb, the main direction of whose course was from north to south (or perhaps from north-east to south-west); other canals also surrounded, or, we 1: iy suppose, traversed it. With the complete change of the water-courses in that region, it is hardly likely that its site will ever be exactly made out.

The inhabitants of this ephemeral capital for the most part, doubtless, drew the necessaries of life from the immediate neighbourhood. Yet they were also dependent to some extent on imports; so that in the end, when the blockade was fully established and all communications cut off, they were reduced to great extremity. Until then traders and Bedouins had ventured to bring provisions to the negro city even in full sight of the hostile army. The dates grown there served, in part at least, as payment for the Bedouins. But as the home consumption of this chief article of produce hardly left much over for trade, we must assume that the dealers who thus risked their lives for the sake of gain must have been paid for the flour, fish, and other provisions which they brought with articles of plunder, and with money that had been accumulated by plunder and taxation, or rather black-mail.

At the pressing entreaty of the terrified Basrans the government sent the Turkish general Jolán. For six months he lay in camp face to face with the Zenj. His troops, consisting mostly of horsemen, could not move freely over the ground, thickly planted as it was with date-palms and other trees, and broken up by water-courses. At last a night attack by the negroes upon the entrenched camp made such an impression upon his soldiers, that Jolán judged it expedient to withdraw to Basra. Previously to this an attack of the Basrans had been victoriously repelled by the Zenj. The latter now grew so bold that they seized upon a fleet of twenty-four vessels bound for Basra; much blood was shed in this action, and the booty, including many captive women and children, was very great. On Wednesday, 19th June 870, they attacked the flourishing town of Obolla, which lay four hours from Basra, on the Tigris (approximately on the site of the modern Bussorah), and captured it after a brief struggle, in which the commandant fell along with his son. The slaughter was great: many were drowned; the city, built of wood, fell a prey to the flames. The fall of Obolla had such an effect upon the inhabitants of Abbádán, a town on an island at the mouth of the Tigris, that they made their submission to the Zenj; in doing so they had to deliver up their slaves and all their arms; the former augmenting the fighting strength of the victors. Hereupon the negro chief sent an army far into

Khúzistán (Susiana), the adjoining country on the east. Wherever submission was not made, fire and sword did their work. On Monday, 14th August, the capital Ahwáz (on the stream now known as the Kárún) was taken. The garrison of this important place had prudently withdrawn, and this doubtless secured for the inhabitants a milder treatment. But, of course, all the property of the government and of the governor, who with his people had remained at his post, was confiscated.

Thus, then, within less than a year an adventurer at the head of negro slaves had taken considerable cities, made himself master of the mouth of the Tigris, and gained control of wide territories. Even the disturbance to commerce was very serious. The communications of Bagdad, the world-city, were broken, and its victualling rendered a matter of difficulty. Basra trembled at the fate of Obolla. Matters certainly could never have gone quite so far, if in the meantime the greatest confusion had not prevailed at the then residence of the Caliph, Sámarrá (on the Tigris, some three days' journey above Bagdad). At the very time of the fall of Obolla the disputes of those in authority had led to the death, after less than a year's reign, of the pious Caliph Muhtadí, and the proclamation of his cousin Motamid as Caliph. But this was the beginning of an improved state of affairs. For though Motamid was not at all such a sovereign as the times demanded, yet his brother Mowaffak, who in reality held the reins of government, leaving to the Caliph only the honour and luxury of the exalted position, had intelligence and perseverance enough gradually to restore the power of the dynasty, in the central provinces at least. At first, indeed, he had too much on hand elsewhere to be able to think of the Zenj, but in the early summer of 871 he had got so far as to send against them an army under the command of his chamberlain Said. Said at first inflicted serious losses on them, but in the end suffered a disastrous defeat through a night attack. He was recalled, but his successor fared no better. Five hundred heads of soldiers of his were exhibited in the immediate neighbourhood of Basra; many were drowned. In Susiana, too, a general of the blacks had fought with success, but their chief called him back to cut off the Basrans anew from communication with the Tigris, which had recently been reopened for them by the imperial troops. This done, the Zenj for some time pressed hard on Basra itself, which had but an inadequate garrison, was torn by party dissensions, and was suffering from dearth. The negroes were joined by a number of Bedouins. Great as is the contempt with which the genuine Arab regards the black, the prospect of plunder, and the plunder of so rich a town as Basra, is an attraction which the hungry son of the desert cannot resist. These Bedouins were not equal to the Zenj, either in bravery or in loyalty; but they were valuable to the chief, as supplying him with a body of cavalry. On the 7th September 871, during the Friday service, the negro general Mohallabí, with these Arab horsemen and with black foot soldiers, penetrated into the city, but retired once more, after setting fire to it in several places. It was not till Monday that the Zenj took full possession. The massacre that followed was frightful. It is even alleged that many inhabitants were induced, by offers of quarter, to gather together at certain places, where they could more easily be cut down. The chief had vowed direst vengeance on the city which had deceived his hopes. His general Alí, son of Abbán, had allowed a deputation from one of the parties of the town to approach his chief with prayers for quarter; but he would not admit them to his presence, and superseded the general by a less soft-hearted man. The brutal negro slaves waded in the blood of the free men. The lowest estimate places the number of the slain in Basra at 300,000. The captured women and children were carried into slavery. The noblest women of the houses of Alí and of the reigning house of Abbás were sold to the highest bidder. Many negroes are said to have received as many as ten slaves, or more, for their share.

But a permanent occupation of the great city was not feasible. It was forthwith evacuated, and the army, which, immediately after the arrival of the shocking tidings, had been despatched from the capital, under Mowallad, against the Zenj, was able, in conjunction with the remains of the troops already in the district, to occupy Basra and Obolla without striking a blow. Many inhabitants who had been lucky enough to escape gathered together once more in Basra. But when Mowallad proceeded further against the Zenj, he was, like his predecessors, defeated in a night attack, and compelled to withdraw again to the neighbourhood of the town. In Susiana likewise the fortunes of war, after some fluctuations, proved favourable to the Zenj.

Mowaffak himself now advanced with a brilliant force to the neighbourhood of the negro city; but this also suffered defeat (29th April 872). The mortal wound of Moflih, the actual commander, seems to have thrown the soldiers into confusion at once. Mowaffak remained in the district of Obolla, keeping the Zenj steadily in his eye. In one of the battles of this period one of their best generals, Yahyá of Bahrein, was wounded and made prisoner. He was brought to Sámarrá, and there, in the brutal and cowardly fashion then customary in the treatment of prominent captive rebels, was led about on a camel for exhibition before being cruelly put to death in the presence of the Caliph.

After Mowaffak's troops had somewhat recovered from the severe sicknesses from which they had suffered in those hot marshy regions, and had repaired their equipment, he again marched against the enemy; but although he occasionally gained some advantage and succeeded in rescuing captive women and children, he in the end sustained another reverse; and, to add to his misfortunes, his camp took fire and was burned. Towards the beginning of full summer, accordingly, he found himself compelled to quit the proper seat of war, and to withdraw to Wásit. His army melted away almost entirely, and he himself, in January 873, returned to Sámarrá, leaving Mowallad behind him in Wásit. The expedition on which such great hopes had been built had come to nothing; yet it had not been wholly vain, for Mowaffak had come to know the enemy more perfectly, and had seen more clearly how he was to be reached.

After the imperial army had left the field, the negro chief again sent considerable forces into Susiana, who, with some trouble, succeeded a second time in taking Ahwáz, the capital (beginning of May 873). Several prisoners of distinction, who had fallen into the hands of the victors there, had their lives spared by the chief, doubtless with a view to heavy ransoms. The expeditions of the Zenj into the neighbouring countries, be it noted, were designed less for the acquisition of permanent possessions than to procure food and booty, perhaps also to inspire terror in the enemy. The Zenj leader may sometimes have dreamt of conquests on the grand scale, but in the end he always recognised that he and his negroes were safe only among their marshes and ditches.

A new army, despatched from the capital, ultimately defeated the Zenj in Susiana, and drove them out of the country. Other armies pressed on them from other quarters, and sought to cut off their supplies. The principal leader in these enterprises was one of the most powerful men in the empire—Músá the Turk, son of Boghá, who had left Sámarrá in September 873. Still nothing decisive took place.

A considerable interval passes, during which we learn

11

nothing of the Zenj. Meanwhile, they were aided by a
rising to which they had not contributed, and which had
not them in view. For when a rebel, who had made himself
master of Persia proper (Persis), had vanquished one of the
subordinates of Músá, the latter found himself uncomfort-
able in Wásit, and begged to be relieved of his post (spring,
875). Provisionally, Mowaffak undertook, nominally at
least, the government of Músá's provinces along with the
war against the Zenj. The latter had meanwhile taken
Ahwáz a third time, and had proved disastrous occupants.
They had to be left alone, for now a quite new and very
dangerous enemy made a diversion in their favour. Yakúb,
son of Laith, the coppersmith (Saffár), who had conquered
for himself a great empire in the East, aiming also at the
possession of the central lands of the caliphate, forced his
way through Persia and Susiana and advanced upon Bagdad.
But between Wásit and the capital he was met by Mowaffak
with the imperial army, and decisively defeated (April 876).[1]

The Zenj, of course, took advantage of the withdrawal of
troops from the lower Tigris, every available soldier being
required against the coppersmith. They extended themselves farther to the north, where the Arab tribes who had
their settlements in the marshy districts to the south of
Wásit lent them a helping hand. Isolated efforts to drive
them back had no result. The negro king now seriously
exerted himself to become sovereign of Susiana. A Kurdish
upstart, Mohammed, son of Obaidalláh, who, under Yakúb
as his superior, had made himself master of part of that
province, became his ally, but with no sincere intentions.
The two armies parted, and consequently the Zenj were
defeated by the imperial troops, especially as a number of
Bedouins had gone over to the latter. The *Societas malorum*
had not held good. Yet the government derived no sub-

[1] See below, p. 191.

stantial benefit; in the long-run the Zenj retained, even
in these regions, the upper hand. All sorts of troubles,
and, in particular, the threatening proximity of Yakúb, who
would not be propitiated by Mowaffak, and who might
break out again at any moment, sufficiently explain why
nothing considerable was attempted against them. For
the inhabitants of those countries this must have been a
dreadful time. Yakúb peremptorily rejected the alliance
tendered by the chief of the Zenj, yet, at last, without
definite agreement, a truce was established between the
two enemies of Mowaffak. But after Yakúb's death (4th
June 879) the imperial regent quickly induced his successor,
his brother Amr, to conclude a peace. Meanwhile, he made
him very great concessions, in order that in his great expedition against the blacks his left flank and his rear might
remain covered.

In 878 the Zenj succeeded in capturing Wásit and other
cities of Babylonia; the customary atrocities were, of course,
not wanting. But in the end not even Wasit was held;
Mowaffak's lieutenant again forced the Zenj back to bounds.
The latter continued to make plundering and devastating
incursions; in 879 they ventured as far as Jarjaráyá, less
than seventy miles below Bagdad, so that the terrified
inhabitants of the country fled for refuge to the capital.

In Susiana, Tekín the general opposed the Zenj with
vigour, and relieved the great city of Shúshter which they
were besieging, but afterwards entered into negotiations
with them. When these became known, one portion of his
army went over to the enemy, another joined Mohammed,
son of Obaidalláh. Such things throw a strange light upon
the discipline and loyalty of the imperial army. After
much fighting and conference the Kurdish Mohammed had
at last to bring himself to recognise the supremacy of the
negro chief, to surrender to him a part of his territory,

along with the important town of Rámhormuz, and to pay
tribute; but even now he continued to act in a thoroughly
untrustworthy manner, and caused all kinds of mischief to
the Zenj.

In any case, the power of the Zenj was now (879) greater
than ever. But it was at this point that the tide really
began to turn. Mowaffak's position had gradually grown
stronger, and the death of Yakúb had given him a free
hand. He now no longer delayed to summon all his
resources for making an end of the black robber-scourge.
In doing so he proceeded with great deliberation and un-
wonted caution. He had learned wisdom at last, from
many failures of the imperial troops, which, in part, had
followed close on brilliant victories. He now knew that
it was impossible to get at these amphibians in the same
way as enemies on firm accessible soil are reached. His
preparations for a decisive campaign against the Zenj
would require to be of a quite peculiar character, and in
the campaign itself it would be of supreme importance,
along with bravery, to exercise all caution. A great
general with similar resources at his command would certainly have annihilated the blacks much more quickly than
Mowaffak did; the latter in the campaign plays the part
rather of the prudent statesman who acts only with hesitation, does not place much at stake, and strives towards his
end slowly, if surely.

The task of expelling the Zenj from the northern territories near Wásit was entrusted by Mowaffak, in the first
instance, to his son Abul Abbás (afterwards Caliph Motadid),
who was now but twenty-three years old. In November or
December 879 the troops and ships of the latter were
reviewed by his father near Bagdad. The fleet consisted
of very diverse kinds of craft, but all of them rowing
vessels. The largest served partly for transport, partly

as floating fortresses; a smaller kind, of which some are mentioned as carrying twenty, and others as carrying forty rowers, seem chiefly to have been used for attack. The young prince justified the confidence reposed in him. He gave battle repeatedly with success, and, though operations had often to be suspended, the Zenj were steadily compelled to give place. One of their captains was taken and pardoned; this is the first instance of the application of a new policy which was to gain over the officers and soldiers of the rebel. This course, more astute than heroic, had great success. In proportion as the situation of the negro chief grew serious, his subordinates were more ready to desert him, and, instead of continuing to endure the dangers and privations of a siege, to accept from Mowaffak amnesty, honours, rewards. Care was taken to make the deserters in their robes of honour conspicuous, so that the rebels might be able to see them. Their prince, of course, did all he could on the other side to check the falling away. Thus, we are told that he caused "the son of the king of the Zenj" to be put to death, because he had heard that he proposed to go over to the enemy. Of this real negro prince we would gladly know more. The prisoners taken by the imperial troops were, as a rule, killed. Abul Abbás distinguished himself personally by his bravery. In one of the battles twenty arrows were found sticking in the coat of felt which he wore over his breastplate. Almost a year passed before Mowaffak in person appeared with a great army on the scene (Tuesday, 11th October 880). The first result of consequence was the capture of the city of Manía, built by the Zenj not very far from Wásit, when five thousand captive women and children were restored to freedom. The liberation of great masses of women and children becomes an occurrence of increasing frequency as one place after another is taken from the possession of the negroes. At every advance Mowaffak was very careful to secure his rearward communications, and to make it impossible for the blacks to attack him from behind. This rendered necessary, among other things, much river-engineering, making and breaking of dams. The regent thereupon again left the campaign for a time in the hands of his son, and marched towards Susiana (Friday, 6th January 881), to clear that portion of the empire. This was quickly done, and without much trouble, for the negro chief himself had given orders to evacuate the territory which was not to be definitively held, so as to concentrate his whole power. On their march back the Zenj continued to loot some villages, although these had made their submission to the chief. Several bands cut off from the main army asked and obtained pardon. That honest Kurd Mohammed naturally made his peace with Mowaffak without delay, and was received into favour. On Saturday, 18th February 881, Mowaffak again joined his son Abul Abbás and his other son Hárún, whom he had sent on before with his army from Wásit towards the south, and the united hosts advanced.

The negroes were now confined to their own proper territory in and around Mokhtára. Before the attack on this place began, Mowaffak sent once more a solemn summons to the rebel calling upon him to surrender, and promising him a full pardon if he obeyed. It need not be said that such a demand had no effect. Bad as the position of the Zenj chief was,—and it grew worse every day, — he could not stoop to become a pensioner of the Caliph. Moreover, it was at any moment possible that troubles in Bagdad or Sámarrá, or the appearance of some dangerous rebel in one of the provinces, might compel the persistent adversary to abandon the siege and all that he had gained. Some of his officers were less steadfast. The desertion of these to the regent, who received them with open arms, began with his first approach, and went on repeating itself to the end of the bloody tragedy. Many soldiers also went over. Mowaffak so arranged that the negroes in his army tempted those of the enemy over to his side. All so inclined were forthwith enrolled in his ranks. Naturally, no one dreamed for a moment of considering the claims of their former masters upon these slaves. In this way the negro chief found many of his best forces gradually drawn away from himself and augmenting the strength of the enemy; this they did less by their direct fighting capacity than by their accurate acquaintance with the localities and with the whole condition of things. To the cause of the Zenj it was, moreover, highly prejudicial that their leader had to become ever more mistrustful of his subordinates. In fact, several of his best colleagues, in whom he had placed perfect confidence, abandoned him, though others held by him to the death. The amnesty was extended also to those Bedouins who should fall away from the Zenj. On the other hand, a leader of the negroes, who had been made a prisoner, when it was proved that he had treated women who had fallen into his hands with singular atrocity, was put to a painful death. In other cases also, cruel punishments were sometimes inflicted on prisoners.

The city of Mokhtára, the siege of which henceforward constitutes the whole war, was protected, not only by watercourses and dams, but also by a variety of fortifications properly so called. It even had catapults upon its walls. During the course of the long siege new defensive works of various kinds continued to be erected, and artificial inundations were also resorted to. Nor was there any lack of boats, and still less of men, though we may take it that the number of 300,000 fighting men claimed for the negro leader is greatly exaggerated. The Zenj may very well have outnumbered their assailants, whose strength is given at 50,000, at least at the beginning of the struggle; but the latter were, on the whole, certainly much better equipped, better fed, and continually recruited by newly arriving troops. Mowaffak, however, had so little thought of taking Mokhtára by sudden attack, that in front of the place, though judiciously separated from it by the breadth of the river, he built for himself on the east bank of the Tigris a city - camp, which he named after himself Mowaffakíya. The matter of supreme importance was to cut off the supplies of the Zenj, and to secure his own. In Mowaffakíya a lively trade sprang up: he even caused money to be coined there. But the Zenj still showed themselves very troublesome enemies, and occasionally captured transports that had been destined for the imperial troops. It was not until a new fleet arrived from the Persian coast that intercourse with the outer world was made almost impossible for the negroes; and henceforward provisions could only be introduced occasionally and by stealth. For the Bedouins, who had still been venturesome enough to supply the Zenj with various kinds of food in exchange for dates, Mowaffak established an easy and safe market in Basra. Thus gradually the scarcity of food began to be keenly felt among the blacks, and the supply of bread virtually ceased. Nevertheless, they held out bravely; and in the numerous collisions which took place, as our authorities make plain, notwithstanding their highly official colouring, the imperialists had by no means always the best of it.

Towards the end of July 881 [1] the troops succeeded in

<hr>

[1] The very precise details of this war occasionally include notices of meteorological facts. In the beginning of December 880 the troops (in about 30° 30′ N. lat. and near sea level) suffered in violent rain from bitter

forcing their way into Mokhtára, and had begun their work
of destruction with fire and sword, but the same evening
they again abandoned their capture. The same thing
frequently recurred; moreover, the invading .troops were
more than once again driven out by the Zenj. At a
comparatively late stage of the siege (end of 882) Mowaffak
found himself under the necessity of again removing his
base, which he had recently advanced to the western bank
of the Tigris, back to the eastern, so troublesome had the
Zenj proved themselves to be. The main action was,
moreover, more than once interrupted; as, for example,
from the end of summer 881 till October of that year.
In their assaults on the town the besiegers specially
directed their efforts to destruction of the defensive works,
so that several approaches lay open in a way that did not
admit of their being again closed; they also set themselves
as much as possible to clear away. the obstacles — bridges,
dams, chains — which the besieged had introduced to prevent the entrance of great ships into the water-ways, and
especially into the main canal—the Nahr Abilhasíb. In
these operations the tide proved sometimes a help, sometimes a hindrance; it frequently happened that the ebb
would leave the vessels high and dry on the sand. As
the opposing parties were often quite near one another,
separated only, it might be, by narrow ditches, wounds
were frequent. In addition to the ordinary weapons of
war, molten lead was hurled against the foe. The besiegers
had also with them "naphtha men," who threw Greek fire
at the Zenj or their works. Fireships were also sometimes
used against the bridges. Occasionally the assailants made
way far into the city; on Monday, 10th December 882,
they in this manner destroyed the building which "the

cold. In December 883 so thick a fog prevailed that a man could hardly
distinguish his neighbour in the ranks.

abominable ones called their mosque," but which the Faithful naturally regarded as nothing better than a synagogue of Satan. But in this particular attack Mowaffak himself was seriously wounded with an arrow, shot by a quondam Byzantine slave; and as he did not spare himself, his wound grew alarmingly worse. Operations were on this account suspended for a considerable time, and many became so filled with fear that they quitted Mowaffakíya. And in the meanwhile an untoward circumstance of another kind arose. The Caliph Motamid manifested an inclination to free himself from the tutelage of his brother, and (in the beginning of December 882) quitted Sámarrá, to take refuge with Ibn Túlún, the vassal prince of Egypt. But the governor of Bagdad, Ibn Kondáj, who held by Mowaffak, intercepted the Caliph and brought him back to the residency (middle of February 883). For this service Mowaffak loaded Ibn Kondáj with honours. The wretched Caliph had even to submit so far as to cause Ibn Túlún, whom he had just been regarding as his liberator, to be cursed from every pulpit as a rebel against the ordinance of God; nay, his own son, designated to be his successor (though afterwards compelled to surrender his right), had to be the first solemnly to pronounce this curse. We can easily understand how in these circumstances Mowaffak was pressingly urged to abandon his camp for a while and betake himself to the centre of the empire: but he continued steadfast in his task. What he had neither heroic courage nor·brilliant generalship to achieve, he effected by caution and perseverance.

The Zenj leader utilised to the utmost the truce that had been thus forced upon his assailants, to place his defensive works in as complete repair as possible, or even to strengthen them still further. It is certain, too, that he was adequately informed by his spies and scouts as to the seriousness of Mowaffak's then position, both personally and politically, and he may well have cherished new hopes; but in February 883 he was again sorely pressed: his own palace was plundered and burnt, and he himself exposed to great danger. In March and April the illness of Mowaffak rendered necessary another cessation of the attack, but from the end of April onwards the struggle was seldom intermitted for any time. The rebel chief transferred the centre of his defence from the west to the east side of the main canal, though without wholly abandoning the former.

The desertions of his officers went on increasing. It is alleged that even his own son opened negotiations with Mowaffak; these, however, we may conjecture to have been quite hollow. But, among others, Shibl, a former slave, one of his most prominent lieutenants, went over to Mowaffak, and allowed himself forthwith to be sent directly against his old comrades. To another of these people, Sharání, whose wicked deeds had been many, there was at first an inclination to refuse pardon; but, in order not to scare his accomplices, he too was at last accepted, and received a rich reward for his treachery. The official account gives us a touching scene, in which Mowaffak, shortly before the last decisive struggle, solemnly admonishes the deserters to make good their evil deeds by bravery and fidelity; and this, deeply moved, they promised to do.

In the actual encounters the Zenj still continued to show great courage. The imperialists were not now, it is true, invariably forced to give up again in the evening the ground they had gained during the day; yet even in the great battle of Tuesday, 21st May 883, in which the harem of the negro chief, with more than a hundred women and children, had been sacked, and Prince Abul Abbás, in his advance, had burned great stores of grain, the assailants found themselves at last so hard pressed by the blacks that Mowaffak judged it advisable to withdraw them to his ships. He did not yet feel himself strong enough to deliver the mortal blow. But now new reinforcements were continually coming in, though indeed, for the most part, these did nothing more than repair the continual losses through battle and sickness. Among the new-comers were numerous volunteers, who, from religious motives, entered upon the holy war against the heretics. An event of very special importance was the separation from his master of Lúlú, the commander in Northern Syria of the forces of Ibn Túlún, the ruler of Egypt mentioned above; he entered into negotiations with Mowaffak, of which the result was that with a considerable army behind him he joined the latter on Thursday, 11th July 883. The preparations for a decisive assault were now complete; transport ships for large masses of troops were in immediate readiness, and the great waterways of the hostile territory were by this time so entirely free of all obstacles as to be passable at all states of the tide. Mowaffak is said to have brought more than 50,000 men into the great battle of Monday, 5th August, while yet leaving a large number behind in Mowaffakíya. After a severe struggle the whole city was taken. The negro chief fled; but as the imperialists, instead of pursuing him keenly, occupied themselves with plunder, and, by becoming scattered, exposed themselves to the danger of surprise, a withdrawal was again in the end found necessary, and Alí returned once more to the city. The respite, however, was but short. The final assault was delivered on Saturday, 11th August 883. From the first the advanced troops broke up the Zenj. Their leader was separated from his companions; Sulaimán, son of Jámi, along with others, was made prisoner. A section of the Zenj, indeed, drove back the enemy once more, but this was of no avail; in a little news was brought that the rebel chief was dead, and one of Lúlú's people almost immediately confirmed this intelligence by bringing in his head. It is not certain how he met his death. Perhaps we may venture to believe a statement [1] that he poisoned himself. According to another story, he perished in flight. That he did not fall in battle is further indicated by the circumstance that none of our authorities, with all their fulness, speak of any combatant as having sought to obtain the royal reward for slaying the arch-rebel. Death by his own hand seems the most appropriate to the nature of the man; at the same time, I am free to confess that we can form a tolerably vivid picture of him only if we bring a good deal of fancy into play.

When Mowaffak saw the head of his enemy, he threw himself upon the ground in an attitude of worship, full of thankfulness to God. The example was followed by officers and troops. It would almost seem as if without the energy of Lúlú the mortal struggle of the Zenj might have been still further protracted. This is not indeed exactly what is said by the history, written as it is entirely in the government sense, but there is evidence for it in a couplet which the soldiers sang, to the effect that—

> " Beyond all doubt, say what you choose,
> The victory was all Lúlú's." [2]

On this and the following days some thousands of Zenj surrendered themselves, and were pardoned; it would have been a senseless thing to have driven the last remnants of the enemy to desperation, especially when they could be utilised as soldiers. Others, again, fared badly who had fled into the desert, some dying of thirst, and some being made slaves by the Bedouins. Yet a number of blacks still remained unsubdued, and from the swampy thickets to the

[1] By Hamza Isfaháni (Leyden MS.; not in the printed text).
[2] Some years later Mowaffak caused Lúlú to be thrown into prison in order to obtain possession of his great wealth—wealth, we may be sure, which had not been quite innocently gained.

west of Basra, whither they had a considerable time before been sent by the negro chief, continued to carry on their robberies and murders.   Mowaffak was on the point of sending a division against them, when they, too, made their submission.[1] When they showed themselves, their good condition struck the beholders; they had not gone through the hardships of the long siege.

The son of the rebel chief and five of his high commanders had fallen alive into the hands of the victors.   They were kept in prison in Wásit, until one day the negroes there once more raised an insurrection, and by acclamation chose the first - named as their chief.   The prisoners were then beheaded (885).   The bowman who had hit Mowaffak was recognised far away from the seat of war at Rámhormuz in Susiana, and brought to Mowaffak, who handed him over to his son Abul Abbás to be put to death.

Mowaffak remained for a considerable time in the city he had founded, to bring matters into order.   A general proclamation was issued, that all who had fled through fear of the Zenj should return to their homes.   Many betook themselves to Mowaffakíya, but this city also had only an ephemeral existence; even the geographers of the following century no longer mention it.   The great trading city of Basra, which once more rose to prosperity, proved too powerful a rival for its neighbour.

Abul Abbás arrived in Bagdad, the capital, with the head of the negro leader displayed on a pole, on Saturday, 23rd November 883.

Thus ended one of the bloodiest and most destructive rebellions which the history of Western Asia records.   Its consequences must long have continued to be felt, and it

---

[1] The Zenj who were received into the service of the Caliph after the death of their leader are described in an original source, dating from the period of his successor, as pure barbarians, who spoke no Arabic, and ate carrion, and even human flesh.

can hardly be doubted that the cities and regions of the
lower Tigris never entirely recovered from the injuries which
they at that time suffered.

Several contemporaries, among them former adherents of
Alí, wrote the story of this rebellion.   Out of their writings,
along with official documents, Tabarí, himself a contemporary,
incorporated in his great Chronicle, a very comprehensive
narrative, especially of the events of the war.   The well-
known book of Mas'údí supplies us with valuable additions
to our information; did we possess his greater works also,
we should doubtless know more as to the person of the
negro chief and the institutions of his State.   Other writers
supply us only with incidental notices.

VI.

YAKÚB THE COPPERSMITH, AND HIS DYNASTY.

IN eastern Irán lies the marshy district of lake Hámún, formed by waters draining from the east and north. The area of water varies greatly according to the season, as the streams rise and fall. These, and notably the Hélmend, which in the lower part of its course is broken up into a number of natural and artificial channels, render a great part of the hot low-lying plain extremely fertile, but the rest of the country is a dreary waste. The plain was anciently called, from the lake, Zaranka ("lakeland"), a designation preserved down to the Middle Ages in the name of the chief town Zereng. From the occupation of the region in the second century B.C. by the Sacæ, barbarians from the north, it was called Sakastán ("land of the Sacæ"), more recent forms of the word being Segistán (Arabic, Sejistán) or Sístán. The low country, which is notorious for its serpents, is almost surrounded by desert; on the east it borders upon Zábulistán,[1] which geographically belongs to the Afghan highlands, and in whole or part often fell under the same government with them, and was included under their name. Sístán was the home of the most heroic parts of the Iránian legends, the stories of Rostam the Strong and his race, of which no trace is to be found in the ancient sacred books. The legend may be taken as reflecting the brave character of the inhabitants,

[1] Approximately corresponding to the upper basin of the Hélmend.

who were plainly separated by strongly marked distinctions from the other Iránians.

Sístán had been conquered at a comparatively early period by the Arabs, but the country was difficult of access, and long remained an insecure possession. Islam soon made great progress in the plain, but among the mountains to the east the new-comers only slowly established a footing. And even in Sístán proper the stubborn spirit of the natives inclined them to adhere rather to the Kharijites[1] than to the State Church. The governors of the first Abbásids had much difficulty with these Independents. The family of Táhir also, which from the days of Caliph Mámún had held the governorship of Khorásán, and of Sístán, which was regarded as an appendage, was unable to put down the Kharijites here, who steadily became more unruly as the power of the Táhirids waned. But in Sístán, as in other desert lands, Kharijite was often little more than a polite name for bandit. We thus understand how it was that, in the midst of this vigorous population, as the power of the State dwindled, volunteer bands were formed for defence against the Kharijites. Like their adversaries they, of course, declared that they were fighting solely for God; with what truth, we need not pause to discuss. At the head of a band of such volunteers one of the name of Dirhem succeeded in seizing Zereng, the chief town, and driving out the Táhirid prefect. Among his people was a certain Yakúb, son of Laith, who had formerly followed the trade of a coppersmith—a prosperous industry in Sístán,[2] whence the surname of "coppersmith" (Saffár) borne by himself and his successors. He, and his equally warlike brothers, belonged to the little town of

[1] See above, p. 80.
[2] A contemporary incidentally mentions the great production of copper and brass work in Sístán.

Karmín, a day's journey to the east of Zereng, in the direction of the notable city of Bust, the ruins of which are still visible. Near his birthplace was, and still is, shown the stable of Rostam's gigantic war-horse.[1] It is possible that the heroic legend had its influence upon him. Yakúb had once before laid down the hammer for the sword. He had fought under Sálih of Bust (852), who had made himself master of Sístán, or at least of a part of Sístán, for a time, but afterwards had been overcome by Táhir, a grandson of the founder of the Táhirid dynasty. Subsequently Yakúb had passed through other adventures. Under Dirhem, his boldness and ability brought him to the front. Thus he killed in single combat a dreaded captain of the Kharijites named Ammán. In this way he rose to such repute among his fellows that Dirhem found it expedient to set out on pilgrimage to Mecca, and afterwards to settle in Bagdad, leaving the leadership to Yakúb.[2] Yakúb having thus risen to a position of command, doubtless assumed the title of Emír, which was vague enough to mean either a general or a local captain, but could also denote a powerful prince by whom even the Caliph was recognised as a merely nominal suzerain. He gradually became ruler of his native land, which always continued to be the central State and the place of refuge of himself and family. His energetic suppression of the robbers, whose villages he destroyed, and the security he obtained for traffic, brought him, it would seem, into high credit, and in any case the brave Sístánese felt themselves drawn to this countryman of theirs who had proved himself a born ruler. Accordingly, the kingdom founded by him is generally designated as that of the Sístánese. That Yakúb

[1] Rostam's stable is pointed out in several other parts of Sístán also.

[2] According to another account the governor of Khorásán had got Dirhem into his power and sent him as a prisoner to Bagdad. Our information as to the earlier history of our hero is at every point full of contradictions.

at every Friday service caused prayer to be offered, in the first instance, for the Caliph as the general commander of all the faithful, need hardly be said. A theoretical dependence such as this, which in fact was rendered necessary by his protest against the Kharijite independence, involved no real restriction of his power, but at most made it necessary to send money and presents more or less regularly to court. At the outset he seems to have recognised, also, the Táhirid Mohammed as overlord. In those times, indeed, it often happened that a lawful governor or vassal and a usurper made appeal to the same lord, and that in that case the usurper, if victorious, was also recognised by the overlord as his faithful subject.[1] The date of these occurrences was about 860.

As early as 867 Yakúb crossed the frontier of his native land, and after hard fighting took from Mohammed's representative Herát, which has often been an object of struggle at many different times, and also Púsheng, ten hours from Herát. For the time he contented himself with this portion of Khorásán; the house of Táhir was still too powerful for him. He brought back with him as prisoners to Sístán some members of that family, restoring to them their freedom, however, when that was demanded by Caliph Motazz. With this Caliph he had already had frequent dealings, sending him magnificent presents, mostly the result of plunder gained in his struggles with the heathen of the East. He was making suit for the governorship of Kermán, which lay to the west of Sístán; but simultaneously a similar application was being made by Alí, son of Husain, who was at that time powerful in Persis (Párs). Kermán is, in fact, essentially a mere appendage of Párs. The Caliph, or rather the Táhirid

---

[1] Something similar happened not unfrequently in the Ottoman empire during the seventeenth and eighteenth centuries.

Mohammed, who had control of the chief towns, Bagdad and Sámarrá, sent a commission to both applicants, in the hope that they would attack and destroy one another. Alí's general, Tauk, promptly seized the capital of Kermán before Yakúb was able to cover the exceedingly arduous desert journey from Sístán. The coppersmith lay encamped for a month or two a day's journey from the capital; he then retired a little, but kept himself accurately informed as to his adversary. When Tauk was now off his guard, Yakúb made a forced march and fell upon him, taking him prisoner (869). In the camp there were found, along with many other valuables, a chest full of necklaces and bracelets intended as rewards of bravery, and another with chains and halters for prisoners. Yakúb decorated his own braves with the contents of the one, and appropriated those of the other to his captives, the heaviest chains being reserved for Tauk himself. When these were being placed upon Tauk, it appeared that shortly before, "on account of the heat," he had had a vein opened. The conqueror made this the occasion of a lecture to the effect that in his luxury he might have thought twice before venturing upon a contest with one who for two months had lain on no bed, had never put off his shoes, and had lived on the hard bread which he had carried while marching in these shoes.[1]

Yakúb immediately pressed forward against Párs, which was much more valuable than Kermán, and indeed one of the richest lands in all the Caliph's dominions. It was in vain that Alí and the leading men of Shíráz, the capital, wrote to represent to him that though his contendings against heretics had been very meritorious, he would fall into the greatest crime if he were to force his way into that country and shed blood without the Caliph's authority.

[1] The details of these struggles are again very variously given.

Alí accordingly, now reinforced by the fugitives from the vanquished army, took up on the river Kur (Kyros), not far from the capital, a strong position, accessible only by a narrow passage between rock and river to one rider at a time. Yakúb halted his followers some distance off from the river while he himself galloped forward, a fifteen-foot lance in his hand, to reconnoitre. The enemy contemptuously shouted: "We shall soon send you back to your pot and kettle tinkering." But he had discovered a passable place, and now caused his horsemen, leaving all encumbrances behind, to enter the rapid stream; the enemy was taken in flank, and fled without resistance. An eye-witness says that Yakúb's horsemen in this movement followed a large dog which he had caused to be thrown into the river; perhaps his object was by this means to determine the force and set of the current. Alí himself was taken prisoner in this action (Thursday, 26th April 869). On the following night, Shíráz was captured. The inhabitants had expected the whole town to be pillaged, but Yakúb seized nothing save the public treasure and the estate of Alí and his officials. Both Alí and Tauk, who had personally offended him, he compelled, by severe maltreatment, to disclose where their treasures were. By 14th May he had again left Shíráz, and set out with booty and captives for Sístán. To the Caliph he sent rich presents, and in addition, we may be certain, the assurance of his utmost loyalty. But for the time it had only been a successful robber's raid. He was not yet in a position so much as to think of taking permanent possession of Párs, which is broken up by very high mountains and other natural obstacles, and abounded in fortresses. On the other hand, he remained master, though not quite completely, of Kermán. The wild and never wholly subjugated inhabitants of the lofty, snow-clad mountain range of Páriz, which intersects the country in a general direction from north-west to south-east, were only gradually forced to submit by himself and his successors.

Yakúb meanwhile enlarged his dominions by conquests in the mountainous region to the east, where it would seem that he had already fought much. He, as well as his successors, made many conquests and plundering raids in these lands, of which, unfortunately, we possess almost no details. In any case they contributed much to the gradual ascendency of Islam in the country now called Afghanistan. In March 871 an embassy came from him to the Caliph Motamid, bringing idols which he had taken in Cabul or in that neighbourhood. Trophies of this kind from the lands of the unbeliever had long ceased to be seen in the capital of Islam. The bold coppersmith thus figured in the eyes of all the world as a champion of the faith. But his embassy had, of course, very practical objects as well; it was to negotiate as to the lands the Caliph would assign as provinces to his faithful Yakúb. The clever regent Mowaffak for his part was anxious, on the one hand, to strengthen the praiseworthy zeal of Yakúb for conquest at the expense of heathens and of distant Moslems, and, on the other, to keep him well away from his own neighbourhood. When Yakúb was again setting out for an invasion of Párs, where at that time, after all sorts of complications, Mohammed, the son of Wásil, had gained the upper hand, and was also recognised as governor by the Caliph, there accordingly came to him a letter which, in addition to Sístán and Kermán, made him lord of Balkh (Bactria) and other eastern countries as far as India. By this means the regent got him away from Párs, left him in possession of what he already had, and pointed him to the lordship over a number of remote regions which he would first have to conquer. Whether he expected Yakúb to make regular payment of the stipulated tribute for these fiefs may be left a question.

Yakúb seems soon to have taken possession of Balkh. We may imagine that the rude warrior chief was not too gentle in his treatment of his new subjects in this doubtful frontier territory, and that he made the most of them in the way of tribute. At least his name, as well as that of his successor, were long held in unsavoury memory among the Bactrians, and we know that oppressive taxes were inflicted on other regions which for a longer or shorter time came under his sway. We have no evidence that he or his successor, outside of Sístán and Kermán, troubled themselves at all about the welfare of their subjects, or even could have done so; but it is beyond doubt that they were very energetic in the matter of tribute. Then, as at all periods of Eastern history, many potentates have distinguished themselves in this line. Nothing else was expected of a military overlord. But that more than a century later the name of Sístánese (Segzí) had evil associations may be taken as an indication that Yakúb and his brother pressed very hardly on their subjects.

Meanwhile the power of the Táhirid Mohammed went on steadily decaying even in Khorásán. The Alid Hasin, son of Zaid, lord of Tabaristán,[1] wrested from him the border-land of Gurgán (Hyrcania, to the south-east of the Caspian Sea). Other portions of Khorásán became the prey of various petty lords. This gave the coppersmith courage to aim at the entire possession of the vast country, some eastern portions of which were already in his hands. We see that he by no means confined himself within the limits of the Caliph's grant. A pretext, if pretext were needed, was supplied by Mohammed. Abdalláh had rebelled against

[1] See above, p. 139.

Yakúb in Sístán, and afterwards fled to Khorásán; after some negotiations he was now induced by Mohammed, instead of seizing upon the capital Níshábúr, to take possession, under him, of certain districts which belonged to the territory of Yakúb. The coppersmith, who had already entered into all sorts of relations with disaffected grandees of Khorásán, accordingly set out from Sístán, whither it was his wont to retreat from time to time, and marched by way of Herát upon Níshábúr. Mohammed sent an embassy to meet him, but in vain. On Sunday, 2nd August 873, Yakúb entered the great and flourishing city of the Táhirids without a blow being struck. Mohammed either could not, or would not, make his escape. He is reported to have thought that he could make a personal impression on the victor, and to have received him with loud reproaches; but Yakúb simply put him into prison with all his kinsfolk, one hundred and sixty males. The continuous rule in Khorásán of the house of Táhir thus came to an end after having subsisted for fifty years. Yakúb now promptly sent an embassy to the Caliph to represent to him that he had set out only upon the request of the Khorásánians, because Mohammed's weak rule had allowed all sorts of disorders to spring up, and that the inhabitants of Níshábúr had come a ten hours' journey to meet him, to deliver their city into his hands. In token of his profound attachment he sent the head of a Kharijite captain, who in the neighbourhood of Herát had dared for thirty years to call himself "Commander of the Faithful." [1] The embassy was honourably received by the Caliph in solemn audience, but received from him emphatic orders to their master that he must quit Khorásán forthwith if

---

[1] The Kharijites considered themselves the only true believers, and accordingly gave this proud title to their own leaders.

he did not wish to be regarded as a rebel. Some of his people, in fact, who were in Bagdad at the time, were thrown into prison. Yakúb, however, was not to be duped, but set about establishing himself as firmly as he could in possession of the country. As Abdalláh his opponent, after the fall of Mohammed, had taken refuge with the Alid rulers of Tabaristán, who refused to deliver him up, Yakúb even resolved to invade that country. On the way he was met by a man who had risen to a kind of religious-political leadership, and who offered to accompany him on the expedition against the heretical Alids. But Yakúb could not accept the services of an independent ally; on the contrary, he put the volunteer in chains. We do not know the details well enough to say for certain that Yakúb's conduct was treacherous, but the suspicion of treachery is grave both in this case and in that of the imprisonment of the Táhirid. Yakúb turned the difficult mountain country to the east by keeping to the sea coast. The old fortifications which barred the access of the northern nomads can hardly have offered a serious obstacle. Soon he arrived in the immediate neighbourhood of Sárí, on the plain bordering the southern shore of the Caspian. Here Hasan met him, but was defeated (Monday, 17th May 874), and fled westwards to the mountains of Dílem.[1] Yakúb occupied the two chief towns, Sárí and Amol, and forthwith levied on both a whole year's taxes; he well knew that it would be impossible for him to hold them permanently. He then set out in pursuit of the fugitive, but in the high and densely-wooded mountains he fell into great danger, especially as it rained for weeks. The moist climate of the northern side of these mountains is as notorious as the drought that characterises the rest of

[1] See above, p. 139.

Irán, and consequently the country is covered with a most
luxuriant vegetation. Yakúb found himself compelled to
desist from the pursuit if he was not to court annihilation
in some one of the narrow passes. He had already lost
the greater part of his baggage and of his beasts of burden,
besides many soldiers. Had he been read in history he
might have consoled himself with the reflection that he
had got off more easily than many another Persian or
Arab general before him who had penetrated into these
dangerous highlands. Returned from Tabaristán, Yakúb
directed his march towards Rai,[1] where, as he had learned,
Abdalláh had now taken shelter with the governor. The
latter, to be rid of the dreaded warrior, handed over the
fugitive. Yakúb killed Abdalláh, and retraced his steps;
perhaps he thought the time had not quite arrived for
conquests in Media. Hasan came back to his own country,
and chastised with extreme severity those who (probably
out of religious ...tipathy to Shíitism) had taken Yakúb's
side. Dur: .g the somewhat lengthened period of Yakúb's
stay in Tabaristán, the Táhirid Husain, a brother of the
captive Mohammed, with 2000 Turks, led by the ruler
of Khárizm (Khíva), had made himself master of southern
Merv (River Merv, or Mervi-Rúd); but we do not know
whether he held his ground there for any time. On the
whole, at least, Yakúb retained his grasp of Khorásán, in
spite of the great losses in his last campaign. Yakúb,
immediately after his first success at Sárí, had sent a most
deferential account of the defeat of the heretics to the
Commander of all true Believers, and had announced to
the Abbásid the joyful news that he now had in his
power sixty members of the family of Alí. But this did
not procure for him pardon for his encroachments. In
November or December of the same year (874) the Caliph,

---

[1] Near the modern Teherán.

through Obaidalláh, an uncle of Mohammed,[1] caused the Mecca pilgrims from the north-east of the empire, who were at that time in Bagdad on their return journey, to be called together to hear a document in which Yakúb was declared a usurper, and his seizure of the lawful governor a grevious crime. Such a communication was the best means of diffusing a knowledge of the Caliph's will in those remote regions, especially as the pilgrims in their religious excitement must have been in a more than usually receptive mood for the words of the head of all believers. Thirty copies of this writing were sent into the various countries.

At this time Abdalláh, son of Wáthik, and thus a full cousin of the reigning Caliph Motamid, and of the regent Mowaffak, died in Yakúb's camp. Unfortunately, we learn nothing more than the bare fact. Perhaps this prince had betaken himself to the coppersmith, that with his help he might gain the throne of his father and of his brother (Mohtadí), and had been put out of the way in their interest; but other explanations of the fact are conceivable.

Whether the solemn repudiation of himself in the presence of his subjects, and the consequent division of Khorásán among the various governors by letters of the Caliph, had proved more than Yakúb could bear, or whether the southern lands had offered a temptation to his love of conquest more than he could resist, we cannot tell; be this as it may, he now once more directed his

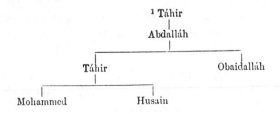

[1] Táhir
|
Abdalláh
|
Táhir — Obaidalláh
|
Mohammed — Husain

energies against Párs, leaving his brothers Amr and Alí along with others to maintain his rights in Khorásán.

Here it may be appropriate to ask whence it was that Yakúb obtained the large bodies of troops required for his campaigns, which often entailed heavy losses, as well as for the occupation of the conquered lands. By levies he can at most have raised only a small number of men. Perhaps also, after the custom at that time, he bought sturdy Turkish boys (Mamlúks),[1] and trained them as warriors; but large masses of men could hardly be procured from this source. The bulk of his armies appears to have consisted of mercenaries. The volunteer, we are told, who offered for Yakúb's service, if he was found suitable, had to give up his whole property; this was sold, and the amount set down to his credit; when he retired, it was returned to him. Obviously we are to understand that the money was retained if he left the service before the expiry of his time, or contrary to the conditions; it was caution-money. Pay and commissariat were adequate, and we cannot doubt that the former was punctually received. In the last resort the expense fell upon the conquered enemies, and still more upon the subject provinces. Yakúb had always a full military chest; mention is often made both of his treasures and of those of his successor. His troops, all of them mounted, and very mixed in their character, he kept together with an iron discipline, about which many stories were current. Thus an officer on one occasion, we are told, who was engaged in a religious ablution at the moment when the order to march was given, did not venture to take time to dress, but put his breastplate upon his naked body. On the

---

[1] The word Mamlúk, meaning something like "purchased slave," was not current in this sense till later; in Yakúb's time, such persons were mostly called Ghulám (plural, Ghilmán), "lads."

other hand, he won his soldiers by his open-handedness; at all events, he possessed the secret of all great *condottieri*, that of creating in his troops a strong attachment to his person. One element in his success may have been that though he was vastly their superior in ability, he was little so in culture. The story was told of this zealous defender of the faith, that on one occasion he had betrayed the haziest ideas about Caliph Othmán,—which is very much as if a good Christian were to have heard nothing about the Apostle John. His personal bravery also, which in one of his earlier battles had left its mark in a great scar slanting right across his face, must have further endeared him to his soldiers. From his best troops he had picked two divisions of Guards, the one of which, one thousand men strong, bore golden, the other silvern, maces on parade.

In the height of summer 875, Yakúb entered Párs. Mohammed, son of Wásil, hastened up from Susiana, sought to throw him off the scent by negotiations, kept back his messengers, and then pressed forward with all speed so as to surprise him. But as-Saffár was duly informed of his movements, fell upon his assailant when exhausted by heat and thirst, and at once put him to flight (August or September). The great treasure of the enemy fell into his hand. It is not to be supposed that the whole country forthwith became his without dispute; but he nevertheless ruled as lord of Párs, and among other things severely punished a tribe of Kurds who had zealously supported the son of Wásil. He did not, however, stay long, but pressed westwards to Susiana. In October he was already at Rámhormuz in the low plain of Susiana, in dangerous proximity to the Tigris. The central Government was in the greatest alarm, for, besides being himself a formidable enemy, Yakúb could cut the line of attack upon the negro rebels, who had brought the empire into great straits.[1] Those of Yakúb's people who had been thrown into prison were accordingly set free with promptitude, and an honour ble embassy was sent to him. As he appeared disposed to treat, Mowaffak called together the eastern merchants then in Bagdad, and told them that Yakúb had been named governor of Khorásán, Tabaristán, Gurgán, Rai, and Párs, as well as military governor of Bagdad—thus conceding to him an extent of power such as Táhir himself had hardly wielded. A new embassy, which included his old superior Dirhem, carried to Yakúb the Caliph's letter with the announcement. But the powerful general knew what weight to give to offers of this kind. His feelings of respect for the imperial Government were long exhausted; he had no scruples about coming to a complete breach with it. He accordingly replied that he would make his decision in Bagdad itself. Certain Arabic verses are put, into his mouth, in which, amongst other things, he says that he possesses Khorásán and Párs already, and that he does not despair of winning Irák also.[2] The man who could hardly speak a little Arabic, and who certainly was not able to use literary Arabic according to the rules of grammar, metre, and style, cannot possibly have made these verses himself; but they well express what his attitude was in the circumstances. He continued, doubtless, formally to acknowledge the Caliph as his overlord. Some years later, a vassal of his undeceived the Zenj, with whom he had entered into relations, by offering public prayers, in the first place, for the Caliph; in the second, for Yakúb. If as-Saffár had conquered, he would perhaps have retained Motamid, but hardly his

---

[1] See above, p. 162 sqq.

[2] In a somewhat different text these verses are given by others as his epitaph; but they are only slightly modified from a much older passage.

vigorous and able brother Mowaffak. For it is rather
improbable, though not altogether inconceivable, that
Mowaffak was in collusion with Yakúb, as was suspected
by the Caliph's "freedmen," the Turkish generals, to whom
the thought that the Sístánese might be bringing their
own hateful power to an end must have been very unwelcome. Yakúb, then, continued to advance, occupying
Wásit on the Tigris, and marching on Bagdad. Motamid
now fell back upon his last resource; he assumed the
mantle of the Prophet, and with the Prophet's staff in
his hand, took command of the holy war against the
godless rebel. He set out with a great army from Sámarrá,
but himself kept somewhat to the rear as the two armies
approached one another, some fifty miles below Bagdad.
Mowaffak took the command in chief. Yakúb's army was
much the smaller; and, moreover, an artificial inundation
hampered his horsemen in their movements. The battle
was keen. An attack upon his camp, made from the
Tigris, and the arrival towards evening of powerful reinforcements for the imperial army, at last compelled as-
Saffár, who had fought bravely and received three arrow
wounds, to yield (Palm Sunday, 8th April 876). With
the camp, rich booty fell to the victors. What was
particularly unpleasant to Yakúb, the Táhirid Mohammed,
whom he carried about with him in chains, made his
escape. The Caliph personally removed the chains, and
named him again military governor of Bagdad on the
spot. This was the first great defeat sustained by the
veteran warrior on the field (for in Tabaristan he had
been compelled to yield to the forces of nature). The
victorious enemy did not venture to pursue Yakúb, who
sulkily withdrew to Gundíshábúr, between Shúshter and
Susa, quite close to Babylonia. His wide dominion was
now in a somewhat precarious state. He could still be

sure of Sístán and Kermán; but in Khorásán his rule
had long had to contend with great difficulties, caused
partly by the imperial Government, and partly by all
kinds of local chiefs; the political state of Khorásán at
that time, as often before and since, must have been most
perplexed.   With the Caliph's sanction, Párs had again
been wrested from the "cursed" Yakúb by Wásil's son,
who, however, was beaten by a general of as-Saffár (876–7),
and himself was made a prisoner, and was carried to the
citadel of Bam, in Kermán, where a number of other state
prisoners were already languishing.[1]

During this period Yakúb himself was at least once in
Párs, where also coins were minted in his name;[2] but for
the most part he resided in Susiana, large portions of
which he held directly, while others were ruled through
his generals.   Other potentates also, with varying fidelity,
stood to him in the relation of vassals.   He sent an
expedition even into the highlands on the north about
the sources of the river Kerkhá; it brought back one
of the chiefs of the region as a prisoner (877–8).   Other
portions of Susiana were, at times at least, occupied by
troops of the Caliph or of the Zenj.   The proposals of
the negro leader for a formal alliance against the common
enemy were brusquely rejected by Yakúb, who would have
nothing to do with unbelievers.   Such an alliance might
certainly have been very disastrous for the empire.   His
troops came even into serious collisions with those of the
Zenj, but ultimately the community of interests made itself
felt, and the territory of each was tacitly recognised, and
mutual injuries ceased to be inflicted.   In September 878
Mowallad,[3] a prominent general of the Caliph, came over

---

[1] This citadel, which is still kept up, has until recently often served as a
place of confinement for political prisoners.

[2] One coinage of the year 877–8 is known.

[3] See above, p. 160.

to Yakúb as a fugitive, and was received, we may be sure, with open arms. The latter, however, still hesitated to make the decisive advance. He had learned to respect Mowaffak's ability and power. But still less did Mowaffak venture to attack the redoubtable hero, especially as the Zenj were still on his hands. Indeed, he made one more attempt to come to a good understanding with him. His messenger, it is related, found as-Saffár sick. When he had delivered his master's proposals, he was bidden take back the answer that Yakúb was ill; should he die then they had peace from one another, but should he recover the sword would decide, either until Yakúb had wiped out the defeat he had sustained, or until, all his empire lost, he was compelled to return to the coarse bread and onions which had been the food of his youth. Inflexible towards his enemies, he was equally intractable with his physicians. His disease was colic; he refused to take their remedies, and died on Wednesday the 5th June 879, at Gundíshábúr. His grave was afterwards shown here, but all traces of it have doubtless disappeared with the complete desolation of the city.

Yakúb was a warrior of iron strength, and certainly also of iron hardness. His enemy, Hasan (with allusion, we suppose, to his former trade), called him "the anvil." He was seldom seen to smile. His successes, in no small degree, were due to the fact that he formed all his plans by himself, and directed their execution personally as far as might be. His main recreation consisted in training boys in the exercises of war. Even when ruler of extensive territories he adhered to the very simplest style of living, probably more from mere habit than, as he himself put it, for the sake of good example. In his tent he slept upon his shield. The dishes set before himself and his attendants, at a time when the art of cookery was highly developed,

corresponded to those which would appear at the table of
a tolerably well-to-do handicraftsman: mutton, rice, a sweet
pottage, and a dish of dates and cream.[1]   Yakúb had no
attendants in his tent; but close beside him he always
had a number of Mamlúks, who were required to be in
readiness at any moment to execute their master's orders.
No traits of gentleness are related of Yakúb, but neither
also of any special cruelty, for, judged by the manners of
the time, his maltreatment of Alí and Tauk can hardly
be so construed.   Fearful atrocities in war were then
mere matters of course.   Yakúb's cunning is often celebrated; without it he certainly would never have succeeded
even so far as to become a captain of volunteers in Sístán.
This subtlety finds its expression in his diplomatic dealings
with the Caliph and other authorities.   As already said,
there is ground for the suspicion that it sometimes made
him treacherous and disloyal to his word; but it is to be
noted that our authorities, though they mainly reflect the
hostile opinion of government circles in Bagdad, make no
point of this; in that age, to be sure, treachery was too
common to excite much remark.   The circumstances of
the time, and still more, by much, the whole character
of the warrior-chief himself, explain why it was that he
established no enduring kingdom.   We meet with no
indication that he combined any higher ends with his
love of conquest.   Certainly he never had the least idea
of binding together, in any organic way, the various
countries which, one after another, fell under his power,
or even of instituting an efficient administration.   Some
buildings he reared, but he hardly devised any far-reach-
ing measures for the common benefit; and, on the other
hand, he certainly taxed his subjects very grievously.   A

[1] In his native Sístán, indeed, a peculiar taste prevailed, asafœtida being
a very favourite condiment.

more ideal intellect would surely have found more efficacious means to prevent the conquered countries from falling into other hands, or at least threatening to do so, as soon as his back was turned. And yet the historian cannot withhold his respect from this powerful personality who, from being a common craftsman in a remote district, raised himself to the position of a great prince, formidable at once to the heathen in Afghanistan and to the Caliph in his palace.

He was succeeded by his brother Amr, who is said to have been in his youth an ass-driver, or, by way of variety, a mason, but as early at least as his first attempts in Khorásán, and probably even at an earlier date, had been a trusty helper of Yakúb. Newly come to power, Amr was naturally indisposed to stake everything on a war with the Caliph, and forthwith he declared himself the obedient servant of the Commander of the Faithful. Mowaffak for his part was delighted to be rid of his worst enemy, and confirmed to Amr all he had offered to Yakúb. The district of Ispahán was also included in his kingdom, which thus towards the east and north extended considerably beyond, though on the north-west and west it in some places fell short of, the limits of modern Persia; but at that time those lands were much more populous and prosperous than they are to-day. In addition to this realm, he held the dignity of military governor of Bagdad and Sámarrá. Amr could not discharge this office personally; he accordingly, as the lords of Khorásán belonging to the house of Táhir had been wont to do, named a deputy, a Táhirid to boot, Obaidalláh, who in autumn 879 was solemnly installed by Mowaffak himself. It is to be presumed that Obaidalláh was on bad terms with his nephew Mohammed, whom Yakúb had dethroned. It even fell to Amr to appoint the governor of the holy

cities Mecca and Medina. But unfortunately for him, it
was only in a few portions of this great kingdom that
Amr's direct or indirect authority was at all sure. Khorásán in particular, in many respects the most important
country of them all, was ready to slip from his grasp.
Here a prominent part was played by Khujastání, a man
who had at first insinuated himself into the confidence
of Yakúb, and afterwards had driven out his brother Alí,
and gained much ground partly on the pretext of winning
back for the Táhirids the territory which hereditarily
belonged to them. Amr hastened to Khorásán, where he
had fought many a battle before, but was defeated by
Khujastání (Thursday, 7th July 880), who took from him
Níshábúr the capital, and slew his adherents. Amr went
back to Sístán, but with no intention of giving up Khorásán.
He might reckon with confidence that Khujastání also
would have enemies enough. In Bagdad he made the
complaint that the latter had been urged on by the
Táhirid Mohammed. In point of fact, Khujastání and
Mohammed's brother Husain, already mentioned, who had
joined him, did retain the public prayer for Mohammed;
and indeed he was in a certain respect the lawful ruler
of the country, and much sympathy was there felt for
the dynasty, which seems, on the whole, to have governed
well. Mowaffak who, as long as the Zenj were still unsubdued, had to keep Amr in good humour, found himself
compelled, in order to oblige the latter, to imprison
Mohammed and some of his kinsmen. In Mecca, also,
Amr asserted his dignity. During the pilgrim festival
in July 881, it came almost to an open fight for the
precedence, in the holiest mosque of all Islam, between
the representatives of Amr and of the Túlúnid ruler of
Egypt. Bloodshed was prevented only by the skilful
conduct of the Abbásid prince, who had the management

of the whole festival. His black freedmen had taken sides for Amr, probably more out of hatred against the Egyptians than from love of the Sístánese.

In 881–2 Amr's governor in Párs revolted. Amr, however, promptly entered the country, defeated the rebel, took possession of Istakhr (Persepolis), once the capital, and gave it up to plunder. The rebel was taken prisoner in his flight. Amr now remained for some time in Shíráz, the capital. He strengthened his rule in Párs more than his 'predecessor had done. Thus, he succeeded in subduing the Arab family which held the eastern portion of the hot coast-land. To accomplish this required indeed two years' severe exertion, and it was at last brought about only with the help of a member of the same family.[1] Amr extracted large sums of money from the lord of Ispahán, and out of these he made handsome presents to the Caliph. He seems once more to have pretty well become master of Khorásán also, especially after the assassination of Khujastání by one of his servants (June–July 882).

He continued to be on good terms with Mowaffak, at whose wish he imprisoned the Kurd Mohammed,[2] son of Obaidalláh, a thoroughly untrustworthy person, who had even on occasions been in treaty with the Zenj. But after the total suppression of the negro rebellion (autumn 883), and after the effects of the exertions it had required had been partially recovered from, the aspect of matters changed. Mowaffak hoped to be able to restore the power of the central government in other parts of the empire also, and especially in Párs. We must assume that he, at least for form's sake, negotiated with Amr, but that the latter rejected every concession. Only thus can we explain the unusually abrupt character of the action taken

---

[1] The precise date of these events is unknown.
[2] See above, p. 162.

against him. On 25th March 885, the Caliph Motamid caused the pilgrims from Khorásán, who were in Bagdad on their way to Mecca, to be called together and personally informed that Amr was deposed from the governorship of Khorásán, and Mohammed the Táhirid restored to his post. He then anathematised the former in their presence, and gave orders that he should be cursed from every pulpit. The deposition applied also, of course, to all the other dominions of as-Saffár. To give effect to these orders was not easy. In the case of the remoter provinces, all that could be done for the time was to detach the people from their lord in the manner indicated. But in the nearer Párs it was possible to take more vigorous measures. As early as the middle of February 885, an army set out from Wásit for that province against Amr. Unfortunately, we know very little about the course of this war. The ruler of Ispahán inflicted on Amr (to whom he had shortly before been tributary) a severe defeat, and plundered his entire camp (probably in August 886). In August 887 Mowaffak himself set out for Párs. Amr despatched several divisions against him; but as the general in command of the vanguard went over to the enemy, he was compelled to evacuate the province. The regent followed him to Kermán; his plan no doubt was to track him to his native seat. Amr withdrew from Kermán also into Sístán; during this retreat his son Mohammed died. But Mowaffak was not in a condition to occupy Kermán even, which was in great part a desert, and the citadels of which were, we may suppose, mainly in the hands of Amr's people; to press on through the frightful wilderness to Sístán was not for a moment to be thought of. Nature had set insuperable limits to the enterprise.

Here begins a course of shifting politics, in which only a few of the leading movements are known to us. Mowaffak must have recognised that he was not yet in a position to subdue as-Saffár, and that it was expedient to come to terms with him. In May or June 889, accordingly, the post of military governor of Bagdad was again conferred upon Amr, and his name inscribed on the standards, lances, and shields in the government office " on the bridge." Some weeks later Amr again appointed Obaidalláh his deputy in this post. This presupposes that a peace had been previously concluded, in which he had received back all, or nearly all, his provinces. That he continued to be ruler of Párs is attested by a series of his coins, extending from 888 or 889 to 898 or 899, better than by any writings of the historians. But as early as February 890 he was again deprived of his dignity as governor. Perhaps he was dissatisfied with the concessions he had received, and this was intended as a punishment. In the East, too, his hands were quite full. He had become suspicious of his youngest brother Alí, and had therefore thrown him into prison along with both his sons, but these had made their escape (890–1) to Ráfi, a rough, unscrupulous warrior of Yakúb's, who had skilfully availed himself of circumstances gradually to become master of a great part of Khorásán, and had also made Rai his own. Alí died while with him, but the breach was not thereby healed. At this point Ráfi came into conflict also with the new Caliph Motadid, who began to reign on 16th October 892, shortly after the death of his father Mowaffak. The Caliph consequently again appointed Amr to the governorship of Khorásán. While Ráfi was inflicting defeat on the Ispahánese, whom the Caliph had at the same time stirred up against him, Amr took his capital Níshábúr (July or August 893). Ráfi, however, did not abandon all hope of his cause, but now allied himself with the Alid prince of Tabaristán ; and when Amr quitted Níshábúr some time afterwards, he stepped into the place, caused the public prayer to be offered

for the Alíd, and professed the Shíite faith. Through force
of circumstances Amr thus became the champion of orthodoxy and of the Commander of the Faithful against the
heretics. How good his understanding now once more was
with the court is shown by the large presents received from
him in Bagdad in May 896. Besides 4,000,000 dirhems
(nearly £75,000), they included a number of blood-camels
and, very particularly, a bronze image, richly decked with
precious stones, of a goddess who (in Indian fashion) had four
arms; in front of the image, upon the car on which it was
borne, were a number of other smaller idols. The whole
were publicly exhibited for three days to the inhabitants of
Bagdad. From this we gather that in the meanwhile Amr had
carried his arms again into the eastern heathen lands which
were subject to Indian influences, and this also is expressly
testified. He had permanent hold of the city of Ghazni,
where, among other works, he built a bridge.

While his presents were arriving in Bagdad, Amr was
already in the field against Ráfi. The siege of Níshábúr
began in the end of May. Ráfi was unable to hold out for
long, and fled, but was pursued and beaten by Amr, whose
account of what occurred, sent to the Caliph, was read before
the grandees of the empire on Tuesday, 22nd December 896.
Within eight days a further dispatch arrived, to the effect
that the miscreant had been again defeated near Tús (north-
east from Níshábúr), had thence fled to Khárizm, and there
had been slain (Friday, 19th November). This letter,
showing, as it did, how the hand of God had once more
annihilated the foes of the house of Abbás, was read in all the
great mosques at public worship on the following Friday (31st
December 896). On Thursday, 10th February 897, Amr's
messenger arrived with the head of Ráfi, which was publicly
shown all that day. Motadid had undoubtedly good reason
for hating the vanquished man. That Ráfi had done homage

to the descendant of Alí was bad enough in the eyes of the Caliph, who assumed a consuming zeal for orthodoxy, but it was much worse that he should publicly have charged Motadid with having compassed the death of his uncle Motamid, in order to hasten his own succession. This reproach was all the less pleasant if, as seems likely, it was founded on truth.

Amr, into whose hands the victory over Ráfi had brought his two nephews also, was now in undisputed possession of Khorásán. In the course of the year 897 there arrived in Níshábúr a messenger of the Caliph, who, besides a variety of complimentary gifts, invested him with the government of Rai. In return for this, Amr sent a large sum for the pious purpose of setting up hospices for the accommodation of pilgrims on the road from Irák to Mecca. He had now reached his culminating point, and was actually stronger than Yakúb had ever been.

Motadid, perhaps the ablest Caliph since Mansúr, a man whose one object was to restore the caliphate to its former glories, could not long endure so powerful a subject. Amr's want of moderation came to the Caliph's aid. He pressingly urged that he might receive the lands beyond the Oxus, which certainly had long been regarded as a dependency of Khorásán, and on which Yakúb, it would seem, had cast longing eyes. The ruling house there for some time had been that of the Sámánids, who had succeeded in raising to high prosperity the extensive oases surrounded by barbarous nomads. The cunning Motadid acceded to this petition, and in February 898 sent to Amr the tokens of his investiture with Transoxania. Simultaneously, it is said, he wrote to Ismáíl the Sámánid to the effect that he had deposed Amr, and now named him (Ismáíl) governor of Khorásán; this, however, is not probable, Amr's investiture with Transoxania having taken place in such solemn form. Even without this he was sure to gain his end, which was to set the two

princes by the ears, and at least to weaken Amr seriously;
for it was a thing of course that Ismáíl should resist.   Amr
now sent an army to cross the Oxus near Amol (approximately
where the straight line drawn from Níshábúr to Bukhárá
intersects the river).   But, on the Sámánid's advancing to
meet it, Amr's army drew back a considerable distance, and
near Abíwerd, where the cultivated part of Khorásán borders
on the desert, sustained a great defeat (Monday, 29th October 898).   Ismáíl thereafter retired.   Amr now resolved,
against the advice of his counsellors, to take the field in
person.   Then, or even earlier, it is said, Ismáíl wrote to
him urging him to be satisfied with his great kingdom; but
he would not listen, and when the difficulty of passing the
mighty Oxus was represented to him, his reply was: " I
could, if I choose, dam it up with money bags."   He betook
himself to Balkh, which lies pretty near the river.   Ismáíl
advanced to meet him with a superior army.   It is expressly
noted that that army included the " owners of the soil;" if
not patriotism, strictly so called, there entered into the
struggle a determination to protect their well-governed land
from the violence and greed of the Sístánese.   Ismáíl was
successful in investing Balkh, and putting it in a state of
siege; perhaps Amr had previously lost a battle.   It was in
vain that he sued for peace.   He was compelled to fight, but
his troops soon fled, and dispersed in various directions; he
himself got entangled in a marsh, was taken prisoner (April
900), and sent in chains to Samarcand.   Ismáíl sent a suitable message to the Caliph; the news arrived on Wednesday,
28th May.   Whether Motadid had continued to recognise
Amr, or whether he had already had due regard to the
successes of the Sámánid, is not known; now at all events
it was matter of course that he should praise the victor as
his obedient officer, and censure the vanquished as a rebel.
Khorásán thenceforward became for a long time a possession

of the house of Sámán; but Párs was given by the Caliph, about the middle of July, to another. Ismáíl is reported to have given Amr his choice between being detained a prisoner with himself or being sent to the Caliph; he is said to have chosen the latter. If this be the fact, he had radically mistaken the character of Motadid.

The friendship that had subsisted between the two since the accession of the latter had never been sincere; at no time had the Caliph seen in as-Saffár anything but a usurper of his lawful rights, who had attained to power only *injuriâ temporum.* But probably it was at the Caliph's own express demand that Amr was delivered up to him. He had sent messengers to bring him; and the fact that these did not arrive in Bagdad till 23rd April 901, indicates protracted negotiations. The Sámánid had sent an attendant along with Amr, with instructions at once to behead him if any movement should occur in his favour. The mighty ruler, whose presents and trophies four short years before had been the finest spectacle that could be furnished to the mob of Bagdad, was now paraded before that mob in procession, as customary at the arrest of great State offenders or heretical princes. From henceforward the Saffárs were now officially designated as unbelievers or arch-heretics, certainly with great injustice. The one-eyed, sun-burnt captive sat upon a great caparisoned two-bunched camel,[1]—one of the animals that he himself had sent in a present on the occasion just alluded to,—clothed in a rich silken robe, and with a tall cap upon his head. The sight touched the very mob in the street, and they refrained from the customary reproaches and curses. A contemporary poet tells—half pityingly, half mockingly—how, during this ride, Amr lifted up his hands to God and prayed to be

---

[1] In other cases delinquents of this kind were set even upon elephants. The two-bunched camel is a foreign creature in these parts.

delivered from this trouble, and to be allowed to become a coppersmith once more. The Caliph caused the unhappy man to be brought into his presence, and curtly said to him: "This comes of thy insolence." He was then cast into prison, where he lived on for about a year. In the beginning of April 902 (the date of Motadid's death) he was murdered. This, perhaps, was done at the instance of one of the grandees, who was afraid that Amr might again return to power by the aid of the successor to the throne, with whom he stood on a good footing. But it is also possible that the dying Motadid[1] may himself have given the order to have him put to death; it was not inconceivable that as-Saffár, should he chance to make his escape in the confusion attending the change of sovereign, might yet become a great trouble to the new Caliph. So long as he lived he was "an object of hope and fear." In fact, rather more than a year before this (February 901), "out of wrath for Amr,"[2] troops which had served under him had raised upon the shield his grandson Táhir, son of Mohammed (who had died in 887), taken Párs from the Government, and threatened Susiana.

Amr was hardly so doughty a warrior as his brother; he was not unfrequently worsted. But his great craft is spoken of with admiration, and the skill with which he watched over his people by means of a careful system of espionage. He was greatly beloved by his soldiers. Like Yakúb, he kept a full treasury. Occasionally his high officers, even those who enjoyed his special favour, were compelled to surrender large sums which they had gained *per fas* or, oftener, *per nefas;* it is only the sovereign exchequer[3] that

---

[1] Motadid once declared it to be a maxim of his, never to let an enemy out of prison except to his grave.

[2] The French translation of Mas' údí renders this expression quite wrongly.

[3] (" Die Kirch' allein, meine lieben Frauen,
    Kann ungerechtes Gut verdauen."—*Goethe.*)

in the East, and most of all in Persian lands,[1] can digest
every kind of unrighteous gain. By good finance and great
cleverness, Amr always came out successfully from his misfortunes, until at last his land-hunger and the double-
dealing of his suzerain completely undid him. Posterity,
for the most part, soon forgot him; only a few considerable
ecclesiastical and other edifices continued to testify to his
power and magnificence.

His grandson Táhir continued to play a part for some
years in Párs and Sístán, until at last he too, in a struggle
with a former Mamlúk of Amr, was taken captive and sent
to Bagdad (908–9). Several other Saffárids, among them
three sons of Alí, came forward in the following years, but
all were overpowered. Three of them, among whom was a
great-grandson of Amr, also named Amr, were subdued by
the Sámánid Ismáíl and his successor; this Amr had been
chosen by the Sístánese as their ruler in 914.[2]

Fifty years later we find Khalaf, son of Ahmed, ruling
Sístán, under an overlordship of the Sámánids, which was
little more than a name. In his elevation he had been
helped by the circumstance that, through his mother Bánó,
he was a descendant of Amr. Contemporaries even desig-
nate him as "descended from Amr." His native country, it
is clear, still held as-Saffár's name in high honour. Khalaf
was a very pious ruler; a protector of poets, who sang his
praises; and of scholars, to whose number he is himself

[1] See above, p. 133.

[2] Laith

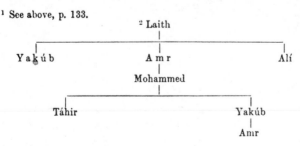

Yakúb — Amr — Alí
Mohammed
Táhir — Yakúb
Amr

reckoned. Amongst other literary works, he caused a commentary on the Koran, in one hundred volumes, to be prepared, the largest of the numerous books of this kind of which we have any information. But yet he, too, cared more for property and power than for piety or culture. Tradition represents him not only as a cunning, but also as a rather untrustworthy person. Out of mistrust he threw his son Táhir into prison, where he died—a suicide, it was alleged. After many vicissitudes of fortune, Khalaf fell into the hands of the great conqueror Mahmúd of Ghazni (1002-3), and died in captivity in March 1008. His son Abú Hafs survived him, and entered the service of Mahmúd. So ended the mighty race of princes of Sístán.

VII

SOME SYRIAN SAINTS.

In the first centuries of our era there was, in the eastern
portions of the Roman empire, a growing tendency to
renounce even lawful worldly pleasures for the sake of
religion.[1] But the inclination to asceticism acquired peculiar
strength after the victory of Christianity, particularly in
Egypt and Syria. Was it not the duty of Christians
(Gal. v. 24) "to crucify the flesh, with its affections and
lusts"? The men of the cloister retained at least a social
life; but many ascetics withdrew into entire solitude to
serve God, remote from the world and its pleasures. They
could not be always fasting; but they contented themselves
with the simplest food, which they either gathered for
themselves or received in gifts from their admirers. Many
exposed themselves, without any protection, to all vicissitudes of weather. Some paid so little attention to the care
of their persons as to give up the practice of washing
altogether; the legends often speak with reverential wonder
of the filth and vermin of these disgusting saints.[2] Among
the number of these Christian hermits there doubtless were
some elevated, if mistaken, spirits, of whom, however, only
a few can actually have found peace and satisfaction in such
a manner of life. But the majority certainly consisted of

[1] For the pagan world compare Jacob Burckhardt, *Constantin* (2nd ed.),
p. 218.

[2] I am told by one who knows, that most Indian ascetics, who in self-
mortification in other respects, as a rule, go far beyond the Christian, pay
strict attention to cleanliness. There are, however (or have been), ascetics
in India, also, who have abjured washing.

petty souls, whom it cost but little to renounce many of
those things by which man is really made man. The men-
dicant who in our day ι ts silent and solitary in the same
spot in all weathers, waiting for the charity of the passers
by, might perhaps, in those times and regions, have become
a holy anchorite. Many of these last may have suffered in
their past lives through fault of their own, or through
innocent misfortune; others had, perhaps, crimes on their
conscience which they sought to atone for. Fastings and
macerations are apt to act on the nervous system and produce visions—now pleasant, now horrible. This must have
been very specially the case with persons of the sort we are
describing—religiously disposed, and brought up to believe
in miracles and manifestations. The saint had at one time
to contend with demons in terrible or in alluring shapes,
whom, in the last resort, he repelled with blows or volleys
of stones; at another time there appeared to him angels
and godly men of old, who exhorted and encouraged him,
or even revealed to him the future. If the actual events
coincided tolerably with what had been previously revealed,
the coincidence would gradually come to appear, in the
dreamer's mind, greater than it really was. A reputation
for prophetic gifts was thus easily acquired. The unfulfilled
was forgotten, or the vagueness of the oracles allowed new
interpretations. Similarly with miraculous healings. Here,
indeed, we must remember that certain nervous diseases can
for the moment, or even permanently, be cured by faith in
the healing power of another; cures of this sort still occur,
and will, perhaps, repeatedly be wrought within the next
few months at Treves, in connection with the exhibition of
the Holy Coat.[1] Other cures were immediately ascribed to

---

[1] This was written in August 1891. As it turns out, the crop of miracles
at Treves has been very poor. This may be explained partly by the strong
light of publicity; partly by the fact that, after all, and even in the lower
classes, there has been a considerable weakening of simple faith.

the blessing or intercession of the ascetics; while cases of failure were attributed to sin, or were forgotten. Once an ascetic had come to be reputed a prophet or miracle-worker, his fame rapidly grew, and often stood highest at a distance from the scene of his activity, or after the lapse of some time.

I have already indicated that the hermit seldom or never lived in absolute solitude. Disciples who learned from him and waited upon him, and other admirers, gathered round him. The looks of admiration which others bent upon the man who had given up all earthly things for God were easily understood and well received; these are not the only devout men in whom an overpowering pride has clothed itself in expressions of the deepest humility.

Once men of this kind had attained high consideration they were often applied to for counsel and advice in matters not strictly religious. Governors and princes occasionally paid attention to them, voluntarily, or to some extent under popular compulsion. Still more had the bishops to do so, to whom it can hardly always have been any particular pleasure to share their power (reaching far into secular matters) with a class of men for the most part uneducated and obstinate. The ascetics, it is true, who did not need to consult worldly interests, often espoused the cause of oppressed innocence, and with success; but there was always great risk of their abusing their authority; for the very conditions of his life often made it impossible for the ascetic to judge fairly of the case laid before him. In the deplorable ecclesiastical controversies of the fifth and sixth centuries, the holy hermits and monks often exerted an exciting, seldom a soothing, influence.

Viewing the subject as a whole, we cannot regard this asceticism as other than a morbid phenomenon. It did little good and much evil. The mania for self-mortification

14

spread among the Syrians like an infection, and, combined with their absorption in hair-splitting dogmatic controversies, had a large influence in giving a false direction to the mind of that people.

In what follows I shall endeavour to exhibit to the reader a few Syrian ascetics. I begin with one of the most famous of them all, and shall afterwards go on to others whose portraits have been drawn for us only by one contemporary, but are characteristic for the whole class.

SIMEON STYLITES.

Simeon was born, towards the end of the fourth century, in Sís, a village near Nicopolis (the modern Islâhíyeh, in Northern Syria).[1] His parents seem to have been fairly substantial people of the lower ranks. He had one surviving brother named Shimshai; the rest of the family died early. While still a child he tended the flocks of his parents, thus becoming accustomed to solitude and privation, and having early opportunity for undisturbed contemplation. He grew up to be a strong and good-looking youth, but of small stature. At this period of his life he repeatedly collected storax, a sweet-smelling resin, and burnt it as an offering without knowing to whom; perhaps in doing so he was unconsciously following some old pagan custom. For, though baptized, he was still at that time without any education, whether religious or secular.

On one occasion, when Simeon accompanied his parents to church in his native village, he was powerfully arrested by the words of the gospel about the blessedness of the poor and the mourner. He had, moreover, according to

---

[1] Sís itself has not been identified. It is not to be confounded with the Sís in the interior of Cilicia.

a not improbable tradition, visions which pointed him to
the path of renunciation; and he gave himself with zeal
to asceticism. Even at this early stage the old Syrian
biography of Simeon makes him a worker of miracles.
The first of these is very peculiar, and deserves to be
shortly told as characteristic for its narrators, and also
for the readers for whom they wrote. Simeon, after a
twenty days' fast, longed for some fish, and went accordingly
to the daughter of a fisherman, who had made a large
catch in a neighbouring lake, and asked her to sell him
five pounds of fish. Untruthfully, but upon oath, she
declared that she had none. Just after he had turned
and gone a mysterious power suddenly seized upon her
and her fish; the latter tumbled out on the road before
him and leapt towards him, while the girl rushed after
them like one demented. All this occurred in presence
of the people, and of the soldiers then in garrison to
defend the place against Isaurian pirates. Simeon finally
quieted the fish and the girl, delivering to the latter a
severe admonition. He then went on his way, but soon
saw a large fish right in front of him, which he took,
after crossing himself; God so blessed it that he and
other shepherds, as well as two soldiers, lived upon it for
three whole days.

Simeon was still but young when he entered the monastery
of Eusebonas at Tel'edá, in the district of Antioch. To this
and other monasteries he handed over his entire fortune,
which had been not inconsiderably increased by inheritance
from an aunt. At the head of its eighty or one hundred
and twenty monks was Heliodorus, who had entered its
cloisters whilst still a little child, and never again quitted
it; he had never in all his life seen a pig or a cock.
Here Simeon remained for nine or ten years, distinguish-
ing himself above his fellows by his severe mortifications.

They fasted only on alternate days, he on every week day;
only on Sundays did he eat a few lentils. In order to
keep awake in his devotional exercises, he supported himself on a round piece of wood, from which he slipped as
soon as he became drowsy; this was a kind of prologue
to his subsequent performances. He girt himself round
his naked waist with a rough cord of palm bast, which
wore into his flesh. After ten days this came to be known,
and his brethren, who already had marked with growing
disapproval that instead of confining himself to their rules
he went far beyond them, succeeded in inducing their
superior to expel their eccentric companion. Simeon hid
himself in an empty cistern, full of poisonous snakes,
scorpions, and other repulsive creatures, as later writers
add. Five days afterwards his superior regretted what
he had done, and caused Simeon to be sought for and
brought back. Soon afterwards, however, he left Tel'edá
finally; he was not adapted for any society. He now
betook himself to the village of Telnishé (somewhat nearer
to Aleppo than to Antioch) to the monastery of Maris,
whose sole occupants were an old man and a boy. Here
he caused himself to be walled in for the great Lenten
fast. Bassus of Edessa, who held the spiritual office of
a periodeutes or visiter, and who happened to be present,
at his urgent request closed up the entrance, after setting
down some bread and water for his use. When, at the end
of the fast, the door was opened, it was found that both were
untouched. This is related by two contemporaries. The
belief that during the great fast Simeon never ate anything was certainly general; but whether the thing be
perfectly true may be doubted even after the performances
of modern fasting men, for, according to the story, we
must suppose that the feat was repeated thirty times,
year after year. During the fast he, at any rate, ate

less than ever; at the beginning of it he stood, then
he sat down as his strength waned, reclining more and
more as he sat, until at last he sank half dead upon the
ground. On the heights of Telnishé he caused a mandra
or "enclosure" to be built for his permanent residence;
the ground for it was given him by a priest named
Daniel. Here he riveted his right leg to a large stone
with an iron chain twenty cubits long. When he at
last took off this chain, at the request of the patriarch
Meletius of Antioch, there were found in the piece of
leather which had protected his skin from the iron more
than twenty fat bugs, which he had left quite undisturbed,[1]
never stretching out a finger against them,—so Meletius
himself informed his biographer Theodoret. The exact
zoological designation of the creatures need not be dis-
cussed; what is certain is, that for the glory of God the
saint allowed himself to swarm with vermin.

In the time during which Simeon sat here in a lonely
corner on the ground, he is said to have wrought various
miracles, mostly healings, such as befit the regular saint.
They were wrought sometimes directly, but sometimes
through the agency of objects which he sent,—such as
water, or even what was called hnáná, or "grace," meaning
thereby a mass of dust or filth of the saint kneaded up
with oil,—an instrumentality much used in those times
in the regions of Syria. Simeon had many visions also,
which were guarantees of his high standing. "Out of
modesty" he related these only to his most trusted disciples,
who were not to speak about them during his lifetime;
but, as was to be expected, many of these fine things about
him spread far and wide. The consciousness which he
enjoyed of his acceptance with God, and the veneration

---

[1] "Where the skin has little feeling, so also has the mind and the soul"
(Hehn, *Culturpflanzen u. Hausthiere*, 3rd ed., p. 472, n. 6).

which men accorded to him, compensated for all the pain which he inflicted on himself.

Simeon's pride finds its most marked expression in the choice of a pillar as his abode. Long before this, at the great sanctuary of the Syrian goddess Attar'athé (or Atargatis), in Hierapolis (Mabbog, Arabic Membij), some ninety English miles distant, there had been a colossal pillar, to the top of which a man twice every year ascended for seven days' converse with the gods;[1] but this practice must have died out long before Simeon's time, and it is highly improbable that such an uninformed person as he should have ever heard anything about it. Moreover, Theodoret, himself a Syrian, and a man of many-sided culture, as well as the other contemporaries of Simeon, all regard this pillar-life as something quite new. We can therefore, at most, attribute both phenomena to similar religious motives; so that Burckhardt—who, so far as I know, has been the first to· bring the two facts together—is, to a certain extent, justified in regarding the use of Hierapolis as " the prototype of the later pillar-saints;" but, historically, they are hardly connected.

Simeon began with standing for three months continuously upon the sill of the hole in the wall, through which the sacrament was handed in to him in his enclosure, because during the great fast he had seen, for three whole nights, an angel performing ritual prayer upon this stone, with bowings and prostrations. Next he caused a pillar to be raised for him to stand on; it was only six cubits high, so that he could still, without difficulty, converse with the people below. The top, a cubit or so square, had probably some kind of balustrade for him to lean on, but had no covering; and was completely exposed to the broiling rays

[1] Lucian, *De dea Syria*, c. 28 sq. The scoffer gravely calls the pillar a phallus.

of the Syrian sun, as well as to the rains and snows of the winter, which in Northern Syria, in such an exposed situation, is often bitterly cold. To live upon a pillar was a grave addition to his self-mortification, but at the same time it served to raise him above the world and above men. Many, it is true, even then asked what good purpose was gained, and others openly scoffed at his folly ; all that his defenders could say in reply was, that he had done so because God had commanded him—in other words, as we would translate the expression, because he had taken it into his head to do so. But on the majority the very singularity of his position made a great impression. Had he kept to the level ground he would never have become nearly so famous. With admiring astonishment his biographers go on to relate how, in the course of seven years, Simeon thrice caused pillars to be set up of increasing height, until at last a maximum was reached of thirty-six or forty cubits, at which elevation he remained for fully thirty years. Of this last pillar the following is related :—When he was standing upon his pillar of twenty-two cubits, he at the beginning of the great fast (during which he always withdrew entirely from mankind) gave instructions to prepare, against the end of the forty days, another of thirty cubits, to consist of two parts. The workpeople set themselves to the task, but somehow it always failed ; four weeks had passed, and nothing had been accomplished. His most intimate disciple ventured one night to shout up to the saint tidings of their ill success. Simeon ordered him to come back the following night, when he told him that, by a revelation he had received, the pillar must be forty cubits high and made in three parts, corresponding to the persons in the Trinity. This high pillar was quickly gone on with, so that it was ready by the end of the fast to be brought within the enclosure for the saint to take his stand on it.

On the top of his pillar Simeon prayed continually, with strict regard to external forms. Once an admirer counted that he had prostrated himself one thousand two hundred and forty-four times in succession in prayer; he then stopped counting, but the saint still went on with his devotional exercise. With a very limited intelligence Simeon must have combined an uncommonly healthy and vigorous constitution to be able to carry on such a life for so long. Even the strength of lung which made it possible for him to speak from that height to the people below deserves our respect. He suffered indeed severely in one of his legs from festering sores with maggots; but latterly this malady seems to have abated somewhat,—the pure, dry air doubtless being favourable to a cure. His biographers revel in descriptions of these bodily troubles. In their pages the maggots become at last huge worms, which his favourite disciple must always replace if they slip away. On one occasion, it is related, one of these fell from the top of the pillar to the ground; an Arab chieftain, a believer, took it up, and, full of fervour, laid it to his eyes and to his heart, whereupon it was turned into a precious pearl. During the night and the greater part of the day Simeon occupied himself in prayer and meditation, except, of course, in the hours of sleep; but his afternoons he gave to mankind, and spent in addressing the multitude below,— instructing, consoling, rebuking, admonishing, and settling disputes. We need not doubt that he often espoused the cause of the oppressed with success. In the Roman empire there were then only too many occasions for such inter- vention. The man who had no one to fear could dare to make his voice heard; and in presence of the great authority which he enjoyed far and wide, many an official must cer- tainly have been compelled to yield, however unwillingly. We still possess the text of a letter in which a priest named

Cosmas, and all the clergy and notables of his village, pledged themselves to a moral and pious life, and, in particular, never to take a higher rate of interest than one-half per cent. per month—that is to say, the half of the then usual interest of twelve per cent. per annum. That he insisted upon this lower rate of interest never being exceeded appears also from other testimony. But in this connection, where the covetousness of the individual is so powerfully supported by the general conditions of trade and commerce, his influence cannot have extended far. On the other side of the account, there was no proper guarantee against abuse of the power which the saint had over the multitude; nor were instances of this wanting. Perhaps the following case comes under the category:—Notoriously one of the worst defects in the constitution of the Roman empire was that the higher municipal officials were weighted with heavy expenses, which often ruined their fortunes; every one therefore, who could, evaded the burden of such charges. It happened on one occasion that the governor of the province wished to bring two young citizens into the Council of the city of Antioch. They betook themselves to Simeon, and represented the conduct of the governor as a piece of vindictiveness. Simeon interfered on their behalf, but without success; the governor immediately afterwards, we are told, was deposed with contumely, summoned to Constantinople, and relegated to exile. This was a divine punishment.

According to the Syriac biography, the powerful minister Asclepiodotus published an ordinance of the emperor Theodosius II., commanding the restoration to the Jews of all the synagogues which had been forcibly taken from them by the Christians. All good Christians were indignant at the idea that buildings where Christian worship had been held should again fall into the hands of "the crucifiers."

Several bishops, accordingly, turned with this complaint to Simeon, who wrote a blunt letter to the emperor. Theo-. dosius promptly recalled the edict, sent to the saint a humble letter of apology, and deposed Asclepiodotus, the friend of Jews and heathen, the enemy of Christians.—The affair cannot, however, have happened exactly in the manner related. We still possess the text of the imperial mandate to the chancellor (*præfectus prætorio*) Asclepiodotus, in which it is forbidden henceforward to take their synagogues from the Jews, and order is made to pay them reasonable compensation for such as had already been used for Christian worship, and so could not be restored. We can scarcely suppose this order to have cancelled another more favourable to the Jews, and, in any case, Simeon can hardly have had a great share in procuring it, for it was issued as early as 423, when he can have been but little known. The story is nevertheless instructive, as illustrating how unfair men can become through fanaticism; for here a simple claim of justice is represented as a shocking crime. It shows, at the same time, how great was the authority attributed to Simeon.

Once and again, on other occasions, Simeon condescended to hold correspondence with the great ones of the earth. Thus, in the closing period of his life (457–459 A.D.), he gave the emperor Leo a written opinion in favour of the Council of Chalcedon (451), which had defined the dogma of the two natures of Christ. In the same sense he wrote also, about the same time, to the patriarch Basil of Antioch. Whether the saint understood—so far as they are at all intelligible—the dogmatic niceties which were dealt with at Chalcedon, may be left an open question. The Monophysites of Syria, who were opposed to the Council of Chalcedon, and who were a majority in that country, afterwards ignored this action of Simeon and reckoned him among their saints; as

was also occasionally done by the Nestorians, although their
doctrine—which refused to call Mary the "mother of God,"
and which had been condemned as early as 431 by the
Council of Ephesus—was held in detestation by Simeon,
and had been expressly repudiated in a letter of his to a
former patriarch of Antioch. Simeon, it may be conjectured, dictated his letters to one of his disciples, who
stood at the top of the ladder by which his confidants
climbed up. Whether he himself could read and write is
uncertain.

The actions of this eccentric saint and the anecdotes told
about him made, as already hinted, a particular impression
on the uneducated. All our informants dwell on the admiration he excited in the wild Arabs. It is credible enough
that many Bedouins were induced by him to receive baptism,
though hardly in such numbers as is asserted. In doing so
they vowed to abstain from the flesh of the wild ass and of
the camel. This vow can have been kept only by tribes possessing sheep or goats; with most Arabs camel's flesh is the
only available meat, apart from game, which is not plentiful.
When Theodoret once, at Simeon's instance, bestowed his
blessing on some newly-converted Arabs, these believers so
crowded and jostled to touch his limbs and his garments (to
secure the blessing properly) that he feared for his life. And
once, in true Arab style, the representatives of two different
tribes had a free fight at the foot of Simeon's pillar, because
each demanded that the saint should send his blessing to its
own chief, and not to that of the other. Simeon, with invec-
tives and threats, had the utmost difficulty in separating the
combatants. This improvised Christianity did not strike
deep root among these Arabs. In some tribes baptism had
certainly already disappeared before the rise of Islam, and
the Arabs of the then Roman dominion who had continued
to profess Christianity, with few exceptions, soon went over

to the new religion. His influence on the inhabitants of
Lebanon, who at that time were still mostly pagans, appears
to have been more permanent; for it is probable that the
Maronites are the descendants of the converts who accepted
baptism after Simeon's intercession, as they believed, had
freed them from the ravages of wild beasts. These beasts
are represented as having been a kind of spectres who
appeared in shifting forms; but as it is said that the skins
of two of them were hung up beside Simeon's pillar, even
the pious editor of the Syriac biography cannot quite free
himself of the rationalistic idea that there must have been
great exaggeration in this, and that the creatures were
actually hyænas.

It is not inconceivable how the fame of the saint, growing
ever from mouth to mouth, should have reached Persia also,
and even the Persian court: superstition does not always
pay heed to differences of religion. Theodoret says only
that the king of Persia is reported to have begged consecrated oil of him, but less cautious writers positively assert
both this and more.

I spare my readers most of Simeon's miracles, which are
mainly of the conventional type. Most of what is related
by Theodoret in this connection may be historical; all that
is required is to allow for some involuntary corrections of
the facts, and to bear in mind the weight of the principle—
post hoc, ergo propter hoc. Thus, Simeon is said to have
predicted on one occasion the coming of a swarm of locusts
as a punishment, but that through the divine mercy it would
not cause great harm; and this actually came to pass. The
story may be essentially true. In these regions locusts are
a frequent plague, and so an obvious element in all preaching
of sin and its punishment; such preaching must also include
some reference to the divine compassion in case of repentance,
and thus an announcement of the kind is always justified by

the event, whether that be the punishment of sin or the compassion that follows repentance. Nor have we any reason to doubt that the wife of an Arab prince had a son after Simeon had prayed for her; it is only a somewhat late biography that connects with this fact an incredible miracle of healing. The appearance or disappearance of local calamities was certainly often ascribed to his curse or blessing. His miraculous cures are covered by the general remarks made above (p. 208).

Superstition, however, did not content itself with such miracles as were wrought by every petty saint, but went on to attribute to Simeon magical powers. Thus it is related that creatures so fleet and so shy as the ibex or the stag could be so charmed by means of his name as to become easy captures; this, however, was regarded as a culpable abuse. On the other hand, it was naturally viewed as very praiseworthy when a cleric, by the same means, took away all power of motion from a great snake which was about to devour a child; in this state it continued for three days, when it was released by Simeon with the command to do harm no more. It is even said that a male snake once came to Simeon to beg healing for his female, which was ill; the application was of course successful; the patient attended outside the enclosure, for Simeon (as we know in other connections) strictly prohibited any female to enter that sacred plot of ground.

But the most wonderful miracle of all is as follows. A ship was labouring in the high seas in a heavy storm. At the mast-head there appeared a black man in token that the vessel was doomed. But it so happened that there was on board a man of the region of Amid (Diárbekr, in Mesopotamia), who had with him some of Simeon's holy dust;[1] with this he made a cross upon the mast, scattering the rest over

[1] See above, p. 213.

the ship, whereupon all with one voice called upon Simeon
to procure their deliverance from God.   Instantaneously,
Simeon himself appeared, vigorously chastising the black
man with a scourge, and driving him away.   As he fled, the
evil one complained of the saint for persecuting him, not by
land only, but also by water.   The sea forthwith became calm.
Let it be observed, that this miracle is effected by Simeon while
he is still alive and standing on his pillar.   An old popular
superstition about the demon of the storm and the heavenly
deliverer [1] is here crassly transferred to Simeon, even in his
lifetime.   According to a shorter version of this story, Simeon
once stood long inattentive to the assembled multitude be-
neath who were imploring his blessing; at last he began to
speak, and informed them that in the interval he had in
person been saving a ship with 300 souls.   That is to say,
his spirit had been absent, and unable to pay attention to
the people below.   He had become a supernatural being,
and could be in two places at once.

   After fifty-six years of severest asceticism (thirty-seven of
them upon his pillars) Simeon died, upwards of seventy years
of age, on Wednesday, 2nd September 459.   His death was
at first kept as secret as possible, that no one might carry off
the corpse, so full of blessing.   The preparations for his burial
were prolonged, and probably the body was embalmed.   On
21st September began a funeral procession of unprecedented
solemnity, which arrived with the body of the saint at
Antioch on the 25th.   Bishops and clergy of every grade,
officials, and innumerable people accompanied it, as well as
the generalissimo of the forces in the eastern provinces,
Ardaburius, son of Aspar, with some thousands of Gothic
soldiers, who indeed, like their commander, were heretical
Arians, but doubtless shared the superstitious veneration of
the Syrians.   For the first hour the coffin was carried by

[1] Compare Leucothea, the Dioscuri, and the like.

bishops and priests; it was then transferred to a car. The burial took place in the great church of Constantine at Antioch. The emperor Leo wished to transport the body to Constantinople, but abandoned the idea on the earnest entreaty of the Antiochenes. It may be conjectured that the function was the more frequented because men's minds were still agitated on account of the two earthquakes (of September 457 and June 459) which had caused dreadful havoc in Antioch. In the body of the saint the Antiochenes hoped to possess a charm against the recurrence of such manifestations of the " wrath of God "—a hope which proved vain. Evagrius, the Church historian, saw the body of Simeon when the Commander of the Forces in the East, Philippicus, son-in-law of the emperor Maurice, caused it to be exhibited (probably in 588). At that time it was still well preserved, though it had lost some teeth, to which believers had helped themselves as salutary relics. I have not found any later writer who notices, at first hand, the grave and relics of Simeon.

A large building was soon erected on the spot where Simeon had lived. The name of this despiser of all earthly things, whose whole life was a scornful protest against all concern for the beautiful, was commemorated in a master-piece of architecture, the only fine art which then flourished vigorously, connecting mediæval and modern art with pagan antiquity by great and original works. On the heights of Telnishé arose a splendid church, described by Evagrius, the ruins of which still leave an impression of grandeur on the traveller. The main building forms a cross, the arms of which, at the point of intersection, enclose an open space. In the centre of this still stands the base of Simeon's pillar. In the time of the historian a great shining star was often seen above, in a gallery of the inner space. Evagrius, a native of Syria, regarded this phenomenon, which he himself had witnessed, as supernatural, just as his pagan countrymen had formerly believed in the divine origin of the light which from time to time was seen above the sacred lake of Aphrodite in Lebanon, or as the Russian pilgrims of the present day still ascribe to a supernatural source the light in the Church of the Holy Sepulchre in Jerusalem, at which they kindled their Easter tapers.

Simeon has had several successors in Syrian lands. Some at least of these must, however, have greatly modified the penance of standing on the pillar, for several authors are included in their number, and one at least, Joshua Stylites, was a very sober-minded and sensible person.

An enthusiastic deacon named Vulfilaicus, somewhere about the middle of the sixth century, set up for himself in the neighbourhood of Treves a similar pillar. But the bishops ordered him down, as he could not possibly vie with the holy Simeon; and his own bishop, when his back was turned, caused the pillar to be broken to fragments. If not so learned as the Syrians, the Frankish bishops had more common sense. Such ridiculous asceticism did not suit the West, where, on the other hand, the early mediæval Church rose to the task of educating the rude peoples in a way that has no parallel in the East.[1]

The famous ecclesiastical writer Theodoret, bishop of Cyrrhus, in Northern Syria, has given us a sketch of Simeon Stylites, with whom he was acquainted, and by whom indeed he was survived. In spite of its somewhat ornate style, this is, on the whole, the most trustworthy biography; the author was a man of education.

Much fuller is the account which was written not long

[1] The horrible rule of the Trappists is of comparatively modern origin.

after Simeon's death by two honest, but rather uneducated
Syrians (probably in 472),[1] and which has incorrectly been
ascribed by the learned Maronites to the Cosmas mentioned above (p. 217). It gives very useful additions to
Theodoret's picture, with a good deal of the legendary
exaggeration which already had begun to gather round
the figure of the saint. It is, however, highly characteristic
for the ideas and manner of expression that prevailed in
the circles where it was written. It became very popular,
and the MSS. present considerable variations of text, as
is usual in such popular books.[2] Evagrius used it. Quite
inferior to both these is the Greek biography which is
said to have been written by Antony, a disciple of Simeon.
It contains so many extravagances that it can hardly be
so old as it professes to be.

Our later authorities about Simeon have no independent
value. There are some Syriac letters of Simeon in the
British Museum which might be worth publishing, but
the editor would have to be on his guard against spurious
or interpolated pieces.

John, Monophysite bishop of Asia (the province so
called), or Ephesus, a Syrian of Amid (Diárbekr), but
who spent great part of his life in Constantinople and
elsewhere in the West, composed in his mother-tongue a
Church history, of which considerable portions have reached
us directly or through other writers, and also a book con-
taining sketches of pious men or saints whom he had met

[1] This is the date of its composition, not of its transcription, as has been
supposed.
[2] This applies even to the Roman and London MSS., which are both very
old. Of the latter I was able to use some years ago a transcript kindly lent
me by Prof. Kleyn, of Utrecht, but in the preparation of this essay I have
had only a few notes from it at my disposal.

in the course of his long life. John was learned, and, as it seems, a man of some activity, but of little enlightenment. Naturally of a mild disposition, he was nevertheless a zealous Monophysite, and hated the Council of Chalcedon with all his heart. All his pious characters accordingly are strict Monophysites. The world brought before us in these sketches is dismal enough, but if we arm ourselves with the needful impartiality, we can learn from them a great deal about the period to which they relate. In presenting a few of these figures to my readers I do not select the most important, but such as exhibit most clearly some of the characteristics of the Syrians of that age.

SIMEON AND SERGIUS.

In the neighbourhood of Amid there were many ascetics about the year 500. One of these, called Simeon (one of the commonest names of the time), lived indeed as a hermit like the others, yet was of a very hospitable spirit. When he was alone he mortified himself with the utmost severity, and ate absolutely nothing for as many as ten days at a stretch; for, since it is written that where two or three are gathered together in Christ's name, there is He in the midst of them (Matt. xviii. 20), it followed that Simeon by himself was not able to secure the presence of Christ, and without this he would not eat. If, however, a strange monk, or monks, arrived, he admitted them over the doorless wall of his enclosure by a kind of ladder, received them cordially, washed their feet, and after further proving his humility by secretly drinking three times of the water with which he had washed them (!), set wine before them, and the produce of his garden. He then ate with them and was happy. To laymen and to women he gave food through a hole in the wall. His garden is said to have grown enough to feed forty people, although it was only twenty cubits long and ten cubits broad, which may be believed if we consider that the climate was favourable and the guests very abstemious. Aided by one or two disciples who were usually with him, Simeon through the hole in his wall, at different times of the day, taught children of various ages to read the Psalter and other holy books. He was evidently a man of cheerful and amiable character, and worthy of a better vocation.

His most notable disciple was Sergius; he was a zealot *pur sang*. His special annoyance was the toleration given to the Jews in the village. "He burned with love for his Lord, and gnashed his teeth" against "the murderers of God." With a handful of younger people accordingly he one night set fire to their synagogue, and burnt it with its books and trumpets and other sacred objects. As the Jews stood under the protection of the great church in Amid, to which they paid dues, they laid a complaint against Sergius before its authorities. But in the meanwhile he and his people had lost no time in planting, on the site of the synagogue, a chapel, which they dedicated to the Mother of God; so that the soldiers sent to restore the Jews to their rights were helpless, a church once consecrated being inalienable. The Jews now, in revenge, burned down the cells of Simeon and Sergius; but these were at once rebuilt by the latter, who also destroyed by night the new synagogue, now near completion, and carried matters so that the Jews were completely terrorised. When at last Sergius withdrew from his master (with whom he had been for some twenty years), to shut himself up in a low and narrow cell, the Jews took courage to begin building once more; but the holy man caused his disciples to set fire to this also, whereupon they desisted from making any further attempt as long as he lived.

In 520 the emperor, Justin I., took strong measures against the Monophysites, to which sect our two anchorites belonged. The agents of the Government left the aged Simeon unmolested, but tried to induce Sergius to acknowledge the Council of Chalcedon. He, however, received them with curses, and swore that if they drove him out he would anathematise them from the pulpit of the great church in face of the congregation. In spite of the threat, they broke through a wall of his cell and did drive him out. He took refuge with the pillar-saint Maron, also a zealous Monophysite, after staying with whom for a short time he addressed himself to the fulfilment of his oath. Armed with the blessing of Maron, who at first had dissuaded him from the enterprise, he went on Sunday to the church when the whole congregation—including many Monophysites, who joined in the service, though they abstained from communicating with the other party—was assembled ; and while the preacher was in the middle of his sermon before the " so - called bishop," the weird figure of the hermit in ragged sackcloth suddenly made its appearance. Planting the cross, which he had carried upon his back, in front of the pulpit, he sprang up the steps, fell on the preacher with cuffs and abusive language, and flung him from his place. He then solemnly pronounced from the pulpit an anathema upon the Council of Chalcedon and on all who accepted its decrees. A great uproar, of course, ensued. Sergius was arrested and taken into custody, his long hermit's beard cut off, and he himself sent in chains to a neighbouring monastery in Armenia, the monks of which, three hundred in number, were all zealous partisans of the Council.[1] The Government, we see, was very gentle with this violent opponent ; if the Syrian Monophysites

[1] The Armenians for the most part were Monophysites, and still are so except those who are "United" to the Church of Rome.

had gained the upper hand, their treatment of a similar
offender would have been very different. Sergius, however,
managed to make his escape three days afterwards, and
finding his way back to Simeon, began to build a cell
beside him. His adversaries, finding themselves unable
to scare him away, left him personally unmolested,—no
doubt out of consideration for the temper of the populace,
—and contented themselves with pulling down what he
had built. He now showed the same determination as in
his contest with the Jews, swearing "by Him who built
up the world, and who was called the carpenter's son," that
he would never cease to renew his task as often as his work
was thrown down; a vow which he kept.

Sergius predeceased Simeon, who, in the closing years
of his life had grown very weak and ill, so as to be no
longer able (greatly to his regret) personally to serve his
guests. He died after forty-seven years of a hermit life.
John of Ephesus testifies that God wrought many miracles
by him, but does not go into particulars.

MÁRÁ.

Márá, a native of a highland village to the north of Amid,
was a huge man of great bodily strength. Although holding
some inferior ecclesiastical office he was still a layman, and
when about thirty years of age his parents wished him to
marry. But after everything had been prepared for the
wedding the spirit came upon him, and constrained him to
make his escape by night.[1] He went to a wonder-working
hermit named Paul, who lived near Hisn Ziyát (Kharput),
in a cave which was reputed a haunt of evil spirits. Márá
remained five years with Paul as his disciple in prayer,

---

[1] An incident that more than once occurs in the lives of Syrian saints,
both legendary and historical. See below, p. 234.

fasting, and other ascetic exercises, and is alleged to have
slept for only one or two hours of the twenty-four. In the
severest cold of winter he went with bare and bleeding feet
through deep mountain snow for firewood. His master
vainly urged him not to overdo his self-mortifications.
In order to be thoroughly free of his family and their
worldly tendencies, he betook himself to Egypt, the chief
school of asceticism, where he visited various penitents,
and himself lived as one for fifteen years.

At this period Justinian's Government was making its
attempt to force the Egyptians, decided Monophysites, to
accept the decrees of Chalcedon. For this end here, as
in Mesopotamia, it particularly sought to win over the
monks and hermits, the most powerful authorities with
the masses, and if they proved obstinate to scatter and
drive them away. Thus Márá, as a firm Monophysite,
was driven from his cell. But instead of simply with-
drawing farther into the desert, he took ship for Constantinople. There, where the majority were thoroughly
" Orthodox," the foreign Monophysites were tolerated by
Government as harmless, and the Empress Theodora was
so much their declared protectress that we must presume
her to have acted with her husband's approval. Justinian
may have had his own reasons for not pressing this
powerful party too hard. Sheltered under Theodora's
wing, many of the Monophysites were not slow to flatter
that clever lady, whose questionable past was in their
eyes fully atoned for by her soundness in the faith. But
our hermit was not of that sort. John of Ephesus declines
to repeat the terms of reproach hurled in the faces of the
imperial pair by Márá when he presented himself before
them in his tattered garb; it would not be fitting to do
so, he tells us; and, besides, he would not be believed.
All this was in execrable taste; yet it is a real pleasure

to see that there still were some people capable of confronting the servile "Byzantinism" of the day in a way that was manly and independent. Neither emperor nor empress was in a condition to meet this holy zeal with violence, if only because they themselves felt a superstitious awe in the presence of such a man. Theodora even sought to keep Márá near herself; perhaps she saw in the rough-tongued saint the confessor her long-borne burden of sin required. She even attempted to win him with a hundred pounds of gold, but he hurled the bag from him with one hand, and said: "To hell with thyself, and with the money wherewith thou wouldst tempt me!" Court and city were astounded at the bodily strength he showed in this, and still more at his contempt for Mammon,—a rare sight in Constantinople.

Márá next retired to the hills immediately to the north of Constantinople, and there lived as a hermit. The empress sent her courtiers to tell him that she would be glad to supply whatever he wished. They had great difficulty in finding him, as he had no fixed dwelling. By way of expressing his thanks, he sent back the message that she need not suppose herself to possess aught that servants of God could use, unless it were the fear of God, if she possessed such a thing as that. With all his rudeness he still maintained relations with the court. He earned his bread by making mats and baskets of palm leaves, but his principal nourishment consisted of wild fruits and herbs. Against winter he erected for himself some kind of a hut in the mountains. Being reputed a saint he had many visitors.

It, of course, came to be well known that Márá was frequently visited by messengers from the empress, and this naturally gave rise to the idea that the hermit's hovel must contain imperial gifts. One night, accordingly,

he received a visit from a robber band. But the saint
wrested from one of them the club with which he had
attacked him, seized him by the hair, and threw him to
the ground; three others he disposed of in the same way,
whereupon the six who were left took to flight. Three
of these also he succeeded in overtaking, and after binding
them all he triumphed over them at his leisure. Next
morning the visitors who came saw what had happened;
naturally they wished to hand the robbers over to the
authorities, but Márá, retaining only their swords and
clubs, dismissed them with a vigorous allocution. The
affair became known, and a chamberlain carried the weapons
to the emperor and empress, thus giving ocular demonstration of what can be done by the power of prayer
when conjoined with strength of arm. There may be
some exaggeration in this story, but the substance of it
as related by John of Ephesus, who was resident in
Constantinople at the time, and knew Márá personally,
is doubtless correct.

After a sojourn of some years among the mountains, Márá
allowed an official of the court to purchase for him a small
villa near the city, where he lived for five years, earning
what was required for the sustenance of himself and his
devout and needy guests by gardening. He often sent
salutary exhortations to the emperor and empress. On
the outbreak of a great plague in 542, he got workpeople
sent from the court to set up a cemetery with vaults and
chapel for poor strangers and for himself. Hardly had
they completed their task when he died. His funeral
was attended by many bishops and inferior clergy, as
well as monks, courtiers, and high officers of State.

Of Márá, whose vigorous and somewhat humorous figure
presents a welcome variety amid the mass of ordinary
ascetics, no miracles are recorded.

THEOPHILUS AND MARY.

About the year 530 there appeared in the streets of
Amid a merry-andrew (*mimus*) and his female companion,
who seemed to be a prostitute. People of the kind were
no rarities even in the pious East, but this couple attracted
special attention by their youth and beauty. The public
witnessed their performances with pleasure, but treated
them, as was also the custom, with brutality; the poor
creatures received many little presents, doubtless, but not
without kicks and cuffs. With nightfall they regularly
disappeared, and no one could find out where they had
gone. Some men of influence, whose carnal passions had
been inflamed, now procured from the governor an order
that the woman should be given over to prostitution; but
a God-fearing lady named Cosmo rescued her, took her
to be with herself, and exhorted her to a better life. She
listened to the advice with penitential mien, but forthwith
returned to her companion. Now, however, a pious man
named John, an acquaintance of John of Ephesus, began
to suspect something extraordinary about the pair. With
much trouble he discovered the retreat where their nights
were spent, and saw them engaged in long-continued prayer.
He now came up to them and asked an explanation. With
great reluctance they consented, but only after he had
solemnly promised upon oath to tell no one as long as
they continued in Amid, and even to treat them with
the usual contumely wherever he should see them in
public. Their story, which they told the following night,
was that their names were Theophilus and Mary, and
that each was an only child of noble and prosperous
Antiochenes. When Theophilus was fifteen years of age,
he went on to say, he one night discovered, in a stall of
his father's stables, a poor man, who had hidden himself

there in the litter against the cold; his mouth and hands emitted a halo, which Theophilus alone could see, and which disappeared whenever the servants entered. The holy man, at his urgent entreaty, confessed to him (but only on condition of secrecy) that his name was·Procopius, a Roman, who had fled from home to escape his approaching marriage. He predicted to Theophilus the approaching death in that year of his parents, and of ·those of his affianced bride, and exhorted him on this event to sell all that he had and give it to the poor, and himself to live a consecrated life in disguise; the lady also was to do the same. They actually did as they had been bidden, and lived in virginity together, while in the eyes of the world they appeared to be living in shameful immorality. For a whole year John held regular communication with this saintly pair; at the end of that time they disappeared, and for seven years he sought for them in vain; but John of Ephesus once afterwards met them near Tella (south of Amid, towards Edessa).

The author says that his informant had assured him upon his solemn oath of the truth of this story; and though one might be tempted to suspect that the pious man had simply been the victim of a couple of impostors, I, for my part, believe the narrative to be accurate in its main features. The light that proceeded from the holy beggar, and his prophecy, need not mislead us. The story, which comes to us through two intermediaries, may unintentionally have received various touches of the marvellous, and, above all, some account must be taken of the religiously excited fancy of the young man himself, which perhaps was full of such figures as that of the Roman "man of God"[1] fleeing from his nuptials, whose double the Procopius of our narrative is. It is indeed the very height of

[1] In later forms of the legend his name is St. Alexius.

unnatural self-abnegation when a virtuous maiden of even excessive spirituality ventures to assume the disguise of a common prostitute so as to bear the full shame of sin for the glory of God.

> " Opfer fallen hier
> Weder Lamm noch Stier
> Aber Menschenopfer unerhört." [1]

These Syrians were too apt to hold everything natural for wickedness; and yet unbridled sensuality was by no means unknown in their circle.

[1] " Sacrifices here are neither lamb nor steer,
But human sacrifice unspeakable."—GOETHE.

VIII.

BARHEBRÆUS.

In the first half of the thirteenth century a great part of the population of Melatia, in the east of Asia Minor, close to the upper Euphrates, consisted of Jacobites, that is to say, Syrians of Monophysite creed.[1] These Syrians were numerous also in the adjacent districts, where they had a number of bishoprics and monasteries. Conspicuous amongst the latter was the great and wealthy monastery of St. Barsaumá, where the Jacobite patriarch often took up his abode, and where synods frequently met; its patron saint was held in high repute by the Moslems of the district also, who presented many gifts in gratitude for miraculous help. The Moslems of these parts seem to have been of Turkish speech; probably there was also an Armenian population. The land belonged to the kingdom of the Seljuks of Asia Minor (Rúm), but, lying on the marches, was much exposed to assaults, on the one hand, from the principalities of Syria and Mesopotamia; and, on the other, from the Christian Armenian State of Cilicia. It had also to suffer from the internal struggles that accompanied the decline of the Seljuk power. The Syrians in this quarter seem, however, to have enjoyed a fair degree of prosperity down to the time of the Mongols; several eminent Syrian prelates and authors came from Melatia, amongst them the subject of the following sketch. His father, a respected physician of the name of Ahrún

---

[1] They derived the name from Jacobus Baradæus, who gave permanent form to the Monophysite Church of Syria in the sixth century.

(Aaron), seems to have been a baptized Jew. This is not inferred from his name, which was common enough among Syrian Christians, and besides would certainly have been changed at baptism, but from the fact that his celebrated son bore the surname of "Son of the Hebrew" (Bar Evráyá, or, according to another pronunciation, Bar Evróyó). From an epigram of his we see that the epithet was by no means agreeable to him, which confirms what has just been said. His Jewish origin is perhaps confirmed by the keen and sober intelligence which appears both in his actions and in his writings. His Christian name was John, but in ordinary life he was known as Abulfaraj, an Arabic name such as Christians living amongst Mohammedans were wont to bear. But in the following pages we shall throughout call him Barhebræus, the Latinised form of his surname, which has long been familiar to European scholars.

He was born in 1225–26. His mother-tongue was, it may be presumed, a vulgar dialect of Syriac; but it is certain that from an early age he was able to speak with fluency the literary Syriac, which had already disappeared from common use, but played a great part in the language of the Church and of learning. Of the youth of Barhebræus we have no details. He must certainly have received in Melatia such a training in learning as was then given to young Syrians destined for the higher service of the Church. But the statement sometimes made, that he also became acquainted with Greek and the ecclesiastical literature of that language, is certainly incorrect; his writings nowhere show any real acquaintance with either. By that time the Arabic language and literature had long superseded its rival with all Syrians who aimed at the higher education.

When the Mongols (Tartars) invaded the country in the summer of 1243, his father Aaron, in common with many others, wished to take refuge with his family in Syria, but was hindered by an accident, and thus he and his escaped the fate of the fugitives, who fell into the hands of the Mongols. The Christians and Moslems of Melatia on that occasion, under the leadership of the Syrian metropolitan Dionysius, came under a solemn mutual obligation to stand by one another. This incident is in the highest degree surprising to one who knows something of the social conditions of the East. The professors of the two religions habitually regard one another as born foes ; but here the terrible danger effected a union, and even a subordination of the proud Moslems under the downtrodden Christians, who were manifestly in the majority, and had for their leader a man of energy, though not over scrupulous. The Mongol chief allowed himself to be bought off, and no battle took place. Falling ill, he asked for a physician ; Barhebræus's father was sent to him, and did not leave him until he had reached Kharput, after being cured of his malady.

Aaron and his family after this removed to Antioch, which was still in the hands of the Franks. Here his son became a monk, doubtless with a view to the episcopal dignity, the higher ecclesiastical charges being in the Oriental Churches accessible only to monks. Soon afterwards we find Barhebræus in Tripoli, also still in the hands of the Crusaders. Along with a companion[1] he here studied dialectic and medicine under a Nestorian. This may have had something to do with the tolerance which he afterwards showed towards Christians of different creed, though indeed it was not unusual for a Syrian to frequent the lectures of a man whose doctrine he regarded as heretical. Barhebræus probably had Moslem teachers also, for he could hardly otherwise have acquired his good knowledge of the Arabic language and literature. He wrote Arabic almost as fluently as Syriac, and not much more incorrectly than most Mohammedan

[1] See below, p. 246.

writers of his time. He could also make use of Persian
books without difficulty, at least in his later years. He
spoke Arabic well, of course; and presumably he had
acquired a colloquial knowledge of Turkish also. But he
seems never to have been brought into close relations with
the Franks.

Talented and industrious, he must very soon have attracted
the notice of the ecclesiastical authorities, and while still a
youth of only twenty he was ordained by the Jacobite patriarch (12th September 1246) to be Bishop of Gubos, near
Melatia, on which occasion he assumed the ecclesiastical
name of Gregory. Not long afterwards he exchanged this
bishopric for that of Lakabín, in the same region.[1]

As bishop he took part in the synod held at the monastery
of Barsaumá, after the death of Ignatius (14th June 1252),
for the election of a new patriarch. At this juncture there
arrived in the neighbourhood of Melatia a body of Mongols,
a detachment of the great hordes which in those years made
an end of the caliphate, and devastated on all hands with
fire and sword. Barhebræus's aged father, who had again
returned to his home, fled with his little son Barsaumá from
the village of Margá to a rocky region beside the Euphrates,
and remained there in hiding for six weeks, until the barbarians had gone. The world was trembling in its courses,
but this made little impression on the Jacobite dignitaries;
they went on intriguing and quarrelling just as usual.
Dionysius of Melatia, who has been already mentioned, and
John, surnamed Barmadeni, the maphrián or primate of
the eastward dioceses,[2] a man of high repute as a scholar,
were competitors for the patriarchate. By the laws of that
Church no valid election could take place without the presence of the maphrián; but Dionysius procured his own

---

[1] I am not sure of the exact pronunciation either of Gubos or of Lakabín.
[2] See below, p. 244.

election in September 1252 in defiance of this rule, and in a very thinly attended synod. The youthful Barhebræus was sent into Mesopotamia to convey to John the apologies of the synod, and to beg his concurrence. But John had meantime gone to Aleppo, where, on 4th December of the same year, he got himself chosen to the patriarchate,—an election which certainly has a greater apparent claim to validity than the other. But the all-important question was as to which patriarch the Moslem rulers would recognise. There began accordingly a scandalous competition between the rivals (not a rare occurrence in the Eastern Churches). On both sides the effort was made to gain over princes and potentates, as well as individual bishops and other ecclesiastics of influence, by money or fair words. Along with his nephew, a monk, Barhebræus was sent into the mountains of Túr Abdín, in northern Mesopotamia, which were mostly inhabited by Jacobites, to collect funds in the monasteries and villages for gaining over to Dionysius the local prince, to whom John had promised a sum of money for recognition, but had as yet failed to pay it. The mission was successful. It is well worth noticing, though not very edifying, to see how coolly Barhebræus, certainly one of the most respectable persons of his class, relates these transactions. It must be remembered that the laity, from whom the money was drawn, were for the most part exceedingly poor; bright prospects of a reward in heaven [1] were, to be sure, held out to them by way of compensation, and all the proceedings

[1] In a little Syriac treatise, which, gross forgery though it is, seems to have been popular, God says: "To every believer who gives of the earnings of his hand to the holy Church, I make it good in this world, and repay him thirty, sixty, and a hundredfold in the world to come, and write his name in the book of life;" and again: "Honour God's priests, who sacrifice the living lamb, so that ye may find mercy in the world to come. He who despises them shall fall under my wrath, for my priests are the salt of the earth." The Jews, who contribute handsomely to their synagogues, are cited as patterns for Christians.

were carried on in the most approved Christian phraseology. The Eastern Churches were, of course, unable to secure immunity from the caprice and violence of the Moslem authorities without a skilful use of the mammon of unrighteousness, but it is a very different matter when the faithful are taxed that one of their own spiritual heads may be able to secure an effectual triumph over another. Occurrences of the kind have not been wholly unknown in the West, but the abuse attained far larger proportions in the East.

Dionysius now proceeded to Damascus, where he was honourably received by the governor, Barhebræus acting as interpreter. In these negotiations, however, Dionysius fell into a stupid blunder, exhibiting the letter of a Mongol magnate which had been intended for his supporters in Melatia. This caused great offence, for the Tartars were regarded as mortal enemies by the Moslems. It was only with great trouble, and through the intervention of Ibn Amíd (Elmacinus), the well-known Coptic author, that Dionysius at last succeeded in obtaining his diploma of confirmation on payment of a large bribe.

Barhebræus was soon afterwards named by Dionysius to be bishop of Aleppo; but on the installation there of a partisan of John's, he withdrew, along with his father, to the Barsaumá monastery, where his patriarch was. John betook himself to the Armenian king of Sís, while Dionysius received recognition almost everywhere. Barhebræus soon again took up his abode in Aleppo. When the Mongols, who in the meantime had taken Bagdad (January 1258), entered Syria he wished to go to meet them, plainly with the object of securing mild treatment for the Christians. The idea was not unreasonable, for their common antipathy to Islam readily predisposed the Mongol chiefs in favour of the Christians, who, moreover, sought only toleration, and did not fight for sovereignty like the Moslems. Some

of those wild Tartars had, moreover, been baptized, for the
Nestorians had successful missions among the Turkish
tribes.   Dokuz Khatun herself, a wife of the sovereign
Hulagu, who formerly had been one of the wives of his
father Tuli, and who in accordance with Mongol custom
had passed with the rest of the inheritance to the son,
was a Christian, and did much for the protection and
advantage of her co-religionists.   But the attempt in this
instance was unsuccessful.   Barhebræus was detained at
Kalat-Nejm, one of the Euphrates ferries; and Hulagu
meanwhile coming to Aleppo, occupied the town, and
inflicted on Moslems and Christians alike all the horrors
of a sack (January 1260).

Diónysius compromised himself seriously.   That he obtained letters of confirmation from the Mongol sovereign
(1259) was not amiss, especially as the Seljuks and the
Armenian Christian king had equally acknowledged the
Tartar as their overlord.   But it was a scandal that he
connived at the robberies of the Christian subjects of the
St. Barsaumá monastery, who had broken loose from all
restraint in this period of general corruption and dissolute-
ness.   And he finally lost the last shred of reputation by
procuring the assassination of a cousin who had been a
great trouble to him, and of his cousin's brother, only a
few days after a reconciliation had taken place; even the
chronique scandaleuse of the history of the Jacobites supplied
no parallel to such conduct.   To escape the consequences
of his deed the patriarch again went to Hulagu, and after
overcoming many obstacles was lucky enough to secure his
special protection, so that he was able to lord it more
tyrannically than ever.   And now the monastery of St.
Barsaumá witnessed an unheard-of scene; the murderous
patriarch was assassinated before the altar as he was holding a night service (17th–18th February) by a monk, a

deacon, and a layman, nephew of one of the abbats. The assassins threw the "disciple" of the patriarch, who had been his instrument in the murder of his cousin, down the rock.

Whether Barhebræus had before these occurrences openly broken with Dionysius is not known; but one of his poems shows that latterly he was no longer at one with him, and some verses upon his death indicate that he regarded his assassination as a righteous judgment.

A Mongolian commissioner, himself a Christian, made his appearance for the punishment of the perpetrators of the deed. One of the abbats, who tacitly, at least, had approved it, was cruelly chastised and driven half-dead from the monastery. He was replaced by a brother of the priest and physician Simeon, who had risen to great favour with Hulagu, had grown very wealthy, and stood out as the main support of the Jacobites, in return for which he exercised influence in extraordinary ways in Church affairs. Some of the murderers and their accomplices were executed, and others committed suicide in prison.

By this shocking occurrence John became sole patriarch, and met with universal recognition; but he remained in Cilicia. Barhebræus now stood on good terms with him; and when he died in the spring of 1263, the bishop of Aleppo wrote in his honour a long poem commemorating his many excellences.

Abbat Theodore now hastened to the court, or rather to the camp, of the Mongolian sovereign to seek the patriarchate for himself. But Simeon the physician declined to undertake his cause, and also persuaded Barhebræus, who was also at that time at court, certainly not by mere chance, to oppose his claims. Barhebræus then proceeded to Cilicia and took part at Sís in the election of abbat Joshua, who, as patriarch, assumed the name of Ignatius (6th January 1264). Forthwith they proceeded to fill up

also the office of maphriàn, or primate of the Jacobites of
the East, which had been vacant since June 1258. The
origin of this dignity may be here explained. The Persian
sovereigns had gradually suffered the Christians of various
denominations in their empire to constitute themselves into
distinct bodies, insisting, however, that while the head of
each was to be independent of every external authority, he
was to be in entire subjection to the throne.[1] These heads
bore the title of " Catholicus." The Syrian Monophysites
did not receive a fixed constitution under a catholicus
until a comparatively late date (in the sixth century);
they stood in much closer connection with the Christians
of the hostile empire of Rome than the Nestorians did,
and, on the other hand, were much less able to compel
recognition than the sometimes very warlike Monophysites
of insubordinate Armenia. The main seat of the Jacobites
of the Persian empire was the considerable town of Tagrít,
on the middle course of the Tigris ; but nowhere in Persia
were they nearly so numerous as the Nestorians. The
Jacobite catholicus bore also the title of maphrián (mafri-
yáná), i.e. " the fructifier," who spreads the Church by
instituting priests and bishops. After the Arabs had
become masters of all the countries in which Monophysite
Syrians were found, the separation of the provinces of the
Jacobite " patriarch of Antioch" and that of the maphrián
was, strictly speaking, no longer necessary ; but the force
of custom, and still more the interest which many of the
clergy had in not allowing so influential and remunerative

[1] The Christians of the Sásánian empire -originally had bishops only,
without any single head. Even after they had placed themselves under the
catholicus of Seleucia and Ctesiphon, the Church of Persia proper, for some
time, continued to maintain its independence. The statement that the
patriarchal authority of Antioch had been delegated from the earliest times
to the bishop of Seleucia and Ctesiphon is, of course, a mere fiction, rest-
ing upon the later conception of the unity of the Church in its outward
organisation.

a post as that of maphrián to go down, were enough to maintain the old arrangement. But many disputes arose as to the boundaries of the two provinces, and the whole relation of maphrián to patriarch; on the whole, however, it was agreed that the patriarch's indeed was the higher rank, but that the maphrián in his sphere was quite independent of him; and further, that for the election of a patriarch the co-operation of the maphrián was indispensable (unless that post also was vacant), and that a maphrián could only be nominated with the sanction of the patriarch. In the choice of a maphrián the wishes of the Eastern dioceses (*i.e.* of the bishops and heads of monasteries there) had to be respected; yet, as a rule, he was taken from the West. Now Barhebræus had already been designated as maphrián by the late patriarch, and, moreover, he seems to have been the ruling spirit in the electoral synod; accordingly he was chosen "maphrián of Tagrít and the East" on Sunday, 20th January 1264. The Armenian king with his suite and officials, spiritual and secular, were present at his consecration on the same day in the church of the Theotokos at Sís. Barhebræus preached the sermon, which an interpreter translated into Armenian. The Armenians, be it noted in passing, were of the same creed as the Jacobites, but differed from them on many points of ritual, and perhaps also in some subordinate matters of dogma. Armenians and Jacobites were thus very ready to suspect one another of heresy, and at best there was little love lost between the two parties.[1] After patriarch and maphrián had received their diplomas of confirmation from the Mongol sovereign (whose assent had doubtless been secured before the election) they withdrew, the one to Asia Minor and the other to Mosul.

The Jacobites of the East had long been without any

[1] The relations of the Jacobites with the Monophysite Copts were better.

proper government; for the predecessor of Barhebræus, his old fellow-student at Tripoli, had failed to establish his authority in the East, and soon withdrew into Syria, and after his death the va. ancy had continued for nearly six years. The lands of the Tigris were terribly wasted. Although the Mongols still were more favourable to the Christians than to the Moslems, they were neither willing nor able to spare them in those wholesale massacres which constantly occurred. Moreover, the position of the Christians, which was one of greater friendliness with the Mongols, and thus gave them a somewhat more self-reliant bearing, repeatedly excited the jealousy and fanaticism of the Mohammedan population, which was greatly superior in numbers and in strength; in the district of Mosul, in particular, many bloody encounters took place. Matters were better in Aderbiján (north-western Media), the favourite seat of the Mongolian rulers. There, until the reaction set in, the Christians suffered little molestation, and monasteries and churches arose in the capital cities of Merághá and Tabríz. The Jacobites were here less numerous than either Armenians or Nestorians. Barhebræus now laboured indefatigably as maphrián for the strengthening of his Church. He made many extensive journeys within his territory, took measures for the erection of ecclesiastical edifices, and consecrated numerous priests and bishops. He succeeded in maintaining good relations with the Mongolian court without coming into too close contact with it. And with all this he studied, wrote, and taught without intermission.

At Mosul the maphrián was met in solemn procession by the officials of the Mohammedan prince as well as by the Christians: the vassal of the Mongols had good reason for treating in a friendly way a man of mark who had just been the recipient of their favour. Still more solemn was the reception of Barhebræus when, at Easter 1265, he came to Bagdad—still an important place, notwithstanding its recent terrible sack. Such was the consideration enjoyed by Barhebræus, that even the catholicus of the Nestorians sent a deputation, including two of his own nephews, to escort ·him into his presence. A harmony like this, between the representatives of two creeds which had been separated by the hostility of eight centuries, is well worth remarking. Many Nestorians took part also in the service held by Barhebræus, at which was wrought the customary miracle of a spontaneous overflow of the chrism at the moment of consecration.[1] The catholicus, indeed, presently became jealous of his colleague's popularity, but no mischief followed, for he died a fortnight after the festival (Saturday, 18th April 1265). After spending the entire summer in Bagdad, and consecrating numerous clergy of various grades, Barhebræus returned again to the district of Mosul, where his proper see was. He usually lived in the great fortified monastery of St. Matthew, which was for the maphrián something like what that of Barsaumá was for the patriarch.

The patriarch Ignatius, in the years immediately following, fell into a violent dispute with the physician Simeon, already mentioned, who had taken possession of the government of the monastery of Barsaumá. As he had done this on the strength of orders issued by the Mongols, Ignatius sought to obtain from these a decision in an opposite sense; and although Barhebræus earnestly urged him to come to some amicable settlement of the difficulty, and not to expose himself before "the barbarian Huns," he persevered in the line he had chosen. The maphrián naturally took this very ill. When, accordingly, in 1268,

---

[1] This miracle recalls that of the liquefaction of the blood of St. Januarius at Naples, and no doubt admits of a similar natural explanation.

in the course of a journey westward to visit his relatives
near Lake Van, he encountered the patriarch on his way
to the Mongol court to complain of Simeon, he sought to
avoid a meeting, and the patriarch obtained one at last
only with difficulty. Abaga, who had succeeded his father
Hulagu in the sovereignty of the Mongols in February
1265, actually promulgated a decree in accordance with
the wishes of Ignatius; but the influential Simeon contrived
that it should straightway be cancelled by another, and
Barhebræus, detained in Cilicia by a serious illness, saw
Simeon return in triumph with the decree in his hand.
But the dispute was further prolonged. The Government
pronounced alternately for this party and for that; neither
reconciliation nor compromise proved permanent. At last,
in 1273, Barhebræus, who had been called in as arbiter,
was successful in composing the difference. On this
occasion he found his native land in poor case. Moslem
troops from Syria had invaded the Mongol territory,
wasting it far and wide, and dragging many Christian
women and children into slavery. The lords of Egypt
and the petty princes of Syria were at that time at
continual war with the Tartars, whom in the end they
succeeded in shaking off; but the struggles in the meantime had completed the ruin of many districts. Additional
insecurity was caused by the presence of robber tribes,
which now could do pretty much as they pleased. Barhebræus, who had taken up temporary quarters in the
monastery of St. Sergius, was escorted thence to that of
St. Barsaumá by a body of fifty armed dependants.

In Easter of 1277, Barhebræus was again in Bagdad,
where some years before a large new Jacobite church
had been built in the neighbourhood of the former palaces
of the Caliphs, mainly at the expense of a rich Christian
official named Safíaddaula. At this period, when the

Christians for a short time were able to raise their
heads under the rule of the religiously indifferent, not
to say stolid barbarians, frequent instances are met with
in which wealthy private individuals devoted money to
building churches. The smaller contributions of the poorer
members of the community — doubtless the main source
of income for the higher clergy — were forthcoming, we
may be sure, in unusual abundance during the term of
a maphrián so respected as Barhebræus. He was again
received with great pomp by the Christians of Bagdad.
The catholicus of that time also, Denhá by name, sent a
deputation to meet him, and received him immediately
afterwards with honour. Jacobites and Nestorians, at such
a juncture at least, felt themselves to be branches of a
common stem.

In autumn of the same year Barhebræus came to Tagrít,
which, although nominally the see of the maphrián, had
beheld no incumbent of that office for sixty years. The
Christian population of the place, to be sure, had been
sadly diminished; for immediately after the fall of Bagdad
the Mongols had put to death the Christians of Tagrít
(whom they had at first spared) in their usual wholesale
manner, for having concealed much property of the
Moslems instead of giving it up to the conquerors (Palm
Sunday, 1258). Barhebræus remained here in his nominal
residence for two months. The following years he spent
partly in the neighbourhood of Mosul and partly in
Aderbiján.

It is characteristic of the time that, in 1281, the
Nestorians, on the death of their patriarch Denhá, chose
as his successor a clergyman deficient in ecclesiastical
learning, whose recommendation was that he belonged to
a nationality of Central Asia which was also largely
represented at the Mongol court. This was Marcus, an

Uigur, or Turk of the farthest East, who had come from China on pilgrimage to Jerusalem, but on account of the insecurity of the roads from war and robbers had been unable to complete the last comparatively 'short portion of the journey. As patriarch he bore the name Yavalláhá, and he distinguished himself alike by his honesty and by his knowledge of the world. He showed great friendliness to the Jacobites; but as he knew little of the old dogmatic controversies, and even in the simplicity of his heart sought relations with the pope, he is hardly entitled to so much credit for liberality of spirit as Barhebræus is, who was well versed in the dogmatic questions which divided the Christians of those countries, but, in marked contrast to the old champions of his Church, sought to minimise their importance. He expressly declared that the one thing needful was not love to Nestorius or to Jacobus (Baradæus), but to Christ, appealing to the words of the apostle : " Who is Paul ? and who is Apollos ? " (1 Cor. iii. 5). Isolated instances of similar irenical tendencies are met with elsewhere in the East during the crusading period.

Barhebræus, in the spring of 1282, wished to go to Tabríz, and, accordingly, owing to the insecurity of the roads through the Kurdish country, attached himself to the caravan of a Mongol princess. News now coming of the death of Abaga, he proceeded to Alatag (also in Aderbiján), where, according to the provisions of Jenghiz Khan's fundamental law, the new sovereign was to be chosen by the Mongolian assembly. Here he paid homage to Abaga's brother Ahmed, who ascended the throne on 21st June. He obtained also a diploma of confirmation. Ahmed, as his Arabic name testifies, had accepted Islam, and is reported to have ruled his conduct expressly with a view to the caliphate; but he was by no means fanatical, and he even renewed to the Christian monasteries, churches,

and priesthood their privilege of exemption from taxation.
And the pagan Argun, Abaga's son, who overthrew Ahmed
in July 1284 and caused him to be put to death, was
again exceptionally gracious to the Christians. The Mongols
had already, indeed, begun by this time to go over
in troops to Islam, which was better suited to their
character than even the crudest type of Christianity;
but Barhebræus did not live long enough to see all the
hopes which the Christians of the East [1] had built upon
these brutal barbarians completely falsified, and Islam
once more restored to undivided ascendency in the wasted
lands.

In the autumn of 1282, Barhebræus received in Tabríz a
letter, in which the patriarch told him of his serious illness,
and besought him to come and relieve him of the cares
of his office; this was clearly intended to convey the wish
that Barhebræus should be his successor. Winter being
at hand, and the roads dangerous, the maphrián, however,
did not comply with this invitation. Ignatius died of
dropsy on Tuesday, 17th November, and the party of
Simeon hastened to elect bishop Philoxenus to the
patriarchate (2nd February 1283). The election was
held in the Barsaumá monastery, and only three bishops,
all belonging to depopulated dioceses in the neighbourhood,
took part in it. But confirmation was obtained without
delay from Alatag. Humble apologies were now tendered
to the maphrián for the uncanonical procedure, and he was
entreated to give it his after-concurrence, without which
the election could not hope for the approval of a majority
of the bishops; but he turned the messengers away. Even
when Simeon the physician came in person, he continued
steadfast. It was not until the son of Simeon, a pupil of
his own, with whom he was on personally friendly terms,

[1] Similar expectations were sometimes cherished in the West also.

had a meeting with him (August 1284) that he condescended
to accept the offered presents and to sanction the appointment.   We can well believe the assurance he then gave
that he was far from wishing to be himself made patriarch,
the secure and influential post he actually held being worth
more to him than the headship of the Jacobite Church in
the West, which had been entirely desolated by war; hard
as the times were, he was better off than his predecessors.
But he had to maintain the maphrián's dignity, and his
self-esteem also had been undoubtedly hurt, for he was
well entitled to consider himself the foremost of the
Jacobite clergy.   The meeting referred to took place as
Barhebræus was once again travelling in the caravan of
a princess from Tabríz to the district of Mosul.

Near the village of Bartellé, not far from the monastery
of St. Matthew, he had built to the martyr "John the
carpenter's son" a new church, which he caused to be
decorated by an artist from Constantinople, one of two
painters whom the widow of Abaga, a natural daughter
of the Greek emperor Michael, had fetched from the
imperial city to adorn the church of her own denonina-
tion (the Greek "Orthodox") in Tabríz.   But the old
church had been searched in vain for the relics of the
martyr.   After every one else had failed it was given to
the maphrián, as he himself tells us, to discover the marble
sarcophagus, in consequence of a vision for which he had
prepared himself by prayer and fasting (23rd November
1284).   How far self-deception entered into this, we can
hardly say.   Barhebræus was a cool-headed person, but
like all his contemporaries he had sucked in belief in
miracles and wonders with his mother's milk; on the
other hand, we shall hardly be doing an injustice even to
the best representative of the Oriental clergy of that day
if we deem him not incapable of a little pious fraud.

In 1285–86,[1] Barhebræus, as we learn from one of his verses, was led by astrological calculations to expect his end; a presentiment which proved true. His brother Barsaumá, who was constantly beside him, and took charge of his building undertakings, sought to withdraw him as far as possible from danger by inducing him to quit the neighbourhood of Mosul, which was now yearly harassed by marauding bands from Syria, and to return to Merághá. Here he continued to labour for a while; but on the night of 29th–30th July 1286 he died after a short illness of three days. He had previously expressed his regret for having left his proper place from fear of the death that was inevitable. It may be supposed that he had felt some warnings of weakness, although his brother declares him to have been at the time in exceptionally good health.

There were then in Merághá only four Jacobite priests to conduct the funeral obsequies. But the Nestorian patriarch Yavalláhá, who happened to be also in the place, enjoined a day of strict mourning on all those in his obedience, and sent the bishops who were with him to the funeral. The Armenian and even the Greek clergy also took part in it; there were altogether about two hundred mourners, and for once the Christians showed a united front in face of the Moslems to do honour to a person so distinguished. With solemnities which lasted over nine hours, Barhebræus was buried at the spot where he had been wont to pray and administer the sacrament; but at a later date his body was removed to the monastery of St. Matthew, where his grave is still shown.

We do not need to make very great deductions from the high praise lavished on the character of Barhebræus by Barsaumá, his brother and successor. Had he not been amiable and humane, he would hardly have stood in such

---

[1] The Syrian Julian year begins with 1st October.

pleasant relations with those of other Christian communions.
And yet he was no weakling, but a thoroughly forceful man,
not without ambition; and in point of character, with all
his imperfections, he certainly stood far above the large
majority of the higher clergy of the East.

His great activity is attested by his ecclesiastical buildings, already begun when he was bishop of Aleppo, and by
his literary works. From his twentieth year down to his
last hour, his brother tells us, he studied and wrote without
intermission. Barsaumá's list, which is not quite exhaustive, enumerates thirty-one writings of Barhebræus, among
which are several works of some compass. They are mostly
in Syriac, but some in Arabic. Manuscripts of most of
them can be found in European libraries, and sometimes
there are more copies than one—a sign that they were
much read. His books embrace almost all branches of
the knowledge of his day. It would indeed be idle to
expect much original thought or independent research in
such a mediæval and Eastern scholar. His principal object
was to make accessible to the Syrians the productions of
Arabian and older science. Most of his encyclopædic and
separate scientific works are for the most part, accordingly,
merely intelligent compilations or excerpts from earlier
treatises in Syriac or Arabic. Some are simply translations;
thus he rendered some works of the famous Aristotelian
Avicenna from Arabic into Syriac. Barhebræus wrote on
philosophy, medicine, astronomy and astrology, geography,
history, jurisprudence, grammar, and so on; among the
subjects treated, the secular sciences are on the whole
more prominent than theology proper. He even compiled
two little books of anecdotes. He earned the respect of
learned Moslems by his writings, and no doubt also by
his skill in oral teaching and disputation. An odd proof
of this is the foolish rumour that Barhebræus on his death-

bed had turned Moslem; the thought was the expression
of the wish to gain for Islam and eternal blessedness so
distinguished a scholar.

Some works of Barhebræus are still of great value,
particularly his Sacred and Profane History, drawn from
older Arabic, Syriac, and Persian works, and especially
from the Syriac Church History of Michael, his fellow-
townsman of Melatia, who was Jacobite patriarch from
1166 to 1199.[1] It is distinguished by an apt selection of
materials, contains much that is not to be found elsewhere,
and is an important authority for the author's own period.
In his very last days Barhebræus wrote at Merághá, at the
request of some Moslems, an Arabic edition of the Profane
History, which is shorter than the Syriac work, but contains
some new matter. Next in importance to the History is
his larger Syriac Grammar, in which he tries to combine
the method not very happily borrowed by the older Syrians
from the Greek grammarians with the Arabian system.
Viewed in the light of modern philology the book shows
great defects, but it is far ahead of the works that preceded
it, and still very instructive. Further, his Scholia to the
Bible, which are more philological than theological, are of
value (especially for the history of the Syriac text); and so
is his collection of Jacobite Canon Law.

Barhebræus wrote metrical pieces also. He has certainly
none of the gifts of the heaven-born poet. These composi-
tions have neither fancy nor passion. He writes them
with his understanding, partly after the pattern of older
Syrians, partly on Arabian and Persian models. The
didactic wordiness of the Syrian poetry is often also
apparent. But the skill and elegance with which he

---

[1] A work hitherto known only by an abridged and interpolated Armenian
translation. The original has been recently discovered, but is not yet
accessible.

handles the unpromising materials of the ecclesiastical language is worthy of recognition, and he shows spirit and taste, especially in the short epigrammatic poems. He is further entitled to the credit of being almost entirely free from the verbal conceits which were so greatly affected in the poetry of that time. Generally speaking, he can fairly be put on a level with the average Arabic poets of his age, and certainly above most of the Syriac. Altogether he was one of the most eminent men of his Church and nation.

IX

KING THEODORE OF ABYSSINIA.[1]

ABYSSINIA, that marvellous mountain land in which the advantages of the tropical and temperate zones are united, was for centuries a single monarchy. The only African country which retained its Christianity, it had not escaped without grievous injury the many external assaults and inward struggles through which it had passed; and the bond which held together its different provinces, ruled by local princes, and in part separated by well-marked physical features, was by no means strong. But, with all this, it still was a powerful kingdom, governed by a race which an alleged descent from Solomon, and still more a rule that had continued without interruption from the thirteenth century, had invested with a nimbus of sanctity. But shortly after the middle of the eighteenth century the power of its sovereigns broke down. Petty princes asserted independence, and sought to extend their own dominions; rude soldiers grasped a royal authority, and there was a constant succession of civil wars. The unspeakable atrocities connected with these contests completed the ruin of the Abyssinian civilisation, which, it must not be forgotten, had never stood very high. The prestige of the Solomonic dynasty was so great that the actual rulers, some of them Mohammedans and Gallas, maintained it in name; but its sovereigns, set up or dethroned at the pleasure of the conqueror for the time being, had not the faintest shadow

---

[1] Originally published in *Deutsche Rundschau*, x. (1884) p. 406 sqq.

of power. When Rüppell visited the capital Gondar in 1833, the reigning "king of the kings of Ethiopia" hardly had the revenue of a tolerably well-to-do private citizen. The clergy, who were extraordinarily numerous, were the only class who continued to flourish; in the never-ending warfare a church might be destroyed or a sanctuary desecrated here and there, but the old endowments were so rich, and the holders so skilful in working upon the superstitions of the people, that their interests never seriously suffered. They themselves were grossly superstitious, and for the most part little superior to the laity in culture. With some worthy exceptions the degenerate clergy have been, and still are, along with a brutal soldiery, the worst curses of this unhappy country, so richly gifted by nature.

Towards the middle of the present century, Abyssinia was partitioned into three main principalities. The north was firmly and strongly held by the cunning Ubié, hereditary chief of the Alpine district of Semyén, who had taken possession of Tigré, the seat of the oldest kingdom of Abyssinia and of the most ancient Abyssinian civilisation. The largest portion of the country was under Ras Ali, a Galla by race. Though a Mohammedan by origin, he had received baptism; but he was regarded as a lukewarm Christian, — not because his life was irregular, for the same could be said of many good Christians, but because he tolerated Moslems: there were even whispers that, dreadful to relate, he had more than once eaten of the flesh of animals that Mohammedans had killed. He was good-humoured and indolent, permitted the local chiefs to do what they pleased, and was never able to bring some of the more powerful princes to obedience. The chiefs of the unruly Wollo-Gallas, some of them related to him, acknowledged his suzerainty on the tacit condition that he should never trouble himself about anything they

did.   In the extreme south was Shoa, completely independent, under a dynasty which had been in power from
the beginning of the eighteenth century, and had at last
assumed the royal title. Shoa, governed with considerable
firmness, had no share in the confusions of the rest of
Abyssinia, from which it is separated both by natural
barriers and by wild Galla tribes.   If, now, these chief
rulers had remained contented with the territory that
each had acquired, the division would have been to the
positive advantage of the country; for Abyssinia, with its
Alpine ranges and deep erosion valleys, which put a stop
to all intercourse during the rainy season (our summer),
is not fitted by nature to be a single State with effective
administration from a single centre.   But each ruler strove
to extend his own authority by violence, or fraud and
perjury, at the expense of his neighbour.   It was only
with difficulty that Ras Ali, the lord of the central portion,
resisted the encroachments of Ubié, and the everlasting
turbulence of great vassals and petty insurgents.

In this condition of affairs a powerful upstart suddenly
arose and overthrew all the princes of Abyssinia.   Few
Europeans had so much as heard Kasa's name as long as
he continued to be a mere governor or rebel against his
lord; and even to them it was a surprise when Kasa
suddenly restored the old monarchy as "Theodore, king
of the kings of Ethiopia," and united the entire country
under his sway.   The kingdom seemed once more to have
a future before it; for the new ruler was a man of exceptional endowments, a mighty warrior, and a friend of
progress.   This anticipation was unfortunately not realised.
Theodore had to carry on a constant struggle for his
authority, and his power had already been restricted
almost to his own camp when the conflict with the
English began.   This conflict, through which his name

first came to be really known in Europe, reduced him to the alternatives of surrender or death; nor did he hesitate in his choice, dying as a king and a hero by his own hand,—a death which in the remembrance of posterity will ever place him in a different category from that of the many other rulers of savage peoples whom the British arms have subdued.

Theodore was a barbarian, a frightful despot, and yet a great man. If ever there was a tragedy, it is to be seen in the story of this child of the wilderness, who was called to, and achieved, the highest position; but after unceasing struggle was overthrown by error, passion, and crime, more than by a foreign power. It will not be unprofitable to look for a little at his life. For his earlier history we are so fortunate as to possess, not merely the notices of various European travellers, but also a consecutive narrative down to the year 1860, written in Amharic (the chief dialect of modern Abyssinia) by Debtera Zenab, a cleric with whom he had personal relations.[1]

Kasa was born about the year 1820 in the land of Quara, in the extreme west of Abyssinia; his mother-tongue was doubtless the non-Semitic Agau there prevalent, and it is probable that his blood was mainly Agau. His origin was not low, as has sometimes been asserted; his father, Hailu (or Haila Maryam), was a great noble, and for some time ruled Quara, in the capacity of governor, for his powerful brother Kenfu. Kasa's mother, however, seems to have been of humble condition. As the loosest kind of polygamy prevails among the nobles of Abyssinia, it is impossible for them to take very great care of all their offspring. But it is not uncommon for the obscurer

[1] The MS. was presented to the Royal Library in Berlin by the worthy missionary Flad, along with a German abridgment. A portion of the abridgment appears in his instructive work, entitled *Twelve Years in Abyssinia* (*Zwölf Jahre in Abessinien*).

children of princely fathers by mothers of lower rank to rise to distinction. Ubié also was the son of a peasant girl. The youthful Kasa had been designed for a modest career; it was intended that he should be trained for the Church in a monastery not far from Gondar, the capital. But he had early experience of war and its desolations. The governor for the time being had rebelled against his master, Ras Imam (uncle and predecessor of Ras Ali), who invaded the province in 1827. In the invasion Kasa's monastery was destroyed, and Imam's Galla soldiers made eunuchs of its forty-eight pupils, Kasa alone escaping. In this he must afterwards have recognised the hand of God, who had designed him for another career than the clerical, and delivered him from danger; for his faith in his "star" scarcely ever failed him to the last. I very much doubt the assertion of many Europeans, that his monkish education deeply influenced him. At an age of less than eight years, the boy cannot have become a theological scholar. His literary acquirements, measured even by Abyssinian standards, were never high. The use of Biblical expressions which he affected is not necessarily to be regarded in a man of his temperament as a result of direct teaching; in words all Abyssinians are excellent Christians.

Kasa now entered the household of his uncle Kenfu, who ruled an extensive territory, and after his death, that of one of his sons. But Kasa's cousins soon came to open war with each other, and in this he also took part. The cousin on whose side he was had the worst of it; Kasa was made a prisoner, but released by the victor in consideration of their youthful companionship. Misfortune upon misfortune now befell Kasa. On one occasion, when he again was unlucky enough to be on the losing side, he had to remain in hiding for a month, and this within the territory that belonged to his own family; as a scion of

a princely house he bore the pretentious title of Ledj
("Youth," *i.e.* "Junker" or "Prince"), and if discovered
he would hardly have been spared by the enemy.   In
later prosperous days he conferred high honour and
princely rewards on the countrymen who had sheltered
him in this strait.   Kasa served under a variety of captains
great and small, and distinguished himself by his boldness
and skill in battle and in the chase.   For example, he once
on horseback killed two elephants; but in doing so he so
roused the jealousy of his less fortunate chief that he found
it necessary to quit his service without delay.   On such
lines zeal and patience might easily have raised him to
high position; but he had a mind to be a master, not a
servant, and became the leader of a robber band.   In
these parts, to be sure, it is difficult to draw the line
between a robber chief and a petty prince.   For years
Kasa conducted plundering raids, great and small, in
Western Abyssinia.   His Abyssinian biographer, a peaceable man, with great seriousness and visible satisfaction,
describes his "first triumph" as follows.   Kasa had come
to a sworn agreement with seventy robbers that all booty
was to be common property.   But on learning that they
had secretly slaughtered for their own use a cow which
they had stolen, he with twelve others fell upon his
perjured "brethren," put them to flight, and cruelly muti-
lated seven of their number who fell into his hands.   In
this he was no doubt already acting in his character as
a God-appointed judge; breach of oath demanded severe
punishment.   But it is too obvious how hardening must
have been the tendency of such a life upon the future
sovereign.   It may be conjectured that he justified his
robber life by the consideration that his energies were
mainly directed against Mohammedans and heathen.   The
great trading caravans are chiefly in the service of

Mohammedan merchants; and the neighbours of Abyssinia are almost all Moslem tribes, partly Arab, partly pure Africans. In these parts the two religions have been at enmity for many centuries. No one dreams of establishing peace between them; and Kasa could not doubt that he served God better the more energetically he fought against the infidel. And he hated Islam all his life with his whole soul. Enlightened as he was in many respects, and profound as was the contempt he ultimately came to feel for the Christian priests of his nation, he was constant in regarding himself as an instrument of God for the humiliation or extirpation of Islam, and in ever looking for the forgiveness of all his sins as the reward of his merit as champion against the enemies of Christ. Yet in the course of his freebooting life he was occasionally led to make alliance with Moslems, especially in undertakings against heathen negroes, who from time immemorial had been the objects of plundering expeditions and slave hunts on the part of Christians and Mohammedans, great sovereigns and petty princelings alike.[1] Of course, in dealing with heathen, no more pity was shown than if they had been wild beasts, or rather less, for the hunted blacks often had the audacity to defend themselves with bravery. Active participation in operations of this kind was no school of clemency or amiable qualities, but it served to train Kasa as a general in prudence, promptitude, and solicitous care for his warriors.

He and his companions were often in great straits, especially for want of food; but he gradually acquired the position of a considerable prince in his native land of Quara. Though the terror of his enemies and of trading

[1] The good-natured Menilek of Shoa (now king of all Abyssinia) has undertaken many similar expeditions against neighbouring peoples on a larger scale than the nefarious slave hunts of the Arabs, and not less inhuman.

caravans, he even thus early gave attention to the cultivation of the soil, and protected the husbandmen.   He further
extended his influence by matrimonial alliances.   His
reputation steadily increased, and the mother of Ras Ali,
Menen, began to see that her best policy would be to put
a good face on a bad business and formally bestow upon
Kasa the governorship of Quara, which he already exercised
in fact.   This energetic and immoral woman ruled Gondar
and its neighbouring lands for her son; in her old age
(1844) she married a member of the old royal family,
whom she caused Ras Ali to proclaim as sovereign, herself assuming the title of Itégé ("great queen" or
"empress").   Soon afterwards Menen even offered her
granddaughter Tewabetch, daughter of Ras Ali, to Kasa
in marriage.   Such unions in the case of Abyssinian
princes are of even less political consequence than they
are in Europe; nevertheless it was a great elevation for
Kasa to be brought in this way into such close connection
with the most powerful family in the kingdom.   He
accordingly dismissed all the wives he had already married
—an ordinary proceeding in Abyssinia, requiring no special
formalities—and espoused Tewabetch, who was still very
young.   The union was solemnised in the face of the
church,—which is seldom done in these parts,—and Kasa
remained faithful to his admirable consort as long as she
lived,—a thing unheard of in the case of an Abyssinian
grandee.   Even after her death he kept her in tender
remembrance; she was his good genius.   But the marriage
had not the effect of making Kasa an obedient subject; in
the autumn of 1846 he became a declared rebel, and defeated
army after army.   In one instance he even made a naval
expedition, attacking an island on Lake Tana, where a
general opposed to him had taken refuge, with five hundred
light reed-rafts, the only craft known in Abyssinia; each

raft carried a musketeer, a spearman, and a slinger. One of Menen's generals had grossly insulted Kasa. All over the country the story went that Kasa's mother had in early life followed the humble calling of a dealer in kousso, the well - known remedy for tape - worm, a very common trouble in Abyssinia. The general in question had boastfully said before Menen and her people: "Never fear; I shall bring you this son of the kousso-seller with a string round his neck like an ichneumon." But it was his evil fortune to be defeated and taken; whereupon his conqueror caused a large quantity of pounded kousso to be brought, and thus addressed him: "My mother has unfortunately not sold any kousso to-day, and so has no money to buy corn; please therefore accept by way of refreshment the kousso that is left." He then compelled the unfortunate man to swallow a large quantity of the nasty stuff.[1]

In June 1847, Menen took the field in person, but was wounded and made prisoner. As a ransom for his mother, Ras Ali handed over to Kasa her whole territory, reserving his own suzerainty. Kasa, who now assumed the title of Dejazmatch or Dejaz, borne by rulers of large provinces, and by those in higher military commands (thus corresponding partly to our "duke" and partly to our " general "), in this way became one of the most powerful princes in the country. As such he followed alike his inclination and his conscience in leading an expedition against the " Turks "—that is, the Egyptians. He penetrated far into Senaar, but learned, in the neighbourhood of Deberki, how powerless the bravest Abyssinian warriors were against soldiers who had European weapons

---

[1] I repeat the story exactly as given in the Amharic biography. D'Abbadie at the time heard a somewhat different version in Gondar (*L'Abyssinie et le roi Théodore*, Paris 1868). D'Abbadie partly differs also in his order of events from the Abyssinian writer whom I follow; perhaps he may in some instances be right, but in others he has indubitably been misled by inaccurate recollection or by false information.

and some elements of discipline. He was beaten, and compelled to retreat—a humiliation he never forgot. His hatred against all Moslems, and especially all Turks, became blind. As our ancestors once used to regard the possession of the Holy Land by the infidel as a personal reproach to themselves, so also did Kasa, along with many of his countrymen; but what vexed him still more was the thought that the coasts bordering upon Abyssinia, as well as so many other lands of Africa which he (in some cases rightly and in others wrongly) regarded as the ancient property of his own country, were in the hands of Turks or other Moslems. He laid deeply to heart the lesson that European arms and European discipline give an army overpowering superiority, and it was always to him a matter of bitter regret that he could do so little to introduce real discipline among his troops.

A new rebellion of Kasa's ended less fortunately than his previous ones. He hoped to be a match for the numerous cavalry of his suzerain by the use of a kind of mines, and of wooden cannons bound with iron rings—his first attempt at gun-making, a pursuit that latterly became a passion with him. But the enemy found out his secret, and he had to submit himself without striking a blow. For two years he kept quiet; but in 1852 a quarrel again arose. Ras Ali stirred up against his son-in-law the powerful Goshu of Gojam, who had often been a thorn in his own side. Doubtless he hoped that the two troublesome vassals would wear out their strength against one another. But on 27th November 1852, Kasa surprised and defeated Goshu by one of those bold and rapid marches over difficult country which were the special terror of his foes. Goshu himself, one of the most distinguished warriors of Abyssinia, perished. The fame of the victor rose to a high pitch. He made as if he desired peace with Ras Ali, but the Austrian vice-consul

Reiz, who was with him in January 1853, saw even then that the ambitious prince would soon be at blows, not only with him, but also with Ubié. And so it fell out. In two bloody battles the power of Ras Ali was utterly broken. From the battle of Aishal (28th June 1853), Kasa's biographer reckons the fall in Central Abyssinia of the Galla power, that is to say, of the dynasty of the Gallas, with their hordes of Mohammedan Galla cavalry. Ras Ali retired to a remote corner of the territory of his tribesmen, the Yeju-Gallas, where, it would seem, by the sufferance of his son-in-law, he continued to live for some ten years, and at last died in utter obscurity.

After this (26th May 1854) a stratagem placed Beru, the son of Goshu, the bravest hero in all Abyssinia, in the hands of Kasa, who thus became master of the whole south-west. Beru, deserted by his army, prostrated himself before Kasa, with a stone on his neck, after the custom of the country ; but his conqueror seated him beside him, and asked, "What would you have done to me, had I been your prisoner ?" "I would not have allowed you to come into my presence, but would have taken good care to have you put to death without an audience," was the answer ; upon which Kasa thanked God aloud for his victory. Beru remained in custody until the death of his conqueror.

Of the same expedition the following anecdote is told. One of his servants boasted, after the fashion of Abyssinian warriors, "No one, O Kasa, can look even thy servants in the face, not to speak of thyself." The prince happened to have in his hand at the moment one of the very brittle glass vessels in use among the Abyssinians. This, by way of confirmation of what the man had said, he dashed upon a wooden dish ; the glass remained unbroken, but the wood fell into pieces. He now drew his sword, and proudly said, " I, Christ's servant, hold by Christ ; who can stand before

my face ? " He then offered prayer, and drank mead from
the glass. The story is no doubt an adorned version of
something that really happened; it is of interest to us as
showing that people had already begun to regard Kasa as
invincible.

In the same summer (1854) Kasa attacked Ubié, the most
powerful of his rivals, resorting not only to arms, but to
cunning and diplomacy. By the favour which he ostenta-
tiously showed to the Roman Catholic bishop, an Italian
named De Jacobis, he contrived to rouse the fears of Abba
Selama, the spiritual head (Abuna) of the Abyssinian Church,
that in the end Kasa's territory was to be withdrawn from
him, and brought into connection with the Roman Church ;
to prevent this the Abuna made a rapid change of front, and
went over from Ubié, his benefactor, to Kasa, promising to
crown him as sovereign. On this Kasa now expelled De
Jacobis [1] and all the other Catholic priests, as Ubié had
previously banished the Protestant missionaries.

On 9th February 1855 a decisive battle was fought, in
which Ubié was made prisoner, and his whole dominions
fell under the power of Kasa. Almost immediately (11th
February) Kasa had himself anointed and crowned in the
church of Deresgé Maryam, by Abuna Selama, under the
name of Theodore, as " king of the kings of Ethiopia." The
choice of the name, which, confident of victory, he had
announced to his soldiers before the battle, was well con-

[1] De Jacobis is highly spoken of by all unprejudiced witnesses. With
regard to all persons and things involving ecclesiastical interests, the judgments of Protestant and Catholic missionaries alike, and their partisans
(D'Abbadie, for example), must be received with caution. It is undeniable
that Abyssinia offers a much less favourable field to Protestant than to
Catholic missions. Even the narrowest type of Protestantism is something
much too high for the Abyssinians, not to speak of negroes. The desires
that occasionally find expression on the part of Russia for a union of the
Abyssinian with the " Orthodox " Church have small prospect of ever being
fulfilled.

sidered. Throughout the country hopes had long been cherished of the appearance of a Messianic ruler, Theodore, who should restore the glories of the kingdom and subdue unbelievers, and this was the character which Kasa now took on himself to represent; but, curiously enough, he did not assume the proper imperial title of Hatsé (or Haté, Até), leaving it to the old and feeble John, husband of Menen, who survived Theodore, and was always treated by him with the greatest respect, doubtless from some superstitious idea. The defect of Kasa's ancestry was made good by courtly genealogists, who soon supplied a pedigree establishing the descent of his mother from Solomon (that of his father was perhaps too well known), and thus making him to some extent a legitimate sovereign in the eyes of the people.

But he attached no value to the outward display of royalty. He dressed like an ordinary officer, slept almost invariably in a military tent, and went barefoot like all his subjects. At the same time, like some other great warrior kings, he had a touch of the theatrical in his character, which doubtless helped to enhance his reputation with the Abyssinians. Thus, for example, he had a fancy for keeping tame lions. There must have been something kinglike in the whole aspect of the man; he was of the middle height, very dark even for an Abyssinian, with aristocratic features, aquiline nose, and fiery black eyes; almost all Europeans who came before him were much impressed by him at first sight. Some of them also detected a trace of cunning in his face, and this was no doubt correct. Of insinuating address in his friendly moods, he could be terrible in the outbursts of his wrath. Possibly this wrath may sometimes have been merely assumed, as in the case of Napoleon I.

One of his first acts as king was to renew the old laws against the slave trade and polygamy. But unfortunately

his constant wars made it impossible to give full effect to
the former prohibition; and a real reformation of the frightfully loose marriage relations which prevail in this very
" Christian " State could not be effected by edicts apart from
a movement of moral reformation. The law 'remained a
dead letter, all the more that he himself personally in after
years violated it grossly.

Theodore threw himself with all his might into the
maintenance of justice. All the oppressed, so far as was at
all possible, betook themselves directly to him. In Abyssinia
the head of the State still personally discharges the functions
of judge. He sought to protect the country folk against the
excesses of the soldiers. His punishments were frightfully
severe, but at the same time often milder than the laws
prescribed. We would not excuse the excessive and shocking severity of Theodore's punishments, such as the chopping
off of hands and feet, and so on; but it is fair to remember
that it is only modern humanitarianism that has finally put
a stop to similar atrocities among ourselves, and that in
Europe revolting corporal punishments were still sanctioned
by law in an age where they were much less in harmony
with the prevailing civilisation than in modern Abyssinia.
It ought to be added, that he not unfrequently pardoned
vanquished foes. In his legal judgments he showed good
sense. Decisions of his are quoted which are much better
entitled to the epithet " Solomonic " than his genealogy is.

Immediately after the subjugation of Ubié, Theodore
marched against the Wollo-Gallas, reduced them to apparent
subjection at the very first onset, and pushed farther to
the south into the kingdom of Shoa, which, as we learn
from the missionary Krapf, feared no assailant from the
north, being covered (as it deemed) by the Wollos. Such
an opinion would have been justified in the case of any
ordinary Abyssinian prince, but not in that of Theodore.

He was soon master of all Shoa, and, the native king dying at the time, nominated a member of the same family, not as king, but as governor. Thus within less than a year Theodore had added to his old provinces all that remained of Abyssinia.

But to conquer and to hold are not quite the same. Had Theodore been a cool-headed and highly-educated European, he would from the first have called a halt at the natural northern frontier of the Wollo country, the valley of the Beshelo. Really to subjugate this people was a much heavier task than he could have supposed. The Wollos have long been Mohammedans, and are proud of their faith, although they know but little of the doctrines of Islam, and have retained much that is of pagan origin. They are divided against themselves in genuine African fashion; tribe is at war with tribe, clan with clan, but they were all at one in their love of independence and in hatred of the Christian conqueror. All the Gallas (all, at least, who live in or near Abyssinia) are savage and bloodthirsty, with all the instincts of the robber, not very courageous in open fight, but dangerous in guerilla warfare. The Wollos have the reputation also of being exceptionally treacherous. Their country, somewhat less, perhaps, than the kingdom of Saxony, is broken up by great mountain ranges rising close to the snow line, and by numerous deep valleys, so as to make the reduction of a recalcitrant population under a united rule an excessively difficult task. On the other hand, it offers abundant cover for rebels and robbers; and any one acquainted with the byways can easily incommode even considerable bodies of troops. The Wollos are born horsemen, and gallop along the steepest hillsides on their hardy ponies. Theodore carried on his war with them year after year. He was never defeated by them, and, in fact, they were afraid so

much as to look him in the face.[1] His generals also were
for the most part successful against them.   Great parts
of the country, and even prominent chiefs, were often
subdued by him, but he never became master of the whole.
Sometimes with kindness, often with severity rising to
atrocious cruelty, he sought to bring them under his sway;
but the result was always the same, that in the end in
Walloland he could call nothing his own except garrisoned
fortresses like Makdala.[2]

Meanwhile arose, now in one province, now in another,
various rebels, some of them members of old princely families,
sometimes bold soldiers of fortune.   None of them was at
all a match for him.   Wherever he made his appearance
the armies of the insurgents were scattered like dust.   By
force or by artifice he succeeded in getting several of them
into his power, and among them one who, as it seemed,
was the most formidable of all—Negusié of Tigré (beginning
of 1861), with whom France had already entered into
relations as " King of Abyssinia."   Others took refuge in
inaccessible deserts, or in steep rocky fastnesses, of which
so many are found in Abyssinia.   Had he not been
hampered by the Wollos, he would doubtless have got
the better of them all; but his war of extermination against
these savages crippled him completely.   He found no
exceptional difficulty indeed in recruiting his armies,
decimated though they were by the sword, and still more
by periodical pestilence; for Abyssinia has no lack of men
with a taste for war and plunder, and Theodore's name
acted like a charm.   The very size of his armies was his
misfortune.   He could not feed them in any regular way.

[1] When the English, immediately after the death of Theodore, showed his
picture to the Wollo princess Mastiat, his bitter enemy, and asked her
whether it was like him, she replied, " How can I tell?   Who has ever seen
him and lived?"

[2] Not Magdala, as it is usually written in England and Germany.

Though at the outset he strictly repressed all plundering
in friendly districts, he soon had to concede everything
to his hungry soldiers, and even to order the systematic
robbery of prosperous regions. In this way the veneration
of his people was turned into hatred; the poverty-stricken
peasants went to swell the ranks of the rebels, or, at least,
robbed and murdered in secret.

Theodore's embarrassments were further increased by his
relations with the ecclesiastical authorities. At the head
of the Abyssinian Church, a branch of the Coptic (the whole
civilisation of Abyssinia, so far as it is Christian, is derived
from the impure Coptic source), stands a bishop, who must
be, not a native, but a Copt, sent by the (Monophysite)
patriarch of Alexandria. This "Abuna," in power and
consideration, stands almost on a level with the king, has
much larger revenues, and is reverenced by the masses
as a god. Since November 1841 this position had been
occupied by Abba Selama, mentioned above, a man of about
the same age as Kasa-Theodore. Having as a child attended
an English mission school, many English and German
Protestants cherished great hopes regarding him; but
other Europeans who happened to be in Abyssinia at the
time of his arrival there,—Ferret and Galinier (French),
and Mansfield Parkins (English),—who had no ecclesiastical
preoccupations, at once perceived him to be an insignificant,
narrow-minded individual. Nowhere, moreover, could a
prelate, with any serious inclination to reformation, have
a more difficult position than in the wretched Church of
Abyssinia: to make any progress with the laity would
be difficult; with the priesthood, impossible. As Abba
Selama at the outset had the immeasurable advantage
over the natives of a somewhat higher education and a
much greater knowledge of the world, he ought certainly
to have been able, in conjunction with such a man as

18

Theodore, to improve many things, had he shown intelligence
and adaptability. But he cared for nothing except his own
spiritual independence. The king was very amenable to
good advice, and had also laid him under special obligations
by forcibly repressing a large party of the priests that for
dogmatic reasons was hostile to him; but instead of exercising a moderating influence upon him, the prelate soon
brought matters to a complete breach. When the German
missionary Krapf met the king in the heyday of his
victorious career, in the spring of 1855, he still appeared
to be in heart and soul at one with the Abuna; but any
one who is acquainted with the quarrels that subsequently
arose can mark the root of them in the jealous temper
which the language of the bishop, reported by Krapf, even
then revealed. Soon afterwards a mutiny broke out in the
army in Shoa, which to all appearance had been stirred up
by the Abuna and the second spiritual authority in the
kingdom, the supreme head of the monks. This was
repressed without leading to an open conflict with the
clerics. But soon a worse controversy arose. The king
began to lay hands on the vast revenues of the Church
to meet the demands of his army,—a measure certainly
contrary to every usage of the country, and dictated only
by sheerest necessity. Further, he required the priests
to uncover in his presence (he being filled with the Spirit
of God), just as they uncovered in presence of the ark
(or altar), which was the Seat of God. In these controversies the king had to give way at first, but soon it went
hard with the clergy. The biographer, though as respectful
in his feeling towards the bishop as towards the king,
accumulates all sorts of details fitted to make plain the
contempt and hatred which Theodore gradually and increasingly came to feel towards the haughty head of the Church
and the entire clergy. Even the supreme head of that

Church, the patriarch of Alexandria, on one occasion when
he visited Abyssinia, had seriously compromised himself
in the king's eyes. Moreover, the Abuna appears to have
been far from exemplary in his private life. Theodore,
accordingly, in the course of time, broke loose from all
clerical restraints. In his later years he deliberately set
fire to sacred buildings, burned down the town of Gondar
precisely because it was "the city of the priests," threw
the Abuna into prison, and finally even, on his own
authority, issued to himself and his soldiers a dispensation
from fasting, perhaps the most important duty of Abyssinian
Christianity; and all this the priesthood had silently to
endure. On the other hand, of course, their hatred helped
to alienate the people from the king, and the Abuna in his
prison maintained close relations with the more important
rebels.

In the first years of his reign Theodore had two faithful
counsellors in Plowden, the British consul, and John Bell,
who had come into the country along with Plowden, had
almost become an Abyssinian, and adhered with touching
fidelity to the master whose service he had joined. These
two had a great influence in stimulating his desire for the
introduction of European manners, or rather of the arts
of Europe; when he compared them and what he learned
from them about Europe with his own Abyssinians, the
latter could not but fall greatly in his estimation, and
perhaps in the end he even came to value his own people
too lightly, and to judge them too severely. Plowden,
unfortunately, was recalled by his Government to the port
of Massowa, and on his journey (March 1860) fell into
the hands of a rebel, a cousin of the king, receiving wounds
of which he soon afterwards died. Theodore at once set
out against the miscreant, who fell in the battle that
followed, slain, it is said, by the hand of Bell, who in his

turn was killed while shielding the king with his own person. Theodore terribly avenged his two friends, whose loss was never repaired to him. Queen Tewabetch, to whom, as we have seen, he clung with all his soul, had died previously on 18th August 1858; Flad tells us that he regarded her death as a divinè judgment on him for having shortly before caused the wife of an arch-rebel who had fallen into his hands to be cruelly butchered.

Continual conflicts left the king no leisure to carry out reforms, however much his heart may have been set on them. Before everything else the construction of roads, bridges, and viaducts was a necessity for the country, and with road-making he did actually make a beginning. The first section was completed in 1858, under the direction of Zander, a German painter. When he complained that the necessary assistance was not being given to him, the king caused the governor of the district to be whipped and laid in irons, rewarding Zander richly. Theodore desired nothing more ardently than the immigration of European artisans and mechanics. With more of these and fewer missionaries, much disaster would have been averted and much good done.

To outward seeming Theodore was at the height of his power between 1861 and 1863. It was only in these years that he actually wielded authority, through his governor, over the whole of Tigré, the one province which has tolerably easy communications with the coast. But his struggles with the Wollos wasted his strength, and continually gave rebels renewed opportunities to rise. From 1863 onwards, his difficulties increased day by day. At the same time the king's disposition steadily became gloomier. From the first he had been capricious, subject to violent outbursts of wrath, and in his passion capable of the most dreadful actions. But now he experienced disappointment after disappointment. Prince Menilek of Shoa escaped from Makdala in 1865, and again set up the kingdom of his fathers; Theodore attempted to dethrone him once more, but was compelled to retire from Shoa without accomplishing his object. One province after another was lost, temporarily or permanently. Even in the earlier years of his sovereignty many of his grandees in whom he had reposed perfect confidence had left him and become rebels. This made him ever more mistrustful, and increased his contempt for his fellow-countrymen. Ultimately, on the slightest suspicion, or even out of mere caprice, he would put in irons, for a longer or shorter time, his most faithful servants, some of whom in the long-run proved their fidelity by dying with him. In his youthful days as robber chief and adventurer he had resembled David, who, secure of his future, had led a freebooter life among the mountains of southern Judah (of course one must remember that the African character is much ruder still than that of ancient Israel); now, in one aspect at least, he often resembled Saul when the evil spirit had come upon him. When Theodore sat gloomily brooding, every one who knew him took care to avoid him; kindly attendants sought to keep off visitors with the transparent pretence that the king was asleep.

It is no more true of Theodore than of any other extraordinary man, that his whole character was suddenly transformed. All his faults showed themselves at an early period, some of them in a very marked way; but in late years his bad qualities became more and more prominent, and overgrew his better nature. Terunesh, the proud daughter of the aged Ubié, whom he married some five years after the death of the beloved Tewabetch, was unable to hold his affections; and with the full consciousness that he was doing wrong he abandoned himself to the usual polygamy of the native princes. Like most of the Abyssinian grandees, he had always been a heavy drinker; but in his last years, contrary to his earlier practice, he often got drunk, and when in this condition gave orders of the most bloody description, which he afterwards bitterly repented. But this man, who sometimes in anger or drunkenness, sometimes with the clear conscience of a ruler or judge sacrificing to the public weal or to the cause of righteousness, butchered thousands of people, and burned churches and cities to the ground—this very man played in the most genial way with little children, in his expeditions was scrupulously careful that the women and children, numbers of whom always accompany an Abyssinian army, should come to no harm, and was ready to assist personally the exhausted soldier who had fallen out of the ranks.

It would serve no purpose to go into details of the embroilment with England in which Theodore ultimately met his death. It was a singular combination of unfortunate circumstances, misunderstandings, blunders, and crimes. Consul Cameron, a man worthy of all respect, was not acquainted with Abyssinia and Theodore as Plowden, his predecessor, had been, neither does he seem to have been a *persona grata* to the king. In the letter of which he was the bearer (October 1862), Earl Russell thanked Theodore courteously and coldly for his treatment of Plowden, when the king felt entitled to expect a direct communication from the sovereign as between equals. Theodore lost no time in expressing to Cameron the hatred he felt against his hereditary enemies, the Turks. But Cameron had instructions to enter into communication with the Egyptian authorities, and this presently made him hateful to Theodore. The king himself, the servant of Christ, had refused all friendly agreement with the unbelieving Egyptians, although the Viceroy Saíd Pasha had taken much pains in this direction, and it was incomprehensible to him how Christian Europe could hold alliance with Turks, or leave them in possession of lands formerly Christian. We smile at his narrowness; but how long is it since similar views prevailed all over Europe? And did not Russia in her last Eastern war succeed in reviving in Europe, and especially in England, the antipathy of Christians against the unchristian Turks, and in making it serve her own policy of conquest? It was inexcusable that Theodore's letter to the Queen, delivered to the consul, received no answer; the neglect was felt profoundly. Incautious oral, written, or printed utterances of Europeans, communicated idly or in malice, further embittered him. He was well aware that Europeans were his superiors in civilisation; but he had a just sense of his personal dignity, and it stung him to the quick to hear that he was spoken of as a savage. What irritated him above all was to learn that his mother, on whom he rested his claim as a legitimate sovereign, had been spoken of as a kousso-seller.[1] The Jewish missionary Stern made himself particularly obnoxious by utterances of this kind. Theodore had never conceded to the foreign consuls the privilege of inviolability, which is quite unknown to the Abyssinians. He claimed for himself a perfect right to treat discourteous guests exactly as he would treat his own subjects. Thus in 1863 he put in irons the French consul Lejean who had offended him, and afterwards expelled him. In like manner, in January 1864, he put consul Cameron in irons. The other Europeans also, who were under his control, were either imprisoned or kept under prison surveillance. These were for the most part Germans, some of them missionaries, others of them artisans, who had been sent into Abyssinia in the missionary interest, but had been employed by

[1] See above, p. 265.

Theodore in cannon - founding and other works not of a particularly evangelistic character; there were, besides, a few travellers and adventurers of various descriptions. Most of them seem to have been worthy persons.

Britain, of course, could not submit quietly to the imprisonment of her consul. But the Government sought, in the first instance, very properly, to win the king to a better temper, and sent Rassam, a born Oriental (of Mosul), and a man of intelligence and address, with a letter from the Queen to Theodore. The latter gave Rassam a very friendly reception (March 1866), and promised to release the captives. But he could never make up his mind to fulfil this promise. Recollections of real or supposed insults continually came in the way. He had, moreover, the idea that in Cameron and the missionaries he possessed valuable hostages whose delivery might be made to depend on the arrival from England of the artisans and implements he so earnestly desired. Personal misunderstandings, and perhaps misrepresentations, did the rest; until, finally, the gloomy despot, hemmed in on every side by manifold straits, caused Rassam also and his suite to be sent to the rocky fastness of Makdala, and there confined. The captivity, judged according to Abyssinian ideas, was certainly of a mild description, and Theodore always maintained friendly feelings towards Rassam, while regarding Cameron, Stern, and some others as his enemies. He tacitly showed his high respect for the Europeans by the immunity for life and limb which he allowed them to enjoy, while he would mutilate or put to death his own subjects on the slightest provocation.

Rassam's imprisonment compelled Britain to declare war. When the troops landed on the Red Sea coast, not far from Massowa, in the end of 1867, Theodore was already in the direst straits. But wherever he showed himself with his army, he still continued to be undisputed lord; for no one dared to meet him in the field. Had he in these circumstances simply retired before the British troops, and withdrawn with his captives into the hot fever-haunted wilderness of his native Quara, he would have involved his assailants in endless difficulties. Fortunately, however, he determined to choose Makdala—to Abyssinians impregnable—as the place where to concentrate all his fighting power. The same stronghold, more than 9000 feet above sea level, and nearly 4000 feet above the river Beshelo, less than five miles off, in a direct line, was also, as being the place where the prisoners were kept, the objective of the British. Theodore's last march was really a magnificent performance. For the transit of the heavy ordnance, cast by his European workmen, with which he proposed to defend Makdala, roads had first to be made, often along dizzy precipices. Theodore personally superintended all the works, and often personally took a share in them. In his heart what he hoped for was a peaceful arrangement with the British, though in moments of excitement he may sometimes have actually thought of their defeat and annihilation as possible. He reached Makdala, which, including its outworks, has accommodation for many thousands, only shortly before the arrival of the British. He had gone into the net almost with his eyes open.

The arrangements for the English expedition, which was commanded by Sir Robert Napier, were not at first particularly skilful; and the final success was mainly due to Colonel Merewether, to the never-to-be-forgotten Werner Munzinger, who had been appointed British vice-consul, and, as intimately acquainted with the land and its people, had charge of the negotiations with the native rulers, and, lastly, to Colonel Phayre. To within a short distance of Makdala the route lay through the territory of princes who were in rebellion against Theodore, and indeed, to some extent, also at feud with each other. To secure free passage everywhere, accordingly, it was never necessary to resort to open force; diplomatic negotiation was enough. To conquer the physical obstacles, once Abyssinia proper had been reached, was no very difficult task for British troops with British resources.

At Arogé, near Makdala, a portion of Theodore's army fell upon the British, and was, of course, scattered (10th April 1868); no Abyssinian bravery could withstand Snider rifles, rockets, and artillery. The king recognised that he could never again bring his troops to face such a foe. Hope alternated with paroxysms of rage. He began to treat with Napier, and at last released all the Europeans unconditionally. It is possible that he may have done this because he had been informed that Napier was prepared to accept a present from him, and so had virtually conceded peace; but it is at least equally probable that he did not wish the Europeans to be involved i his ruin. Shortly before this, at any rate, he had made an attempt (prevented by his grandees) at suicide, without previously giving orders that he should be avenged on his prisoners. The intelligence he had received soon proved to have been false; the British pressed forward, and his army deserted him. The proud king could not yield to Napier's demand that he should surrender; with a few of his faithful followers he went to meet the foe, and after some of those beside him had fallen, he shot himself with his own pistol (Easter Monday, 14th April).

The British soldiers showed little respect for the body, but their commander afterwards caused it to be buried after the rites of the Abyssinian Church. The conquerors liberated all the captives in Makdala,—scions of ancient families, rebels, robbers, officials, and officers in disgrace,—people for the most part of very questionable antecedents. The young queen Terunesh, along with the boy Alem-ayehu, Theodore's only legitimate son, accompanied the British on their return. She died of consumption before she could leave Abyssinia, the boy not long afterwards in England. The army quitted the country as promptly as might be, in view of the approach of the rainy season, which makes all communication impossible. It is to be regretted that so little care was taken to utilise the opportunity offered by the expedition for a more exact scientific survey of the country.[1]

Thus lies Theodore in the mountain fastness of the Wollo-Gallas. I do not know whether these savages have desecrated the grave of their mortal enemy, or whether, perhaps, their awe of him still keeps them at a distance. Legend is certain ultimately to glorify the memory of Theodore among the Christians of Abyssinia; songs will long be sung and stories told of the mighty king who restored the kingdom, triumphed over the infidel, and at last, worsted by the magical arts of strangers, preferred death to surrender.

The task of permanently uniting Abyssinia, in which Theodore failed, proved equally impracticable to John, who came to the front, in the first instance, as an ally of. the British, and afterwards succeeded to the sovereignty. By his fall (10th March 1889) in the unhappy war against the "dervishes" or Moslem zealots of the Soudan, the path was cleared for Menilek of Shoa, who enjoyed the support of Italy. The establishment of the Italians on the Red Sea littoral, and their policy there, which, though not free from many mistakes, has been on the whole very intelligent and

[1] Of works upon the campaign that are not purely military, by far the best, so far as I know, is that of Markham (*A History of the Abyssinian Expedition*, London 1869). The writer is a keen observer, and an impartial judge.

effective, according to all appearance, promises a new era for Abyssinia. If Italy perseveres with firmness, prudence, and moderation on the laborious path on which she has entered, and if the policy represented by Count Antonelli and others is not frustrated by party exigencies or excessive parsimony, she may derive great advantages from her African enterprise. But Abyssinia will profit still more, though there be an end to the proud dream of an independent kingdom of all Abyssinia.

INDEX.

---o---

285